THE HISTORY OF PIN-UPS

An Illustrated Guide Through Art, Meaning, Psychology and Women Liberation

To Simone,
my never ending inspiration.

First Printing Edition, 2024
ISBN - 978-65-984082-2-0

Published by Gargoyle Collective
Created by Ziggy Quinete
Illustrations by Satoshi Watanabe, Andy K. Moore and Dick Warren

Table of Contents

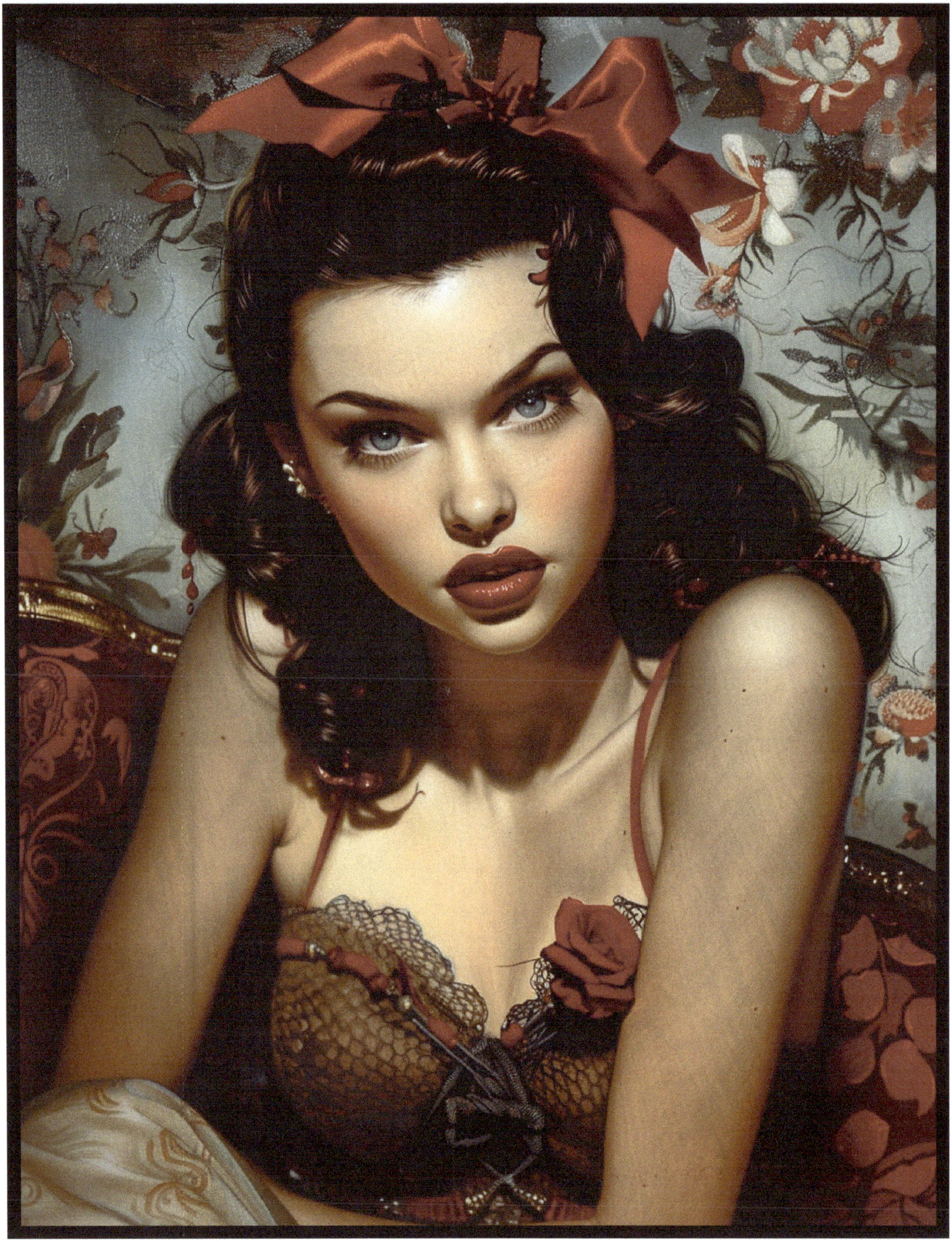

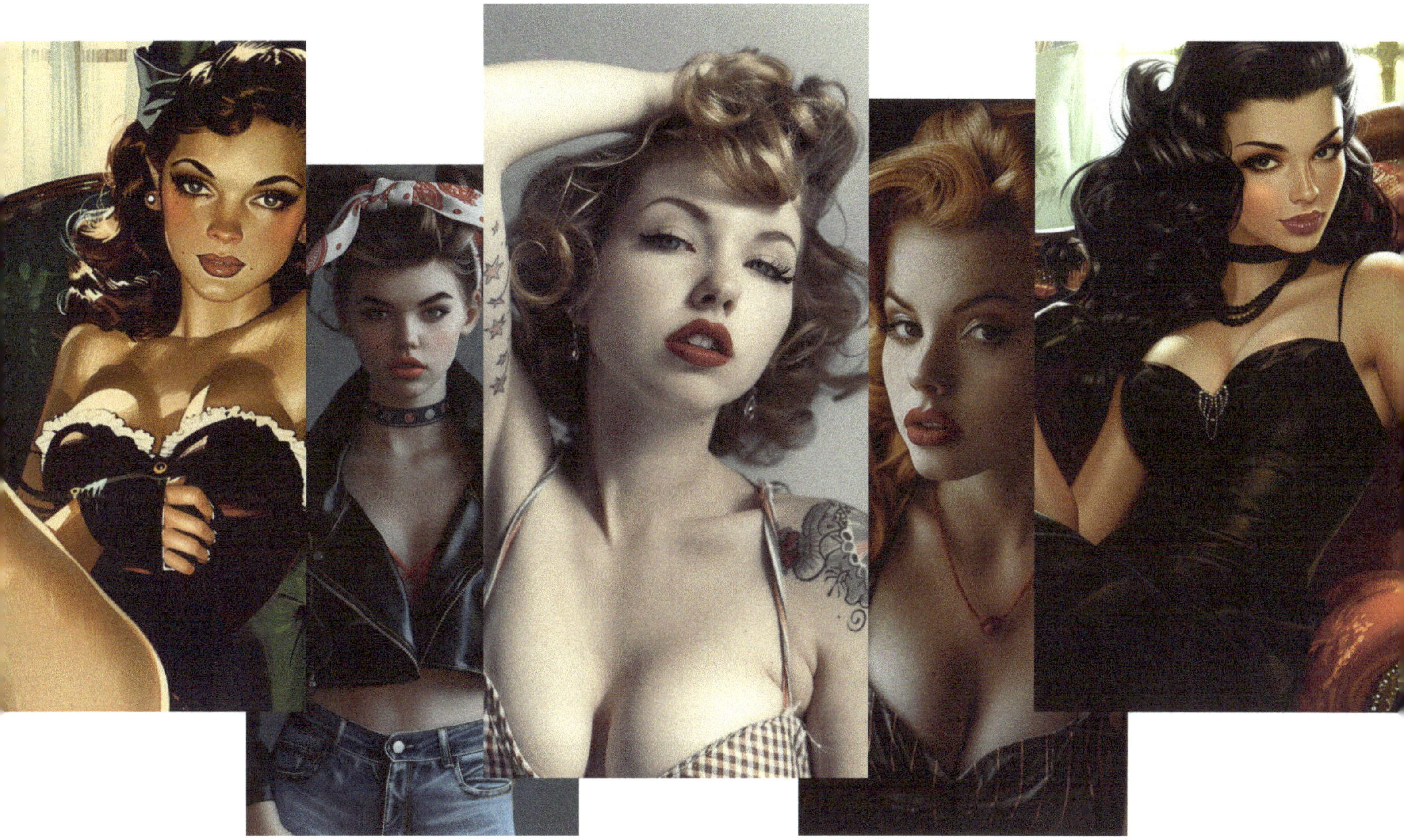

Preface

If you've ever admired a classic pin-up illustration, you might have noticed an enduring allure and captivating charm that transcends time. These images, though united by themes of beauty and femininity, each tell a unique story, much like a gallery of diverse muses from different eras. What is it about pin-ups that have enchanted the hearts and imaginations of so many? What cultural threads weave through these illustrations to create a tapestry that is both nostalgic and ever-evolving? What shared experiences and ideals connect the artists and audiences of pin-ups across decades?

Pin-up culture stands apart from any other artistic phenomenon in modern history. Its essence is not merely contemporary; it is rooted in the artistic expressions of the late 19th and early 20th centuries, flourishing through the illustrations of artists like Charles Dana Gibson and Gil Elvgren. This culture spans over a century, yet its imagery and philosophy have evolved, continually resonating with new generations. From the early days of the Gibson Girl to the glamour of the 1950s pin-ups, these images have celebrated beauty, confidence, and femininity in a way that is both timeless and distinctly captivating.

Pin-up culture celebrates life through art, fashion, and individualistic expressions. Some may call it misogyny or objectification of the woman's body, but this is a 21st-century interpretation of an art form that is over 100 years old. Pin-ups were, for quite a long time, a form of emancipation for working women in the 1940s and for the professional woman of the 1950s. Yes, they were sexy, but let's not forget that they were also free from the bondage of being mere housewives. As time went by, pin-ups continually assimilated new influences while maintaining their core essence. Other cultural expressions were reactions to external events: the flappers to the Roaring Twenties, the beatniks to post-war disillusionment. In contrast, pin-up represents an idealized vision of beauty and confidence that exists within the human spirit, timeless and universally admired across generations.

As I delved into the century-old pieces of what is now understood as pin-up art, I learned about its origins and development and how they have transformed over decades. Pin-up culture can assimilate an ever-growing number of references—from the classic elegance of the Gibson Girl to the bold, playful depictions of mid-20th-century pin-ups, from the burlesque stage to the pages of modern magazines. These elements fuse together, creating something bigger and more complex, with endless room for new interpretations without altering its core essence.

This project has evolved into a versatile and intense exchange of images, ideas, and profound discussions on the symbolism, art, and psychology underlying pin-up as a cultural movement. My journey as a curator has been one of discovery and admiration. Navigating through the vast ocean of pin-up art was more challenging than anticipated, and the selection process was painstaking, with many exquisite images reluctantly set aside for this edition.

As you dive into this book, I hope you discover the rich history of pin-up culture and create new connections between styles from different eras. Through it, I hope you will be able to see beyond the images to understand how women evolved and took their rightful place in society, and how this revolution has helped them to claim their own sexuality and freedom of expression.

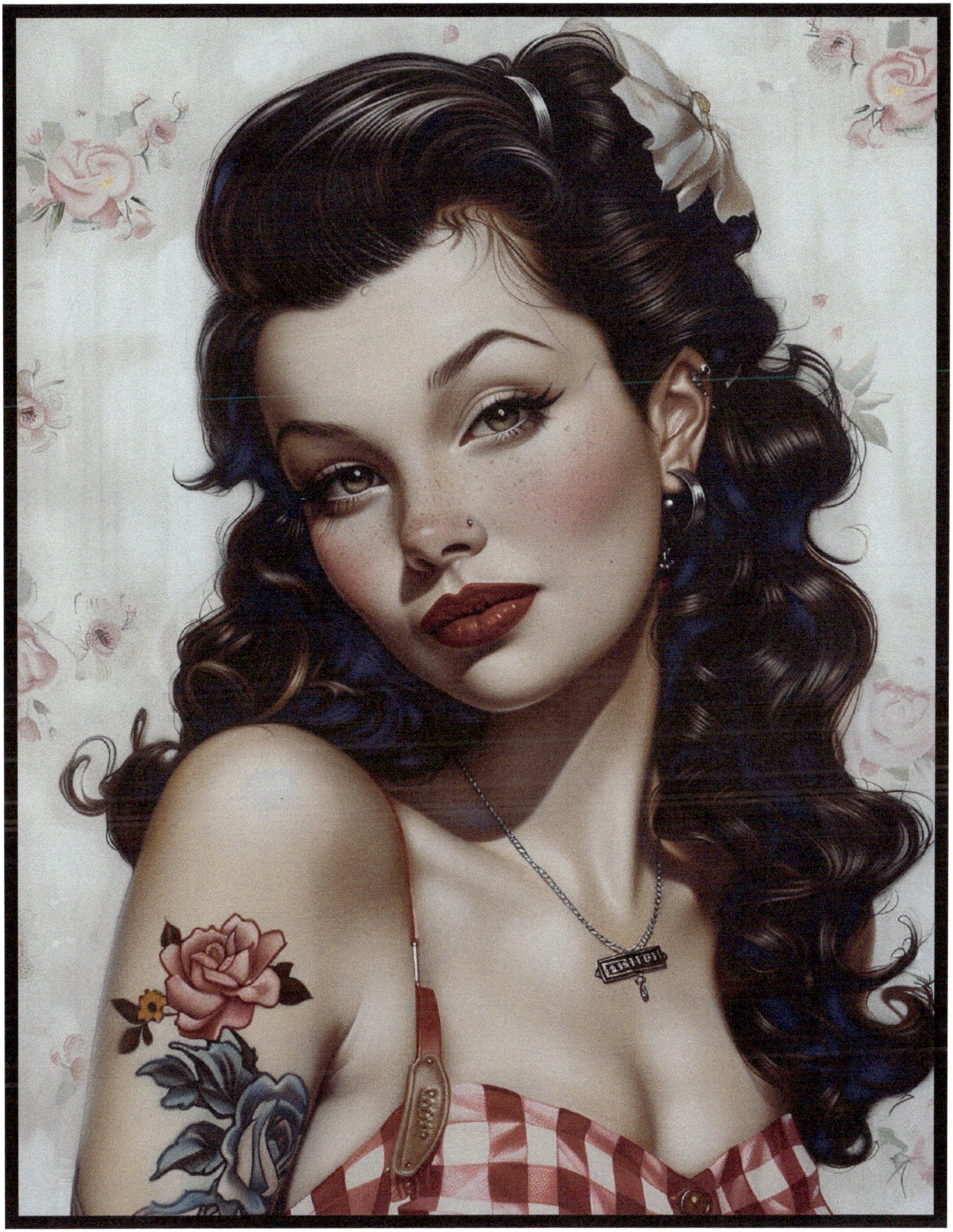

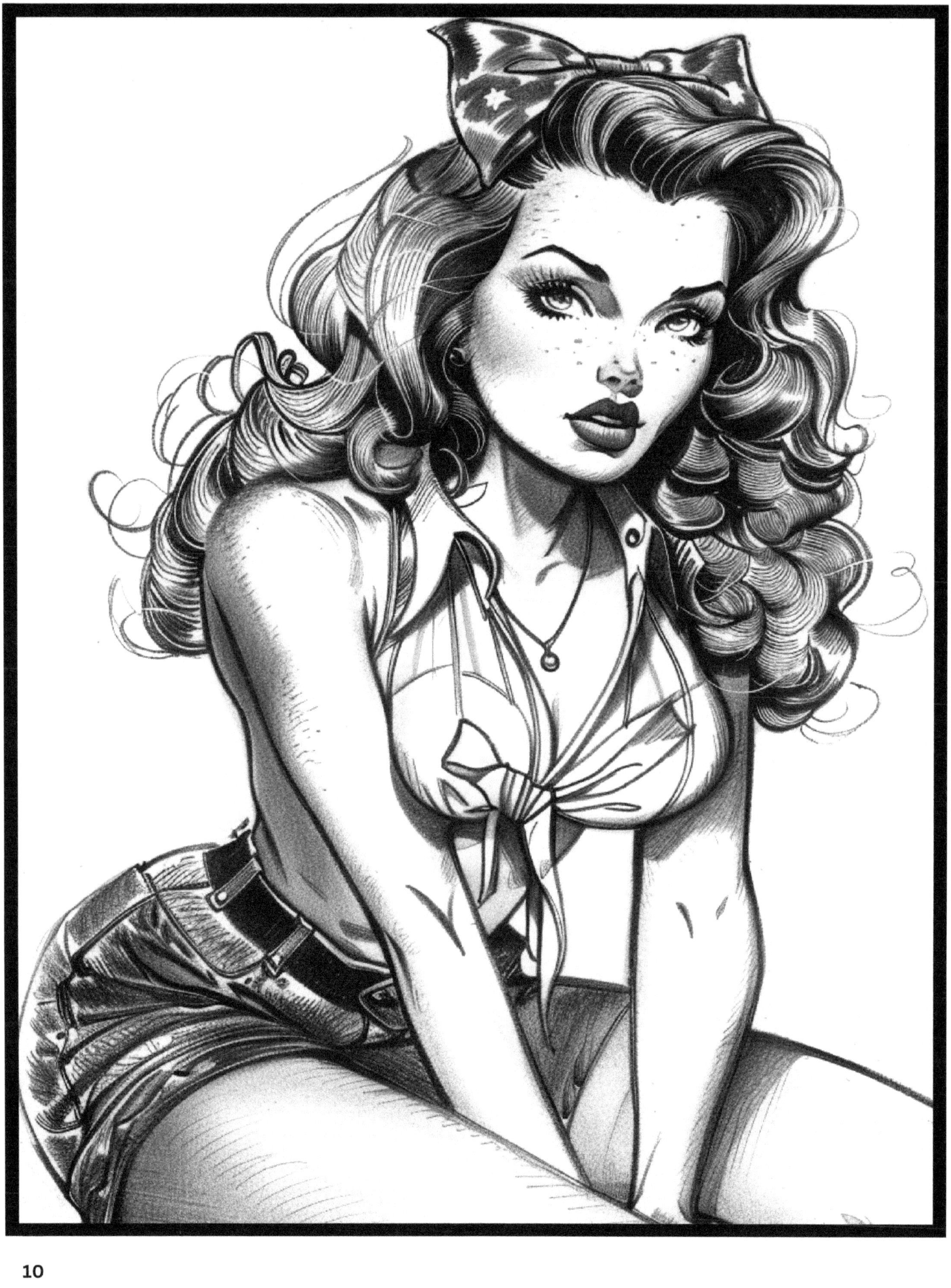

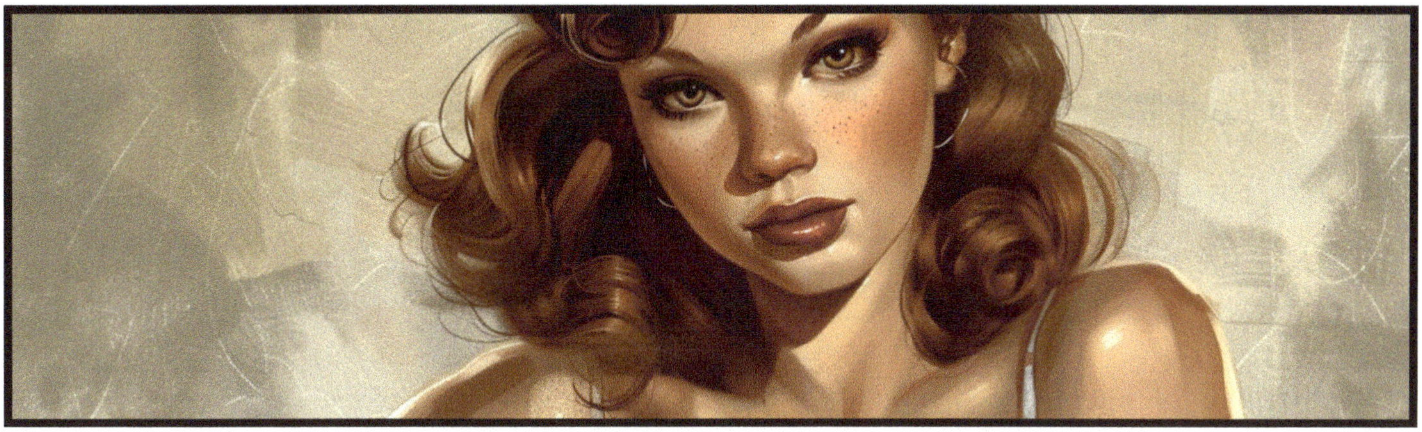

DEFINITION OF A PIN-UP

Pin-up art, a quintessential aspect of 20th-century popular culture, refers to illustrations, photographs, and other forms of visual art that depict idealized and often glamorized images of attractive women. These images, known as pin-ups, were originally created for mass distribution, typically intended to be "pinned up" on walls as decoration. The term "pin-up" itself originates from this practice, capturing the essence of how these images were enjoyed and displayed.

Pin-up art encompasses a variety of styles and mediums, ranging from painted illustrations to photographed models. Despite the diversity in execution, pin-ups share common characteristics: they often portray women in playful, flirtatious, and suggestive poses, exuding confidence, charm, and allure. These depictions are not merely about beauty but also about a certain attitude and presence that made pin-ups iconic.

The roots of pin-up art can be traced back to the late 19th and early 20th centuries, evolving alongside advancements in printing and mass media. It gained significant momentum during the 1920s and reached its zenith during the 1940s, particularly during World War II, when pin-up girls became symbols of morale and inspiration for soldiers. Over the decades, pin-up art has continuously adapted to cultural shifts, reflecting changes in societal norms, fashion, and attitudes towards gender and sexuality.

Today, pin-up art remains a beloved and influential genre, celebrated for its aesthetic appeal and its impact on fashion, advertising, and pop culture. It has also been reclaimed and reinterpreted in contemporary contexts, serving as a medium for empowerment, body positivity, and artistic expression. As we explore the rich history and evolution of pin-up art in this book, we will uncover the stories behind the images, the artists who created them, and the cultural forces that shaped this enduring phenomenon.

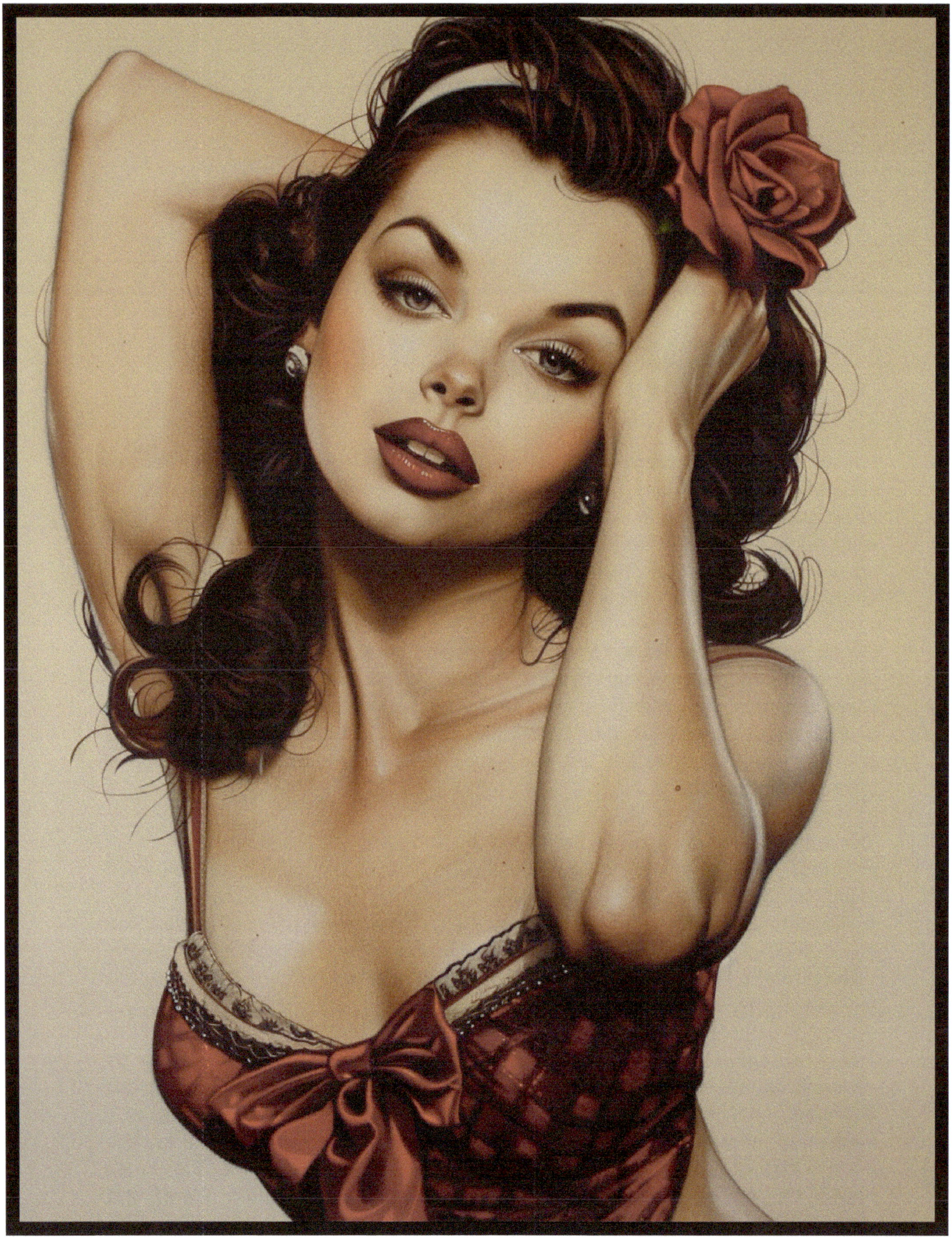

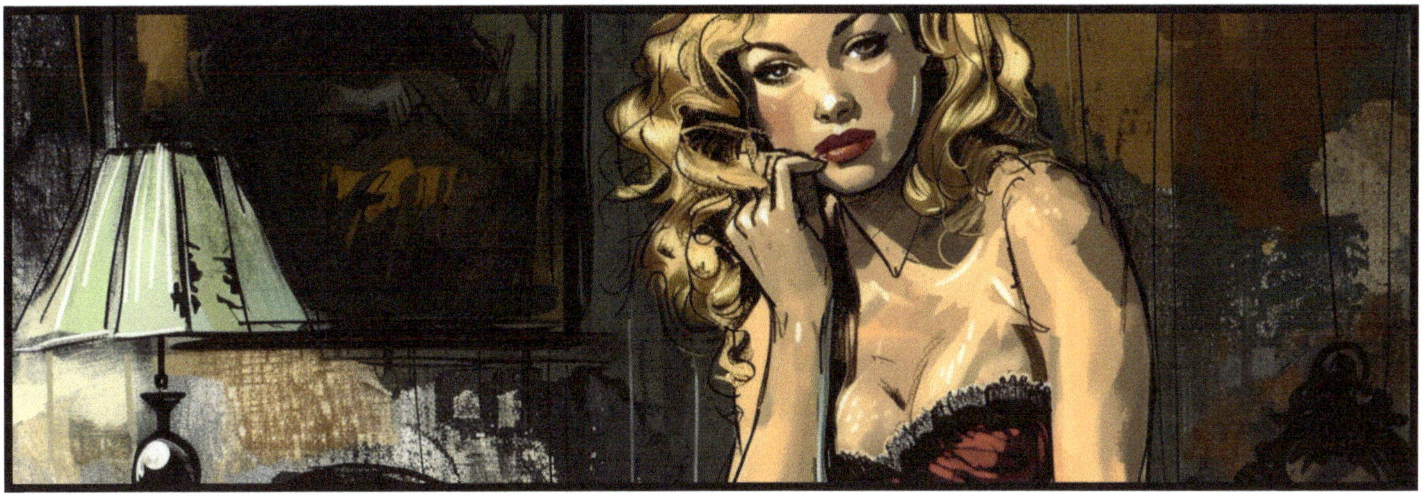

IMPORTANCE IN POP CULTURE

Pin-up art holds a significant place in the tapestry of pop culture, symbolizing more than just an era of glamorous imagery; it represents a multifaceted influence that spans art, fashion, media, and social movements. Its impact has permeated various aspects of society, contributing to the shaping of cultural norms and aesthetic values.

Aesthetic Influence

Pin-up art has played a pivotal role in defining beauty standards and fashion trends. The idealized, often exaggerated features of pin-up models - from their hourglass figures to their flawless makeup and stylish clothing - set benchmarks for beauty and style that influenced generations. The classic pin-up look, characterized by bright red lips, winged eyeliner, and vintage hairstyles, remains iconic and continues to inspire contemporary fashion and beauty industries.

Media and Advertising

The proliferation of pin-up art in media and advertising during the mid-20th century marked a significant shift in marketing strategies. Pin-up girls were used to sell a wide range of products, from household items to automobiles, leveraging their appeal to capture consumer attention. This practice laid the groundwork for the modern advertising industry's reliance on attractive imagery to promote products. Additionally, pin-up art's integration into posters, calendars, and magazines contributed to its widespread recognition and popularity.

Symbolism and Morale

During World War II, pin-up art became a powerful symbol of hope and morale for soldiers. Images of pin-up girls adorned the walls of barracks, airplanes, and ships, providing comfort and a reminder of home. These images were more than just decorative; they embodied the spirit of the times, offering a sense of normalcy and aspiration amidst the hardships of war. This role cemented pin-up art's place in history as a morale booster and cultural icon.

Cultural Reflection and Evolution

Pin-up art has mirrored societal attitudes towards gender, sexuality, and femininity. In its early days, pin-ups often depicted women in roles that emphasized their charm and allure, reflecting the gender norms of the times. However, as societal attitudes evolved, so did the portrayal of pin-up girls. Modern interpretations of pin-up art celebrate diversity, body positivity, and empowerment, challenging traditional notions and promoting inclusivity.

Artistic Legacy

Many renowned artists, such as Alberto Vargas, Gil Elvgren, and George Petty, became famous for their contributions to pin-up art. Their work not only defined the genre but also influenced other artistic fields, including comic books, graphic design, and pop art. The distinctive style of pin-up art, characterized by its vibrant colors, playful poses, and meticulous attention to detail, continues to inspire artists across various mediums.

Subcultural Movements

The enduring appeal of pin-up art has also fostered subcultural movements, such as the rockabilly and retro scenes, where enthusiasts embrace vintage fashion, music, and lifestyles inspired by the mid-20th century. These subcultures celebrate the aesthetics and ethos of the pin-up era, keeping its legacy alive and relevant in contemporary contexts.

Pin-up art is more than a collection of pretty pictures; it is a cultural phenomenon that has left an indelible mark on art, media, and society. Its journey from the walls of soldiers' barracks to the digital age of social media reflects its adaptability and enduring charm. As we delve deeper into the history and evolution of pin-up art, we will uncover the layers of significance that make it a timeless and influential aspect of pop culture.

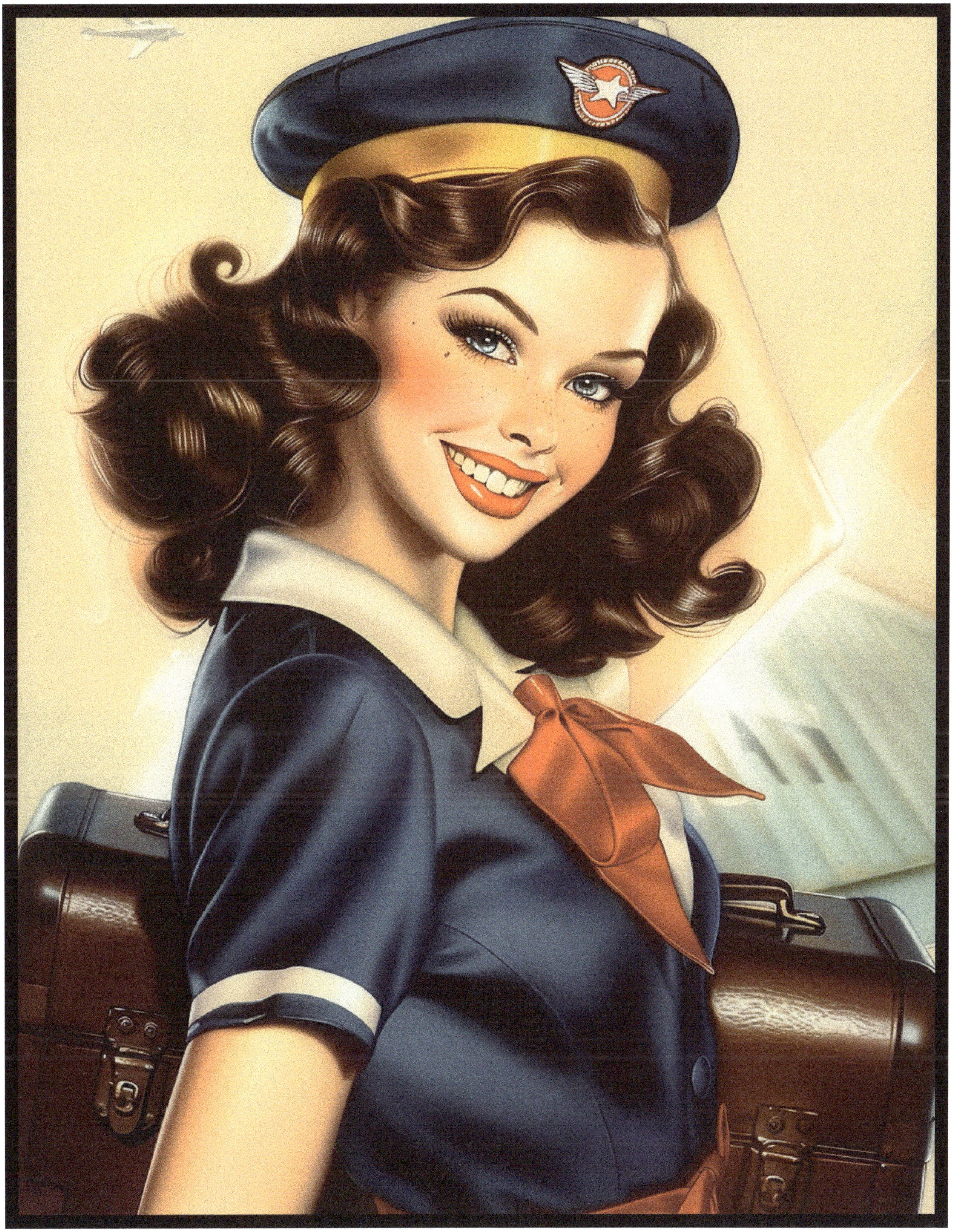

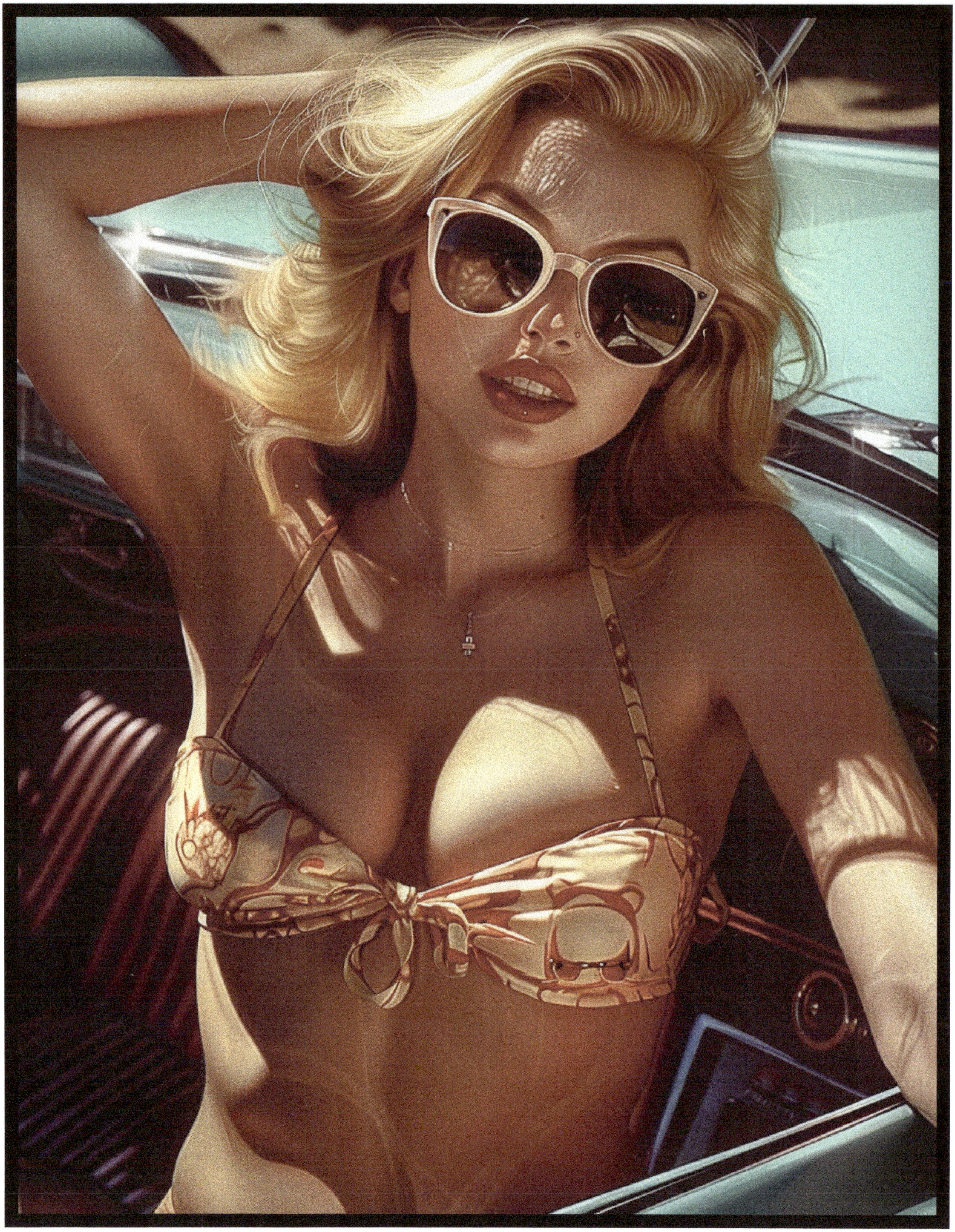

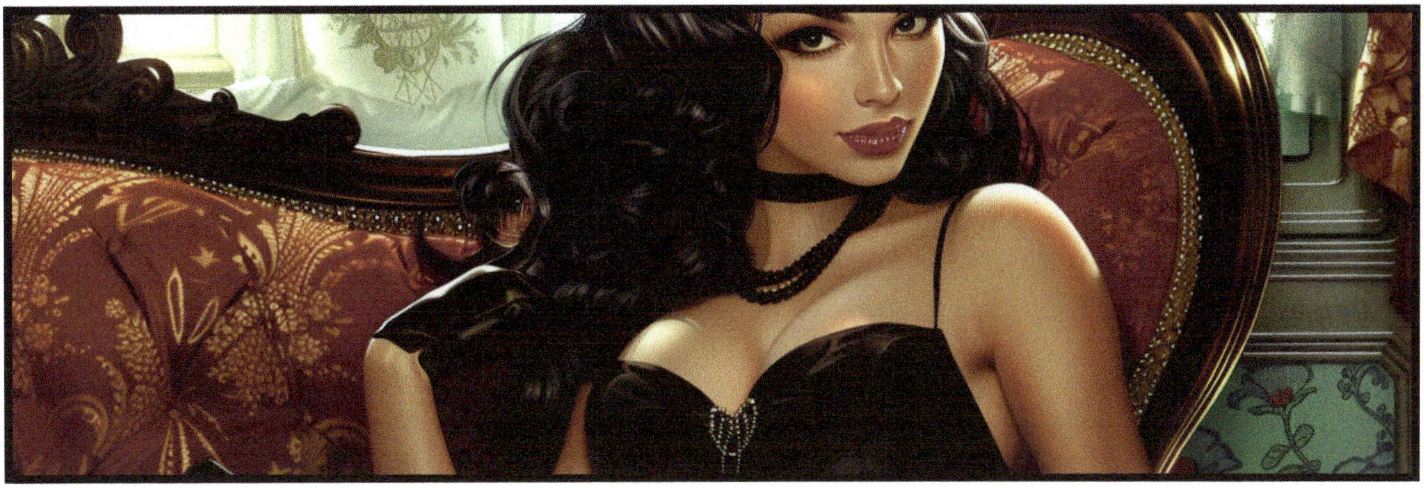

THE PSYCHOLOGY OF PIN-UPS

The allure of pin-up art has captivated audiences for decades, not merely as an aesthetic phenomenon but as a complex interplay of psychological factors that reflect and shape societal values. From the 1940s onwards, the psychology behind the fascination with pin-ups can be understood through several lenses, including human behavior, gender dynamics, and cultural symbolism.

In the 1940s, pin-up art reached a pinnacle of popularity, particularly during World War II. The psychological drive behind this surge can be linked to the concept of morale and the human need for escapism. During the war, pin-up girls served as a symbol of normalcy and hope for soldiers stationed far from home. The images provided a comforting and familiar presence, embodying the idealized version of femininity and home life that soldiers longed to return to. This use of pin-up art as a morale booster highlights the psychological principle of emotional regulation, where individuals seek out positive stimuli to counterbalance stress and anxiety.

Pin-ups during this era were imbued with a sense of idealism and aspiration. The women depicted were often portrayed in playful, confident, and glamorous poses, representing an ideal that transcended the everyday hardships of wartime. This aligns with the psychological concept of idealized self-images, where people are drawn to representations of what they aspire to be or what they admire. Pin-up girls epitomized a perfect blend of beauty, charm, and confidence, creating an aspirational figure that both men and women could admire.

The 1950s saw the continuation of pin-up popularity, but with shifts in its psychological underpinnings as society moved towards peacetime and economic prosperity. In this decade, the pin-up girl became a symbol of the American

Dream. She represented not only physical beauty but also the ideals of domestic bliss and consumer culture. The post-war boom brought about a renewed focus on traditional gender roles, with an emphasis on women as homemakers. Pin-up art of the 1950s often depicted women in domestic settings, elegantly dressed and exuding happiness and contentment. This reflected societal norms and reinforced the psychological drive for stability and order in a rapidly changing world.

The psychology of pin-ups also includes a more complex layer of gender dynamics and power. The depiction of women in pin-up art has always walked a fine line between empowerment and objectification. On one hand, the confident and assertive poses of pin-up girls can be seen as a celebration of female agency and sexuality. These images provided a space where women could express their femininity and allure in a manner that was bold and unapologetic. This aspect of pin-up art aligns with the psychological concept of self-expression and identity formation.

On the other hand, pin-up art has been criticized for perpetuating unrealistic beauty standards and objectifying women. The idealized and often exaggerated portrayals of women in pin-ups can contribute to societal pressures on women to conform to certain physical ideals. This reflects the psychological phenomenon of social comparison, where individuals measure their own worth against the images they see in media. The impact of these comparisons can lead to issues of self-esteem and body image, particularly among women who feel they cannot meet these idealized standards.

The 1960s and 1970s brought about significant cultural shifts, including the sexual revolution and the rise of feminist movements. These changes also influenced the psychology of pin-up art. The liberation movements challenged traditional gender roles and called for greater sexual freedom and equality. Pin-up art during this period began to reflect more diverse and nuanced portrayals of women. The images became more varied in style and context, sometimes embracing a rawer, more candid approach. This evolution mirrors the psychological drive for authenticity and individuality, as society moved away from rigid norms and towards greater personal freedom and expression.

In contemporary times, the psychology of pin-up art continues to evolve. The neo-pin-up movement celebrates body positivity and diversity, challenging traditional beauty standards and embracing a wider range of body types and identities. This shift reflects a broader cultural and psychological trend towards inclusivity and self-acceptance. Modern pin-up art often seeks to empower rather than objectify, focusing on themes of confidence, strength, and individuality. The psychological impact of this evolution is significant, as it fosters a more inclusive and supportive environment for people to appreciate and engage with pin-up art.

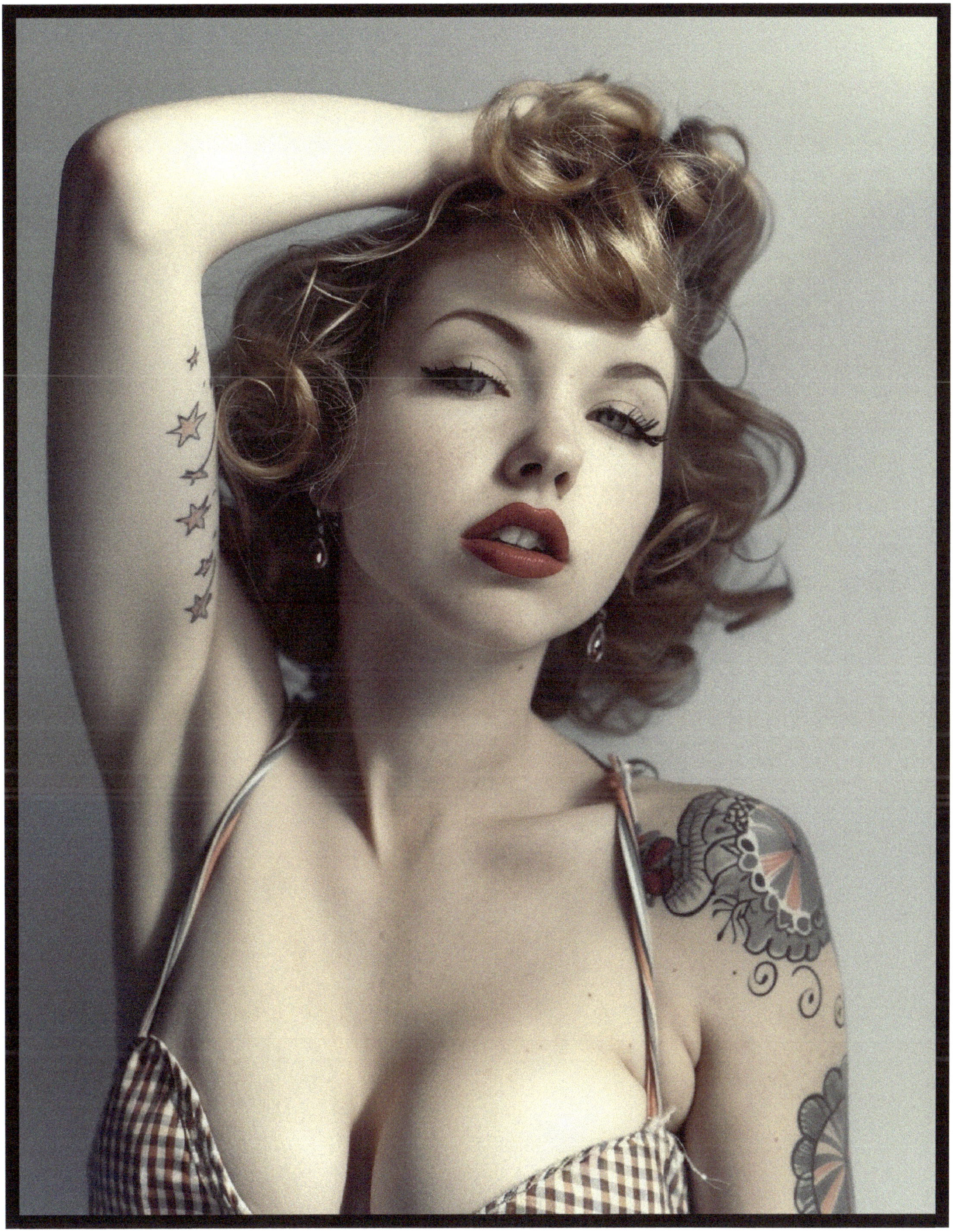

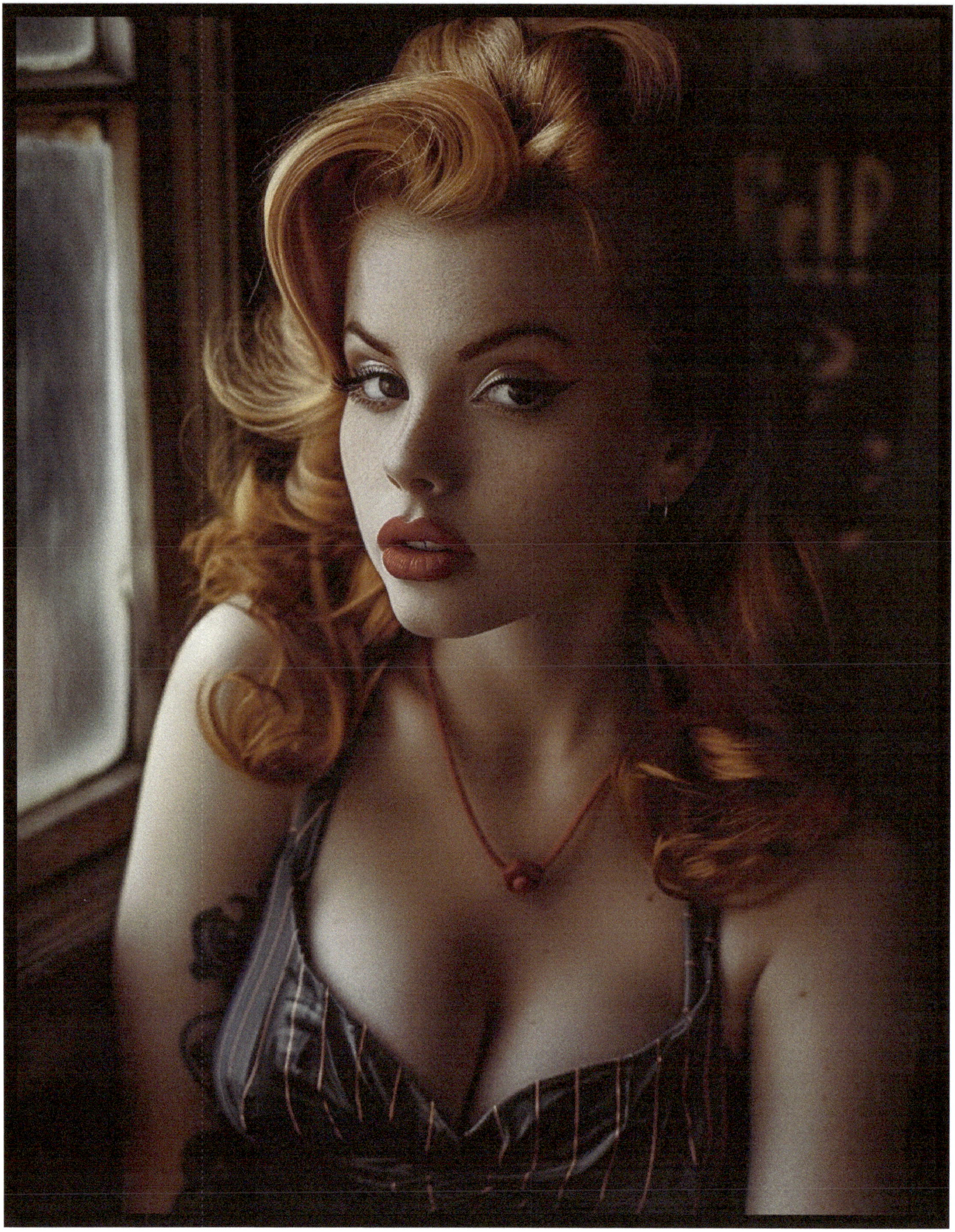

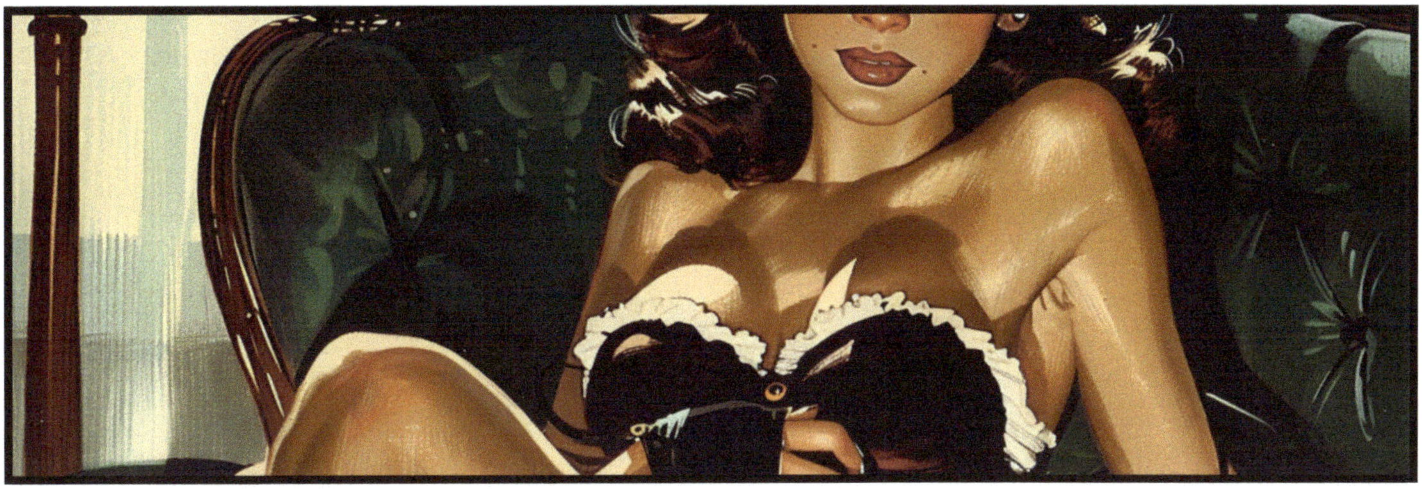

FEMINISM AND MISOGYNY

Pin-up images have been both celebrated and criticized, reflecting broader societal tensions around gender roles, sexuality, and power dynamics. This chapter explores how pin-up art intersects with feminist ideals and the ways in which it has been seen as both empowering and objectifying women.

Pin-up art emerged in a time when traditional gender roles were dominant, and women's primary societal roles were often limited to domestic spheres. In this context, pin-up images, which typically depicted women in flirtatious, confident, and often scantily clad poses, could be seen as a form of rebellion against these restrictive norms. For some, these images represented a celebration of female beauty and sexuality, allowing women to assert their desirability and confidence in a way that was both public and unapologetic.

From a feminist perspective, the idea of women taking control of their own image and embracing their sexuality can be seen as a form of empowerment. This aligns with the concept of bodily autonomy and the right of women to express their sexuality on their own terms. The confident poses and playful expressions of pin-up girls challenged the notion that women's bodies should be hidden or controlled, instead presenting a bold declaration of feminine allure and independence.

However, the celebration of pin-up art within feminist circles is not without controversy. Critics argue that pin-up images often perpetuate unrealistic and narrow standards of beauty, focusing on an idealized, often unattainable version of femininity. This can contribute to a culture of objectification, where women are valued primarily for their physical appearance rather than their abilities or character. The emphasis on youth, slimness, and conventional beauty traits in pin-up art reflects and reinforces societal pressures on women to conform to specific aesthetic standards, which can have damaging effects on self-esteem and body image.

The commercial and often male-dominated context in which pin-up art flourished raises questions about agency and exploitation. Many of the most famous pin-up images were created by male artists for predominantly male audiences, particularly during the 1940s and 1950s. In this light, pin-up art can be seen as catering to male fantasies and reinforcing a patriarchal view of women as objects of desire. This perspective aligns with feminist critiques of the male gaze, which argues that women are often portrayed in ways that satisfy male viewers' desires rather than reflecting women's own experiences and perspectives.

The duality of pin-up art—its potential for both empowerment and objectification—reflects broader societal tensions around gender and power. On one hand, pin-up images can be seen as empowering when women reclaim them and use them as a tool for self-expression and confidence. Modern interpretations of pin-up art, which often celebrate diverse body types and challenge traditional beauty norms, can be empowering by promoting body positivity and inclusivity.

On the other hand, the historical context and pervasive influence of the male gaze in pin-up art cannot be ignored. The objectification inherent in many traditional pin-up images underscores the ways in which women's bodies have been commodified and controlled within a patriarchal society. This tension is at the heart of feminist critiques of pin-up art, highlighting the need to critically examine the power dynamics and cultural messages embedded in these images.

The feminist reclamation of pin-up art in contemporary times offers a way to navigate this complex terrain. By embracing pin-up imagery while also challenging its traditional constraints, modern feminists can transform it into a vehicle for empowerment and self-acceptance. This involves recognizing and celebrating the historical significance of pin-up art while also pushing for greater diversity and representation in its portrayals of women.

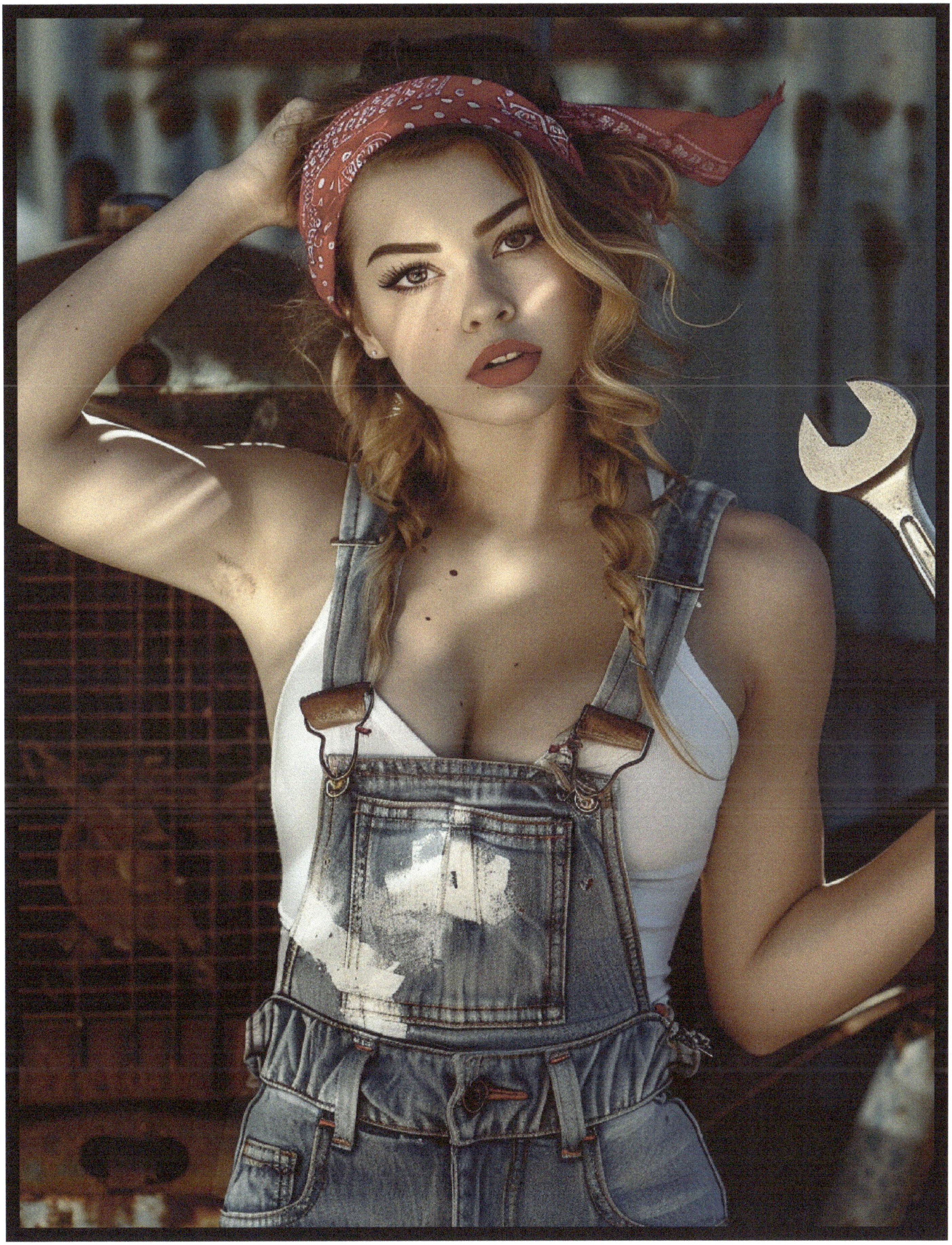

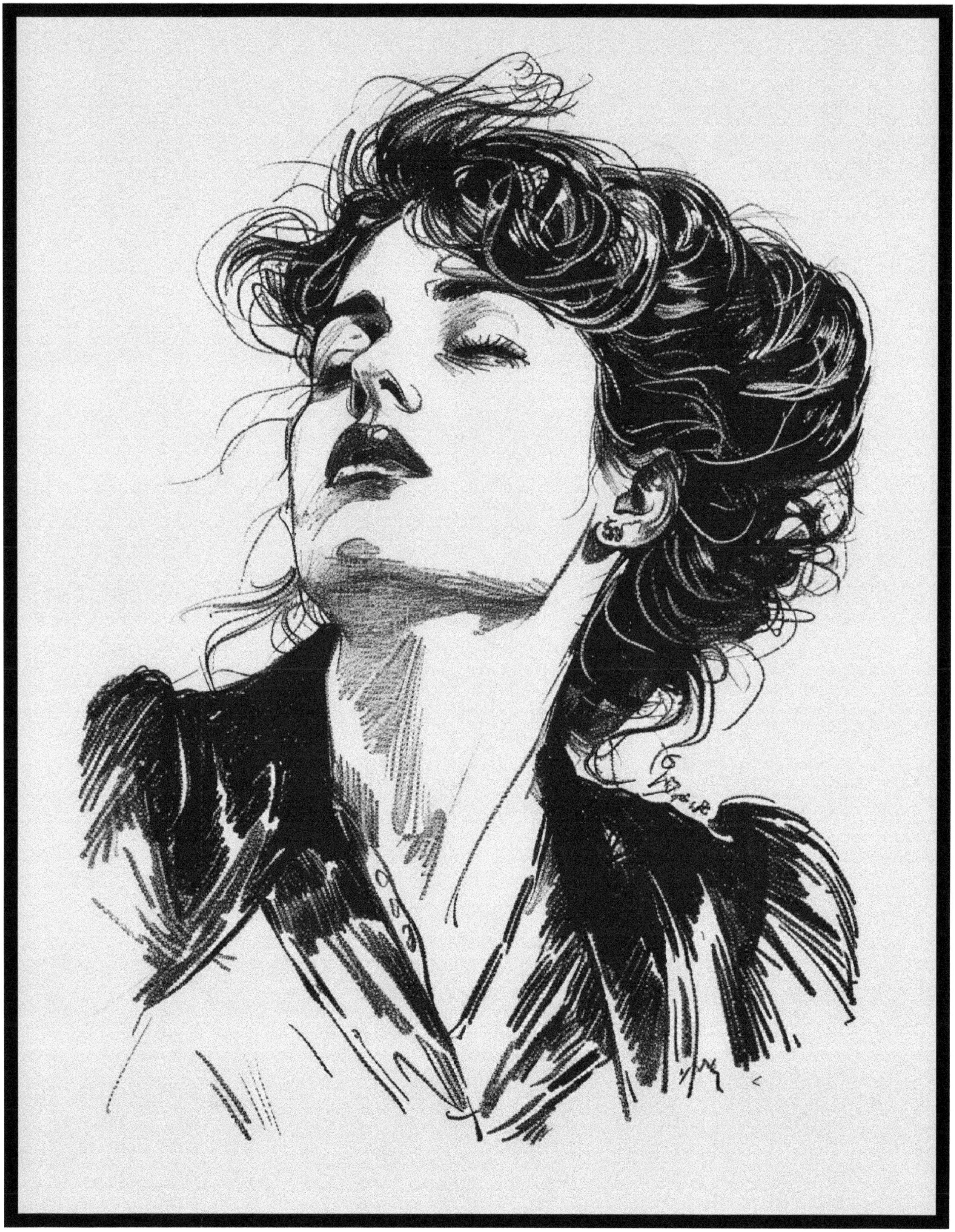

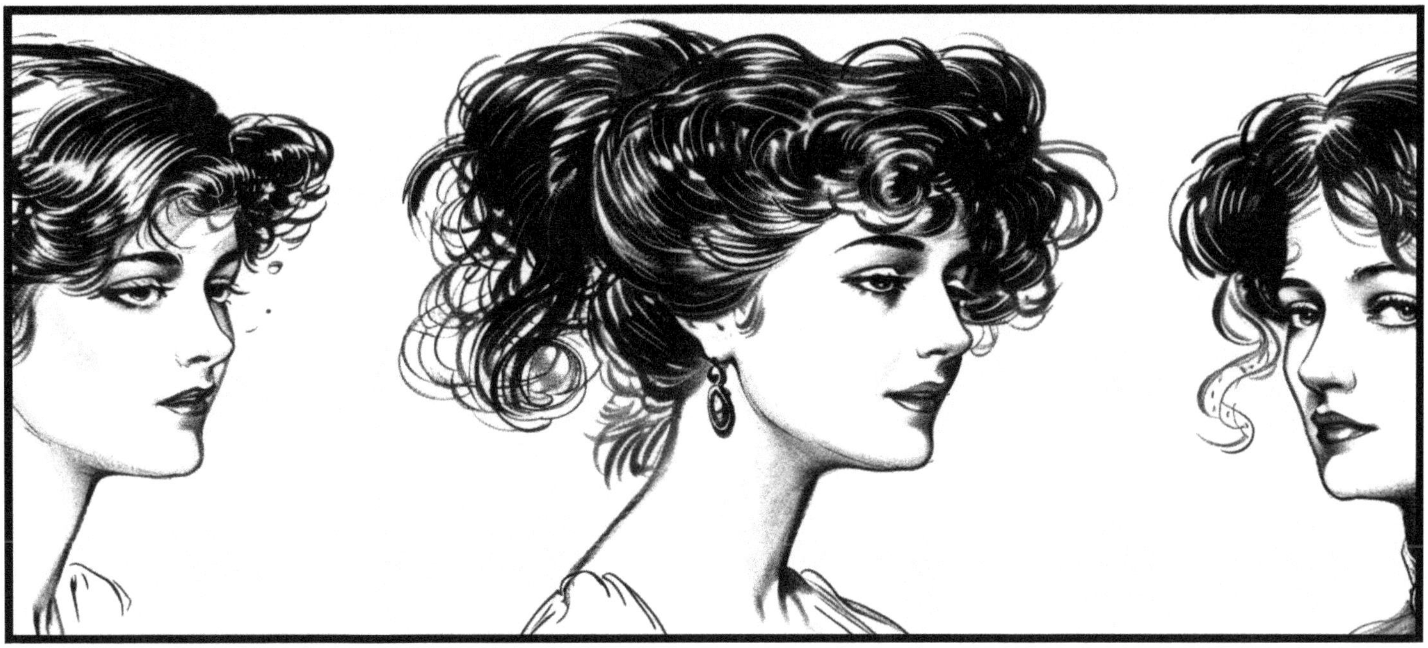

EARLY INFLUENCES

The origins of pin-up art can be traced back to various influences and artistic movements that predate its emergence as a distinct genre. Understanding these early influences provides a foundation for appreciating how pin-up art evolved into a cultural phenomenon.

One of the earliest precursors to pin-up art can be found in the artistic tradition of the Gibson Girl, created by illustrator Charles Dana Gibson in the late 19th and early 20th centuries. The Gibson Girl was an idealized depiction of the American woman, characterized by her poise, beauty, and independence. She became a cultural icon, representing the new woman of the era who was both fashionable and assertive. The popularity of the Gibson Girl set the stage for the visual style and societal fascination with idealized female forms that would later define pin-up art.

The development of printing technology during this period allowed for the mass production and widespread dissemination of images. Advances in color lithography and offset printing made it possible to produce high-quality reproductions of artwork and photographs, bringing images of beautiful women into the public domain. This technological progress enabled the creation of affordable, visually appealing pin-up images that could be easily distributed and displayed.

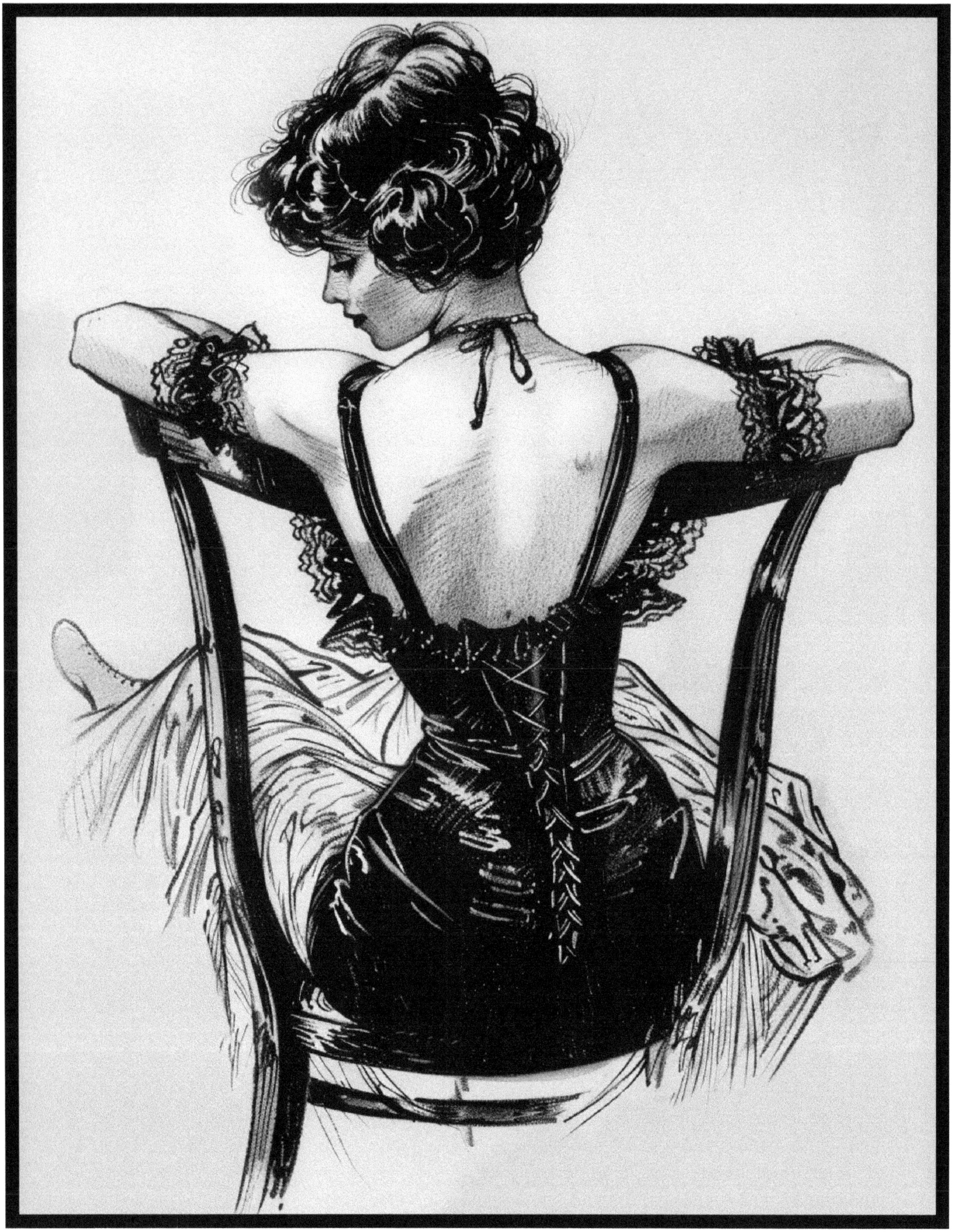

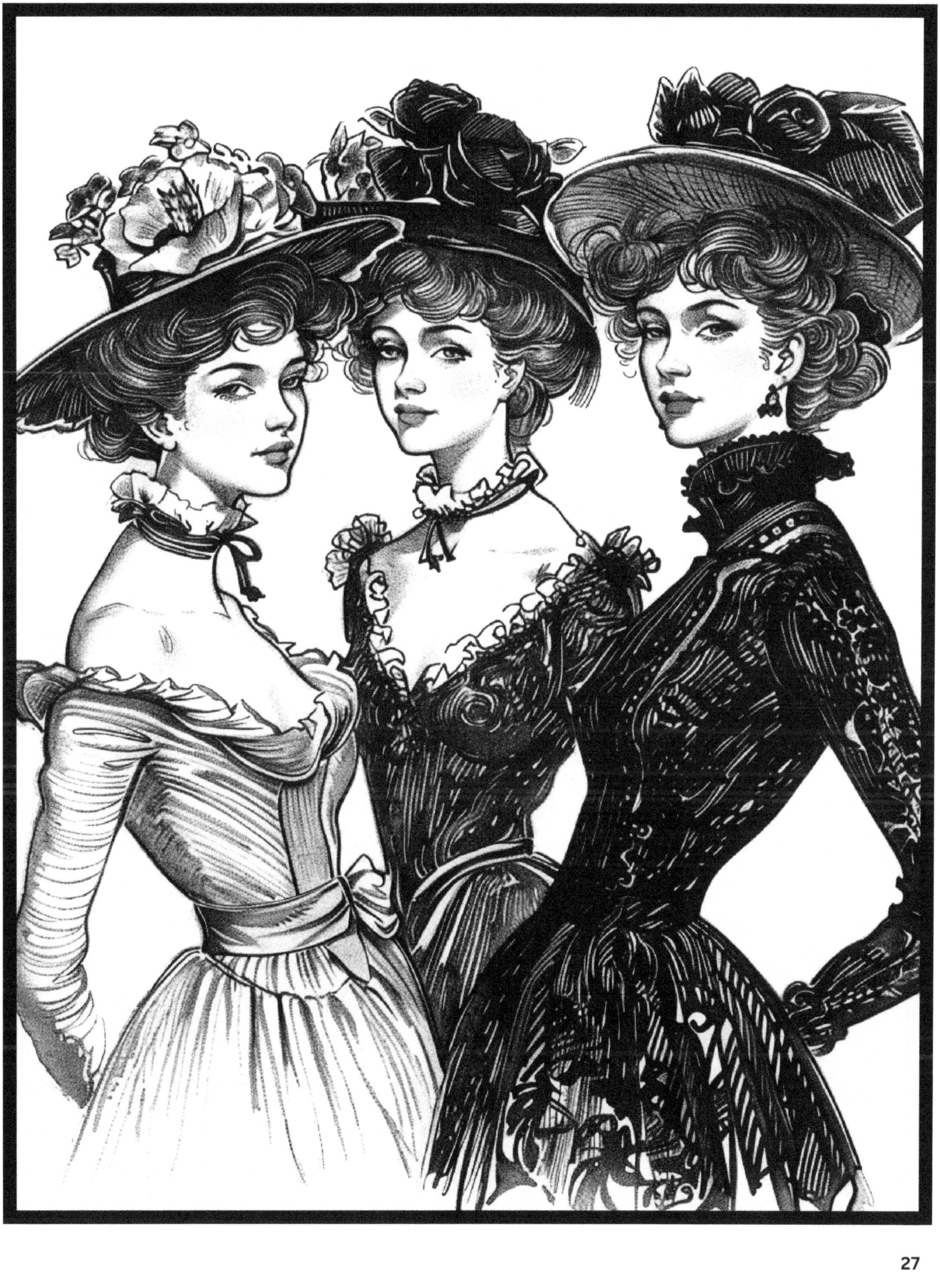

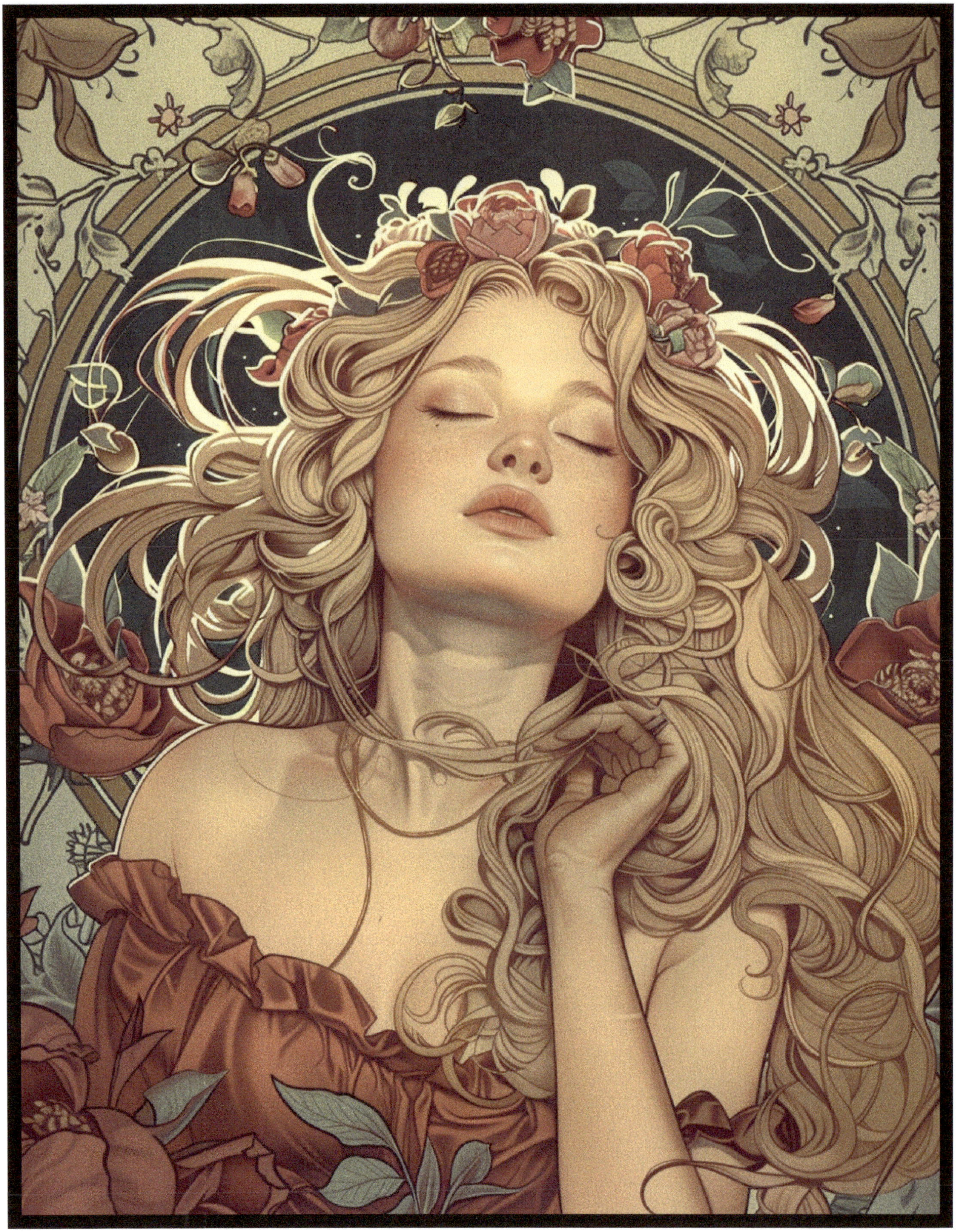

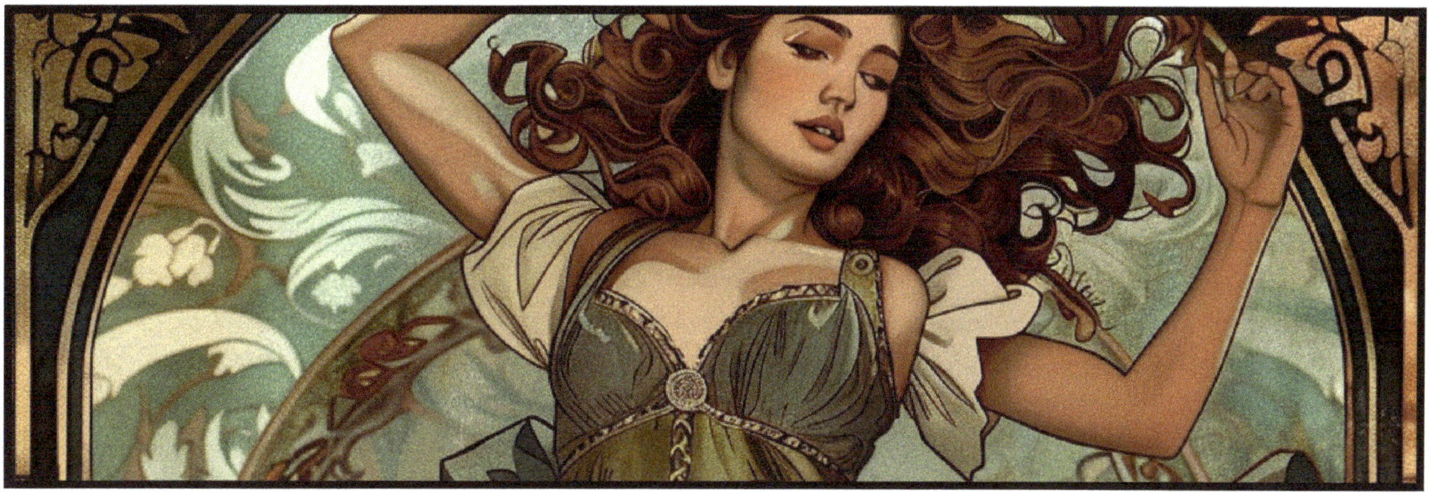

THE BIRTH OF PIN-UP: 1890-1910

In the late 19th century, the concept of the pin-up began to take shape through the work of illustrators and artists who created idealized images of women for mass consumption. One of the most notable early figures in this movement was Charles Dana Gibson, whose creation of the "Gibson Girl" in the 1890s captured the imagination of the public. The Gibson Girl was depicted as a tall, elegant, and self-assured woman, embodying the ideal of American femininity. Her image appeared in magazines, advertisements, and postcards, becoming one of the first widely recognized examples of pin-up art. Gibson's illustrations set a precedent for the portrayal of women as both glamorous and aspirational figures.

Another significant influence during this time was the Art Nouveau movement, which flourished between 1890 and 1910. Art Nouveau emphasized decorative arts, organic forms, and intricate details, often featuring women in graceful, flowing poses. Artists like Alphonse Mucha became renowned for their posters and advertisements that showcased women as ethereal and captivating figures. Mucha's work, characterized by its elaborate designs and sensual depictions, contributed to the visual language that would later define pin-up art. His posters for theatrical productions, commercial products, and calendars often featured women as the central focus, celebrating their beauty and allure.

The turn of the 20th century also witnessed significant advancements in printing technology, which played a crucial role in the proliferation of pin-up imagery. The development of color lithography and offset printing made it possible to produce high-quality, full-color illustrations and photographs in large quantities. This technological progress allowed for the mass distribution of pin-up images, making them accessible to a broader audience. Magazines, postcards, and calendars featuring attractive women became popular, bringing pin-up art into homes and workplaces.

The early 1900s also saw the rise of illustrated magazines and pulp fiction, which frequently included images of beautiful women on their covers to attract readers. These publications, such as "The Saturday Evening Post" and "Cosmopolitan," featured cover art by prominent illustrators like J.C. Leyendecker and Howard Chandler Christy. Christy's "Christy Girl," much like the Gibson Girl, became a symbol of contemporary beauty and sophistication. These cover illustrations further cemented the popularity of pin-up art and its role in shaping public perceptions of femininity.

In addition to commercial and decorative art, early cinema began to influence the development of pin-up imagery. Silent film actresses like Theda Bara and Clara Bow became early sex symbols, with their publicity photos often circulating as pin-up images. These actresses embodied the allure and mystique that would become hallmarks of pin-up art, capturing the attention of audiences and contributing to the genre's growing appeal.

The cultural and social context of the 1890s to 1910s also played a significant role in the birth of pin-up art. This period was marked by significant changes in gender roles and attitudes towards sexuality. The late Victorian era's strict moral codes began to give way to more relaxed attitudes in the Edwardian period. The growing women's suffrage movement and increased participation of women in the workforce also contributed to evolving perceptions of femininity. Pin-up art, with its emphasis on confident and attractive women, both reflected and influenced these shifting societal norms.

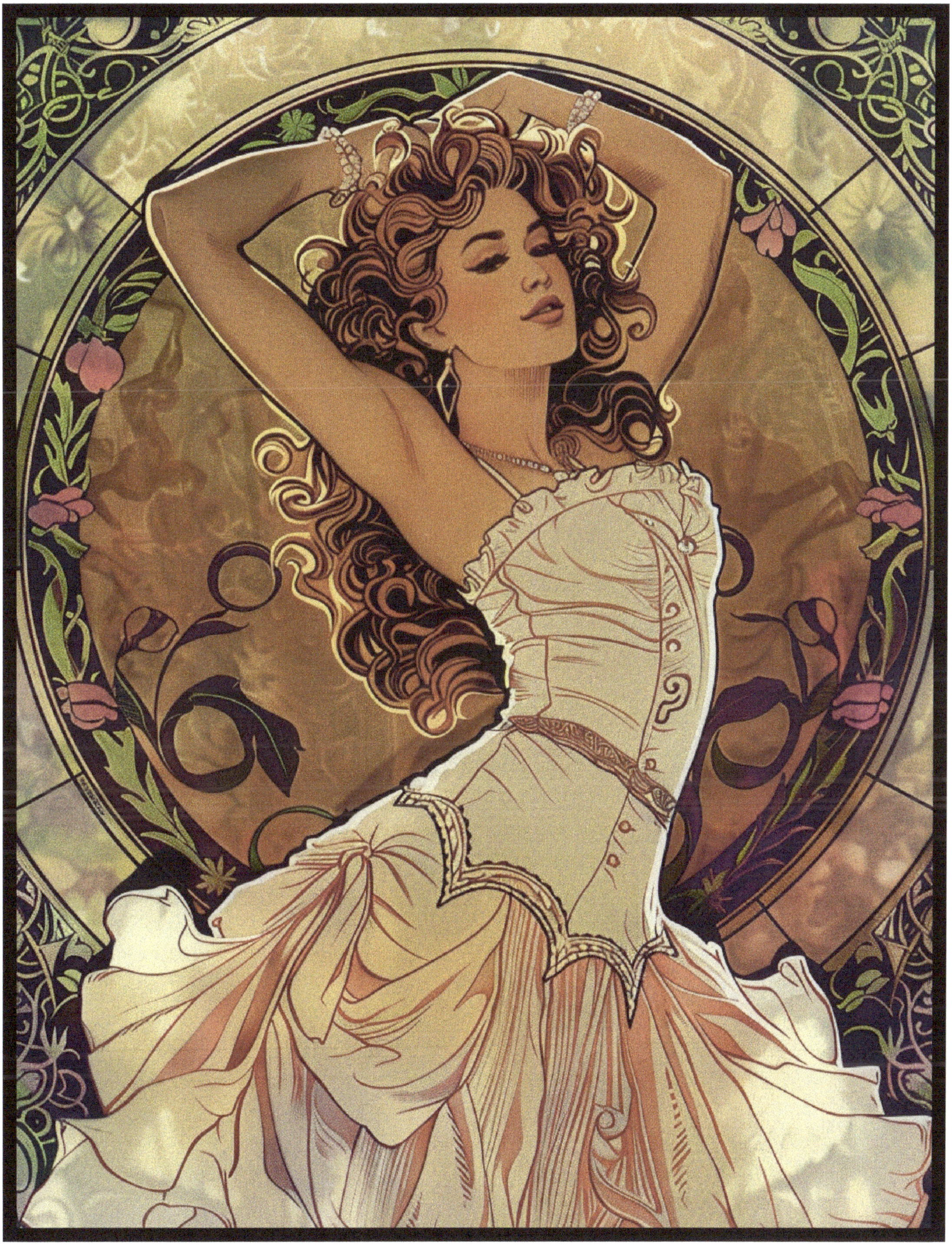

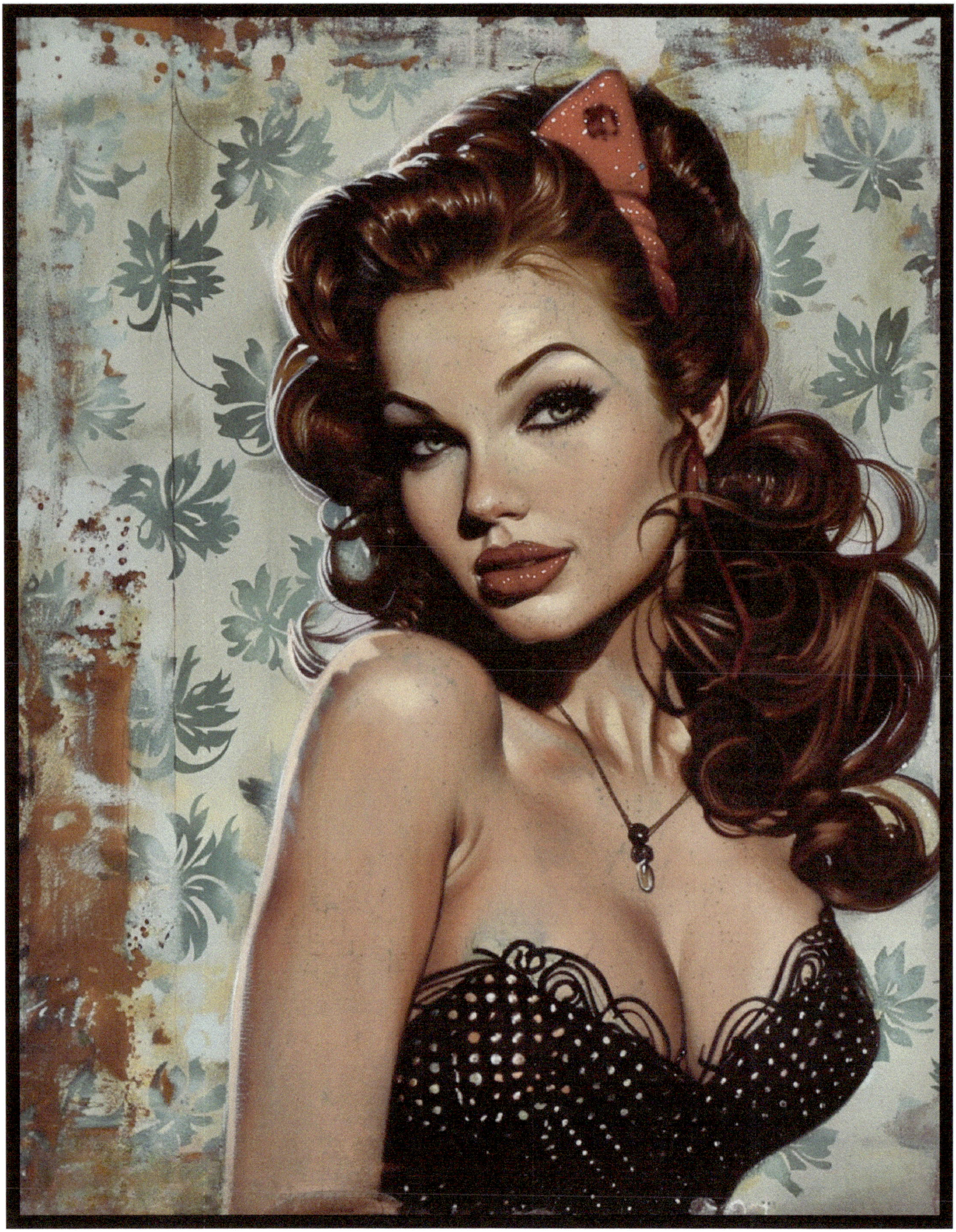

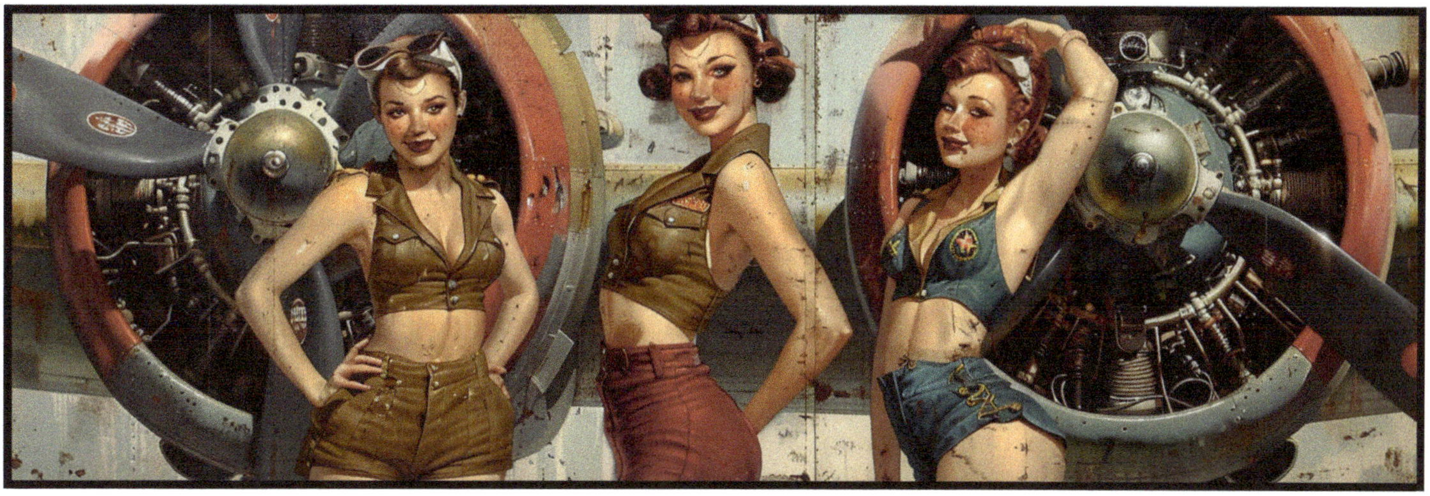

THE RISE OF PIN-UPS 1920-1940

The period from the 1920s to the 1940s, often referred to as the Golden Age of pin-up art, witnessed the genre's rise to prominence and its establishment as a significant cultural phenomenon. This era was marked by a confluence of social, technological, and artistic developments that propelled pin-up imagery into mainstream popularity.

The 1920s, known as the Roaring Twenties, was a decade of dramatic social change and cultural innovation. Following World War I, there was a sense of liberation and excitement, reflected in the flapper culture that emerged. Flappers, young women known for their bold fashion, short haircuts, and liberated attitudes, became icons of the era. Their carefree and confident personas were frequently depicted in pin-up art, embodying the spirit of modernity and rebellion against traditional norms. Artists like Russell Patterson captured the essence of the flapper in their work, creating glamorous and provocative images.

The advancements in printing technology and the growth of mass media during the 1920s also played a crucial role in the rise of pin-up art. Magazines such as "Esquire," founded in 1933, became key platforms for pin-up illustrations. Esquire featured works by renowned artists like George Petty and Alberto Vargas, whose "Petty Girls" and "Vargas Girls" became iconic representations of the idealized American woman. These images, with their sophisticated yet sensual appeal, were widely circulated and contributed significantly to the genre's popularity.

As the 1930s unfolded, the Great Depression brought about significant economic and social challenges. Despite the hardships, the demand for escapism and entertainment remained strong. Hollywood cinema, radio, and magazines provided much-needed distractions, and pin-up art flourished in this environment. The glamorous portrayals of women in pin-up art offered a form of visual escapism, allowing people to momentarily forget their troubles and indulge in fantasies of beauty and romance.

The onset of World War II in the late 1930s and early 1940s marked a turning point in the history of pin-up art. During the war, pin-up images became a powerful tool for boosting morale among troops. Pin-up girls, often featuring popular actresses and models, were used in military propaganda to provide comfort and motivation to soldiers. These images were printed on posters, postcards, and aircraft nose art, becoming a ubiquitous presence in military life. The famous Betty Grable pin-up, with her iconic over-the-shoulder pose, became one of the most recognized images of the era, symbolizing hope and resilience.

Artists like Gil Elvgren emerged during this time, bringing a distinctive style to pin-up art that combined realism with a touch of fantasy. Elvgren's work, characterized by its vibrant colors and playful compositions, captured the imagination of the public and further solidified the genre's appeal. His illustrations often depicted women in dynamic poses, exuding confidence and charm, and became synonymous with the pin-up aesthetic of the 1940s.

The Golden Age of pin-up art also saw the genre's integration into various forms of media and advertising. Pin-up images were used to sell a wide range of products, from household goods to automobiles, leveraging their appeal to capture consumer attention. This commercialization of pin-up art helped to cement its place in popular culture and contributed to its enduring legacy.

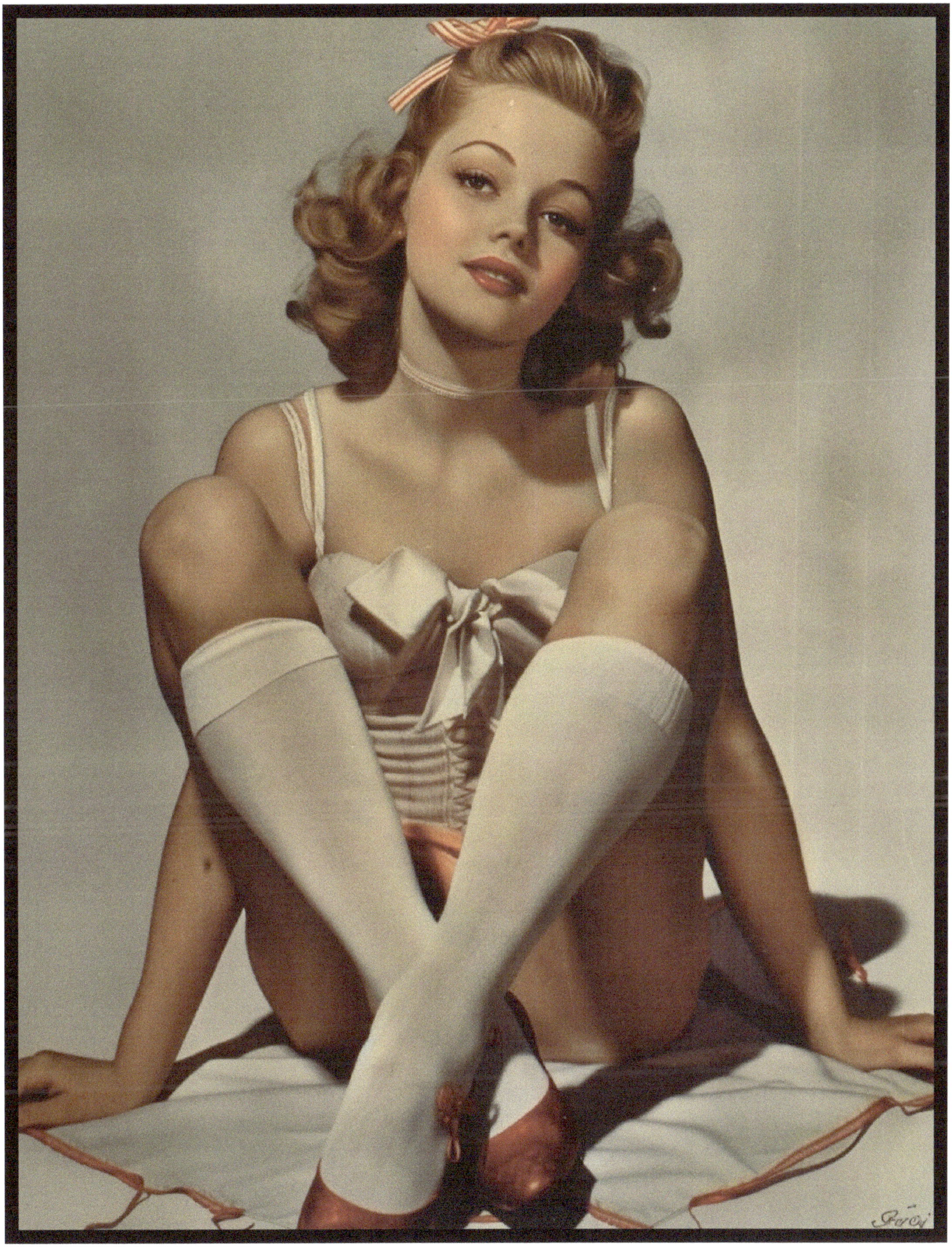

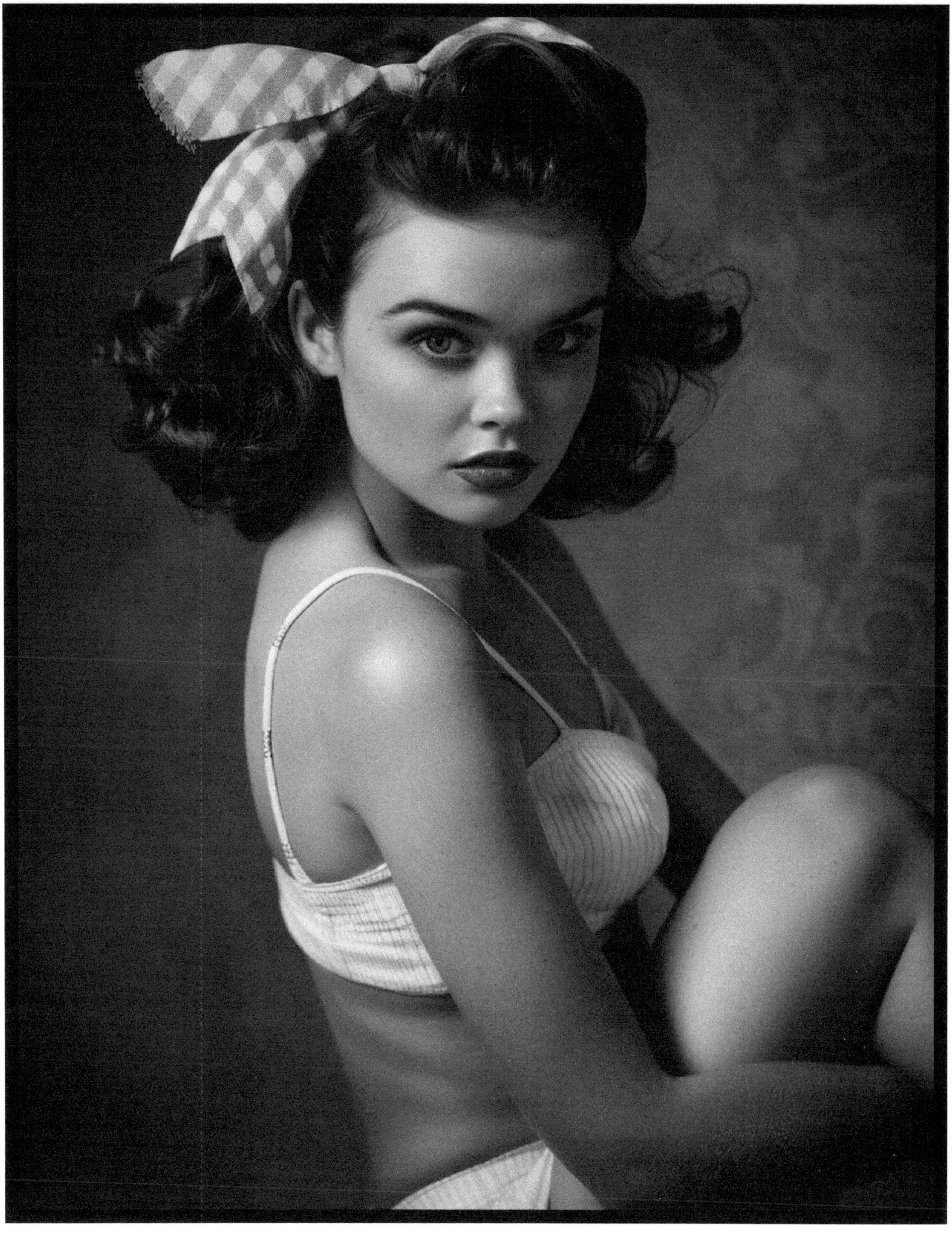

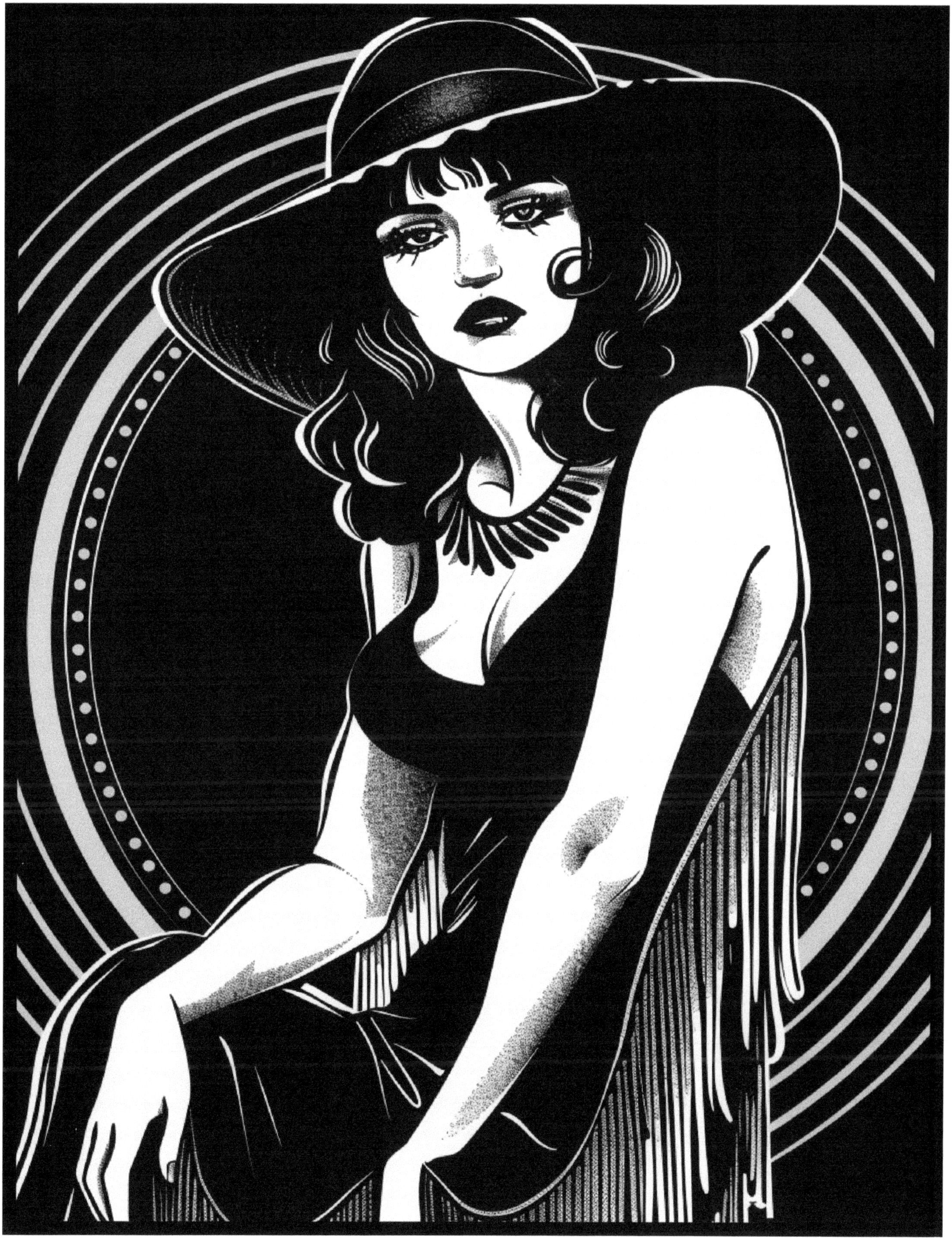

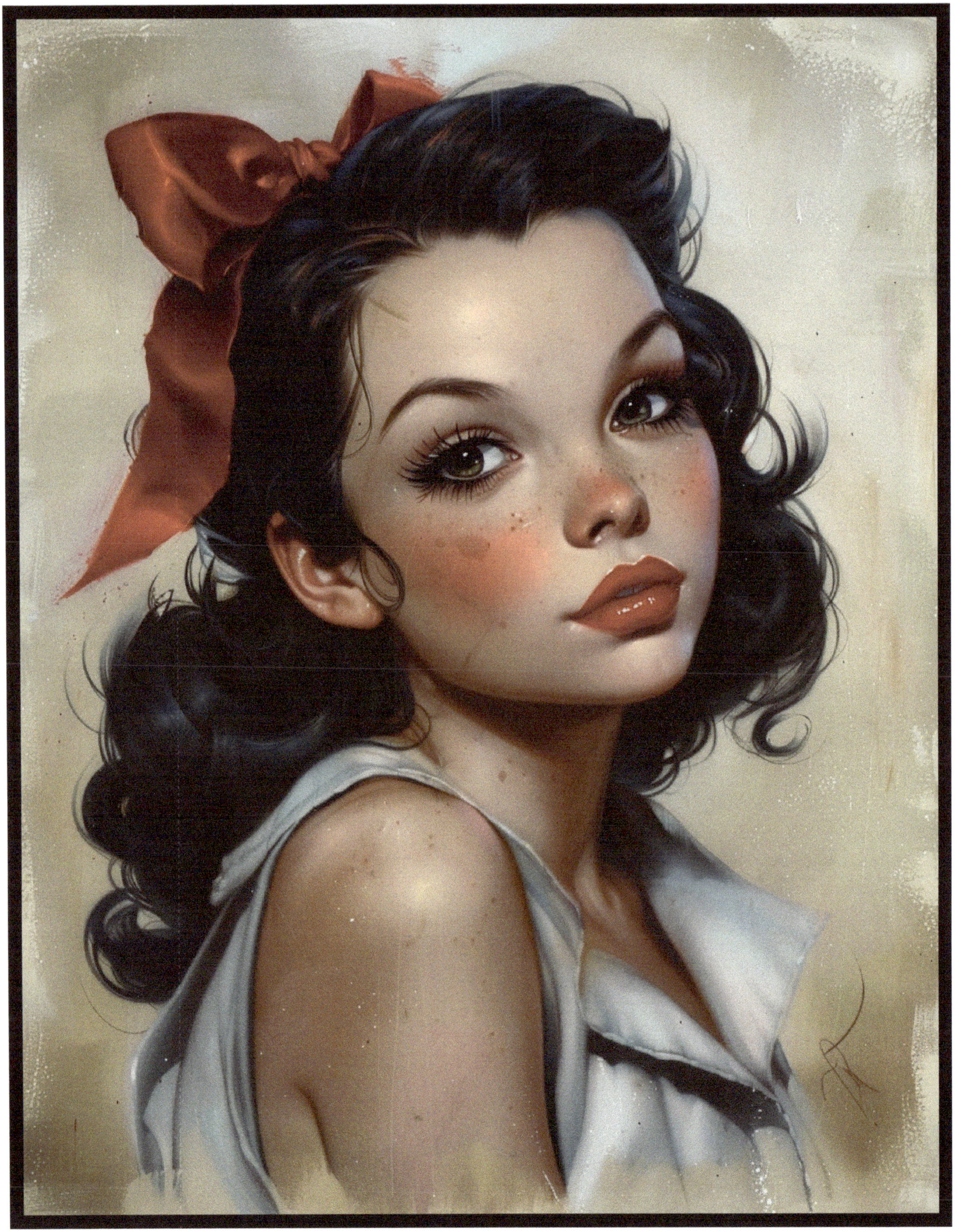

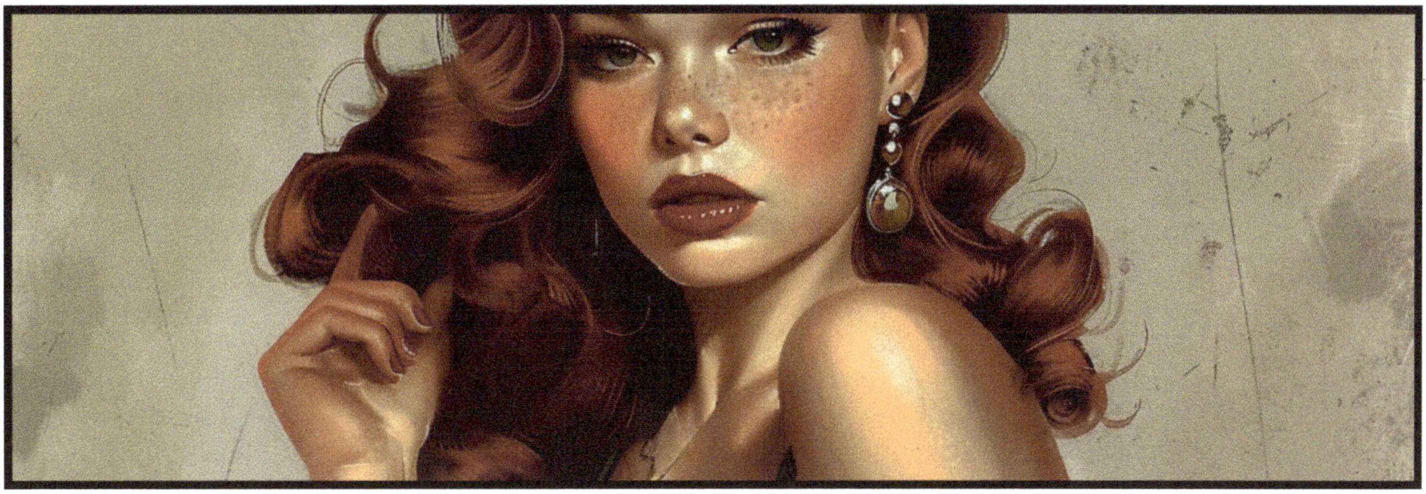

THE ROARING TWENTIES

The Roaring Twenties, a decade marked by dramatic social, economic, and cultural change, played a significant role in shaping the development of pin-up art. This era, characterized by its spirit of liberation and modernity, provided fertile ground for the rise of pin-up imagery, which reflected the shifting attitudes and aesthetics of the time.

The post-World War I period brought about a sense of newfound freedom and optimism. The war's end led to economic prosperity in many parts of the world, particularly in the United States. This economic boom facilitated a cultural renaissance, as people sought to enjoy life and embrace new forms of entertainment and self-expression. The Roaring Twenties saw the proliferation of jazz music, dance halls, and speakeasies, all of which contributed to a vibrant and dynamic social scene.

Central to the cultural shifts of the 1920s was the emergence of the flapper, a new archetype of modern womanhood. Flappers were young women who defied traditional expectations by adopting bold fashions, bobbed haircuts, and a carefree attitude. They embraced behaviors previously deemed inappropriate for women, such as smoking, drinking, and dancing provocatively. The flapper's image was one of independence and rebellion, challenging the established norms of femininity.

Pin-up art of the 1920s often featured flappers, capturing their spirit and style. Artists depicted these modern women in glamorous and playful poses, highlighting their fashionable attire and confident demeanor. The flapper's image in pin-up art was not only a celebration of beauty but also a symbol of the changing roles and perceptions of women in society. These images resonated with a generation eager to break free from the constraints of the past and embrace a more liberated and progressive lifestyle.

The advancements in mass media and advertising during the 1920s also played a crucial role in the spread of pin-up art. The rise of illustrated magazines and advertisements provided new platforms for artists to showcase their work. Publications like "The Saturday Evening Post" and "Life" magazine featured cover art and illustrations that often included attractive, stylish women. These images were widely circulated, reaching a broad audience and solidifying the popularity of the pin-up aesthetic.

Technological innovations in printing allowed for the production of high-quality color images, making pin-up art more accessible and visually appealing. The ability to reproduce vibrant, eye-catching illustrations contributed to the genre's commercial success. Advertisers quickly recognized the appeal of pin-up imagery and used it to market a variety of products, from cosmetics to automobiles. This commercialization of pin-up art helped to integrate it into everyday life and popular culture.

The influence of Hollywood also cannot be overstated. The 1920s saw the rise of the film industry and the creation of the first major movie stars. Actresses like Clara Bow, known as the "It Girl," embodied the flapper persona on screen and off. Their promotional photos and film stills often served as pin-up images, further blurring the lines between celebrity culture and pin-up art. The glamorous and alluring depictions of these actresses captivated audiences and reinforced the association between pin-up imagery and modern femininity.

The Roaring Twenties also saw pin-up art begin to explore themes of sexuality and desire more openly. The decade's liberal attitudes towards sex and relationships were reflected in the more provocative and suggestive poses found in pin-up illustrations. This exploration of sexuality was a departure from the more conservative portrayals of women in earlier art, signaling a shift towards a more open and expressive approach to female beauty and allure.

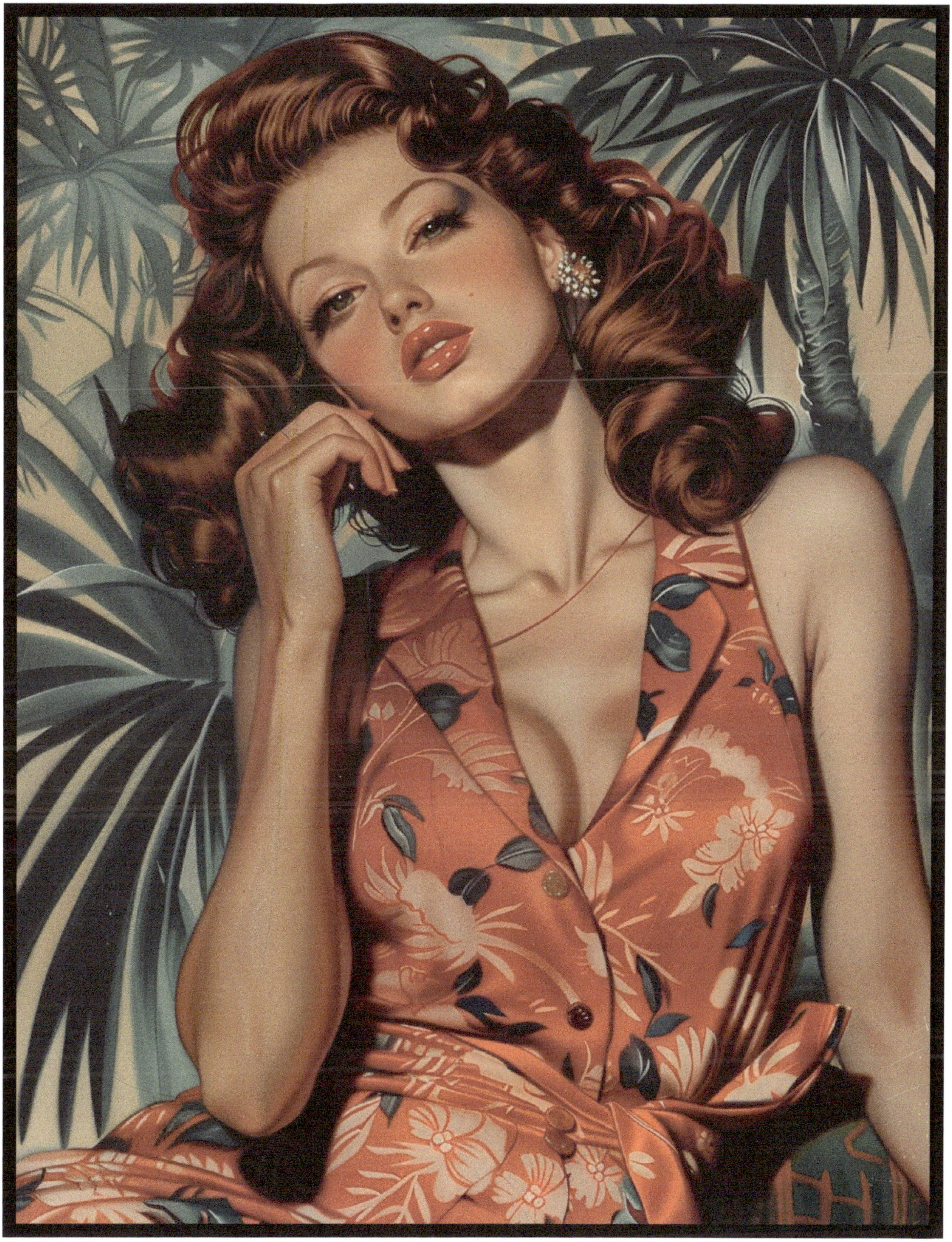

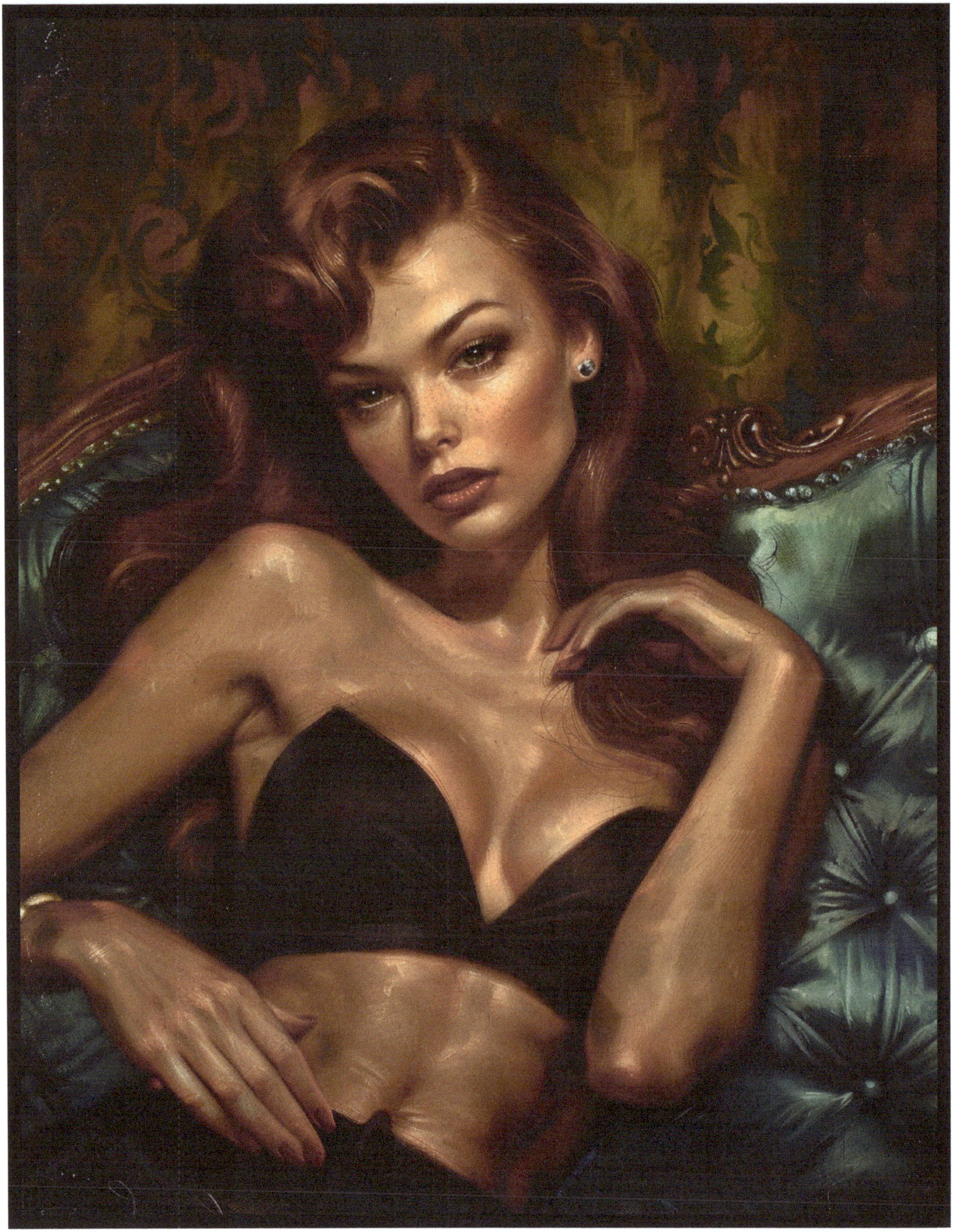

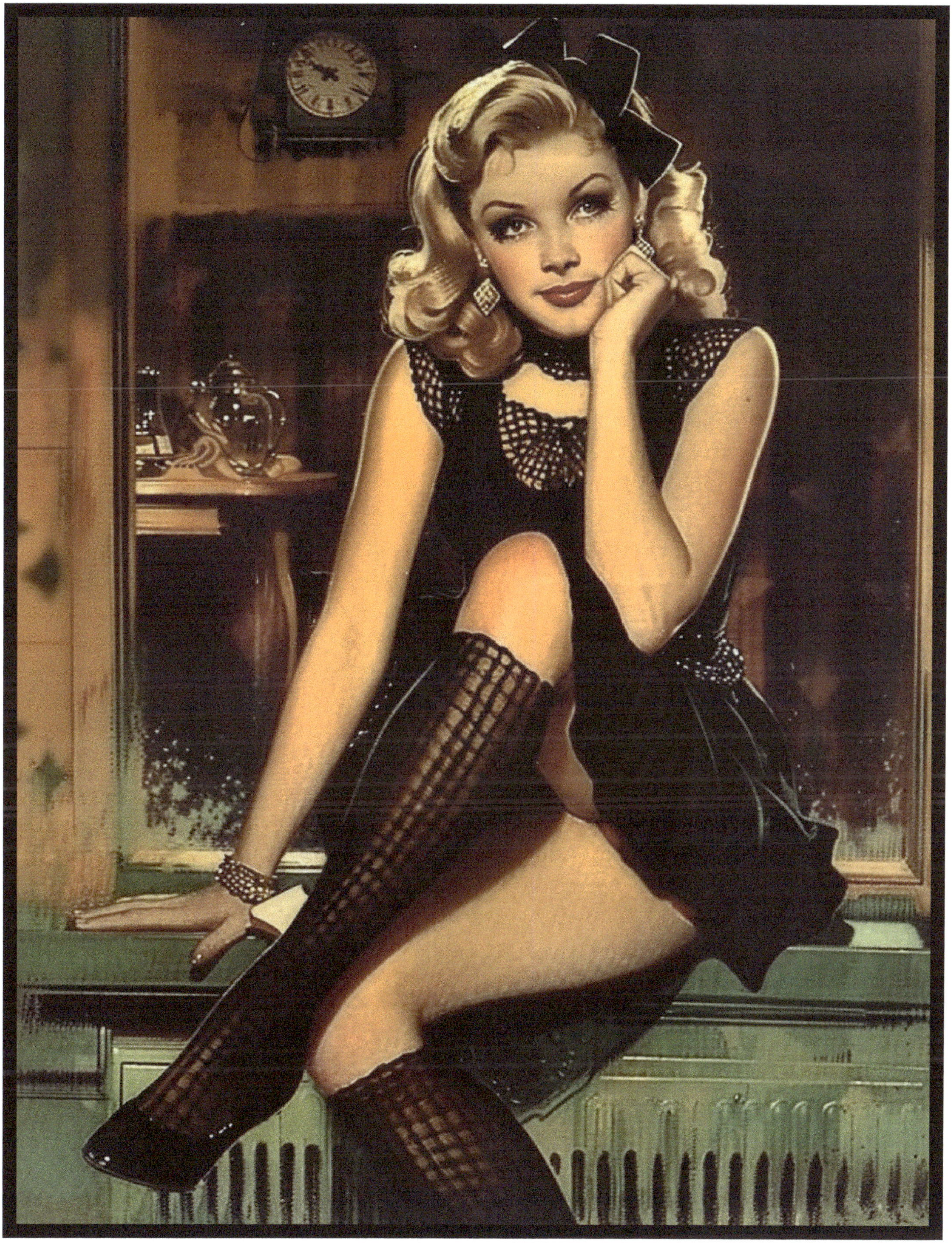

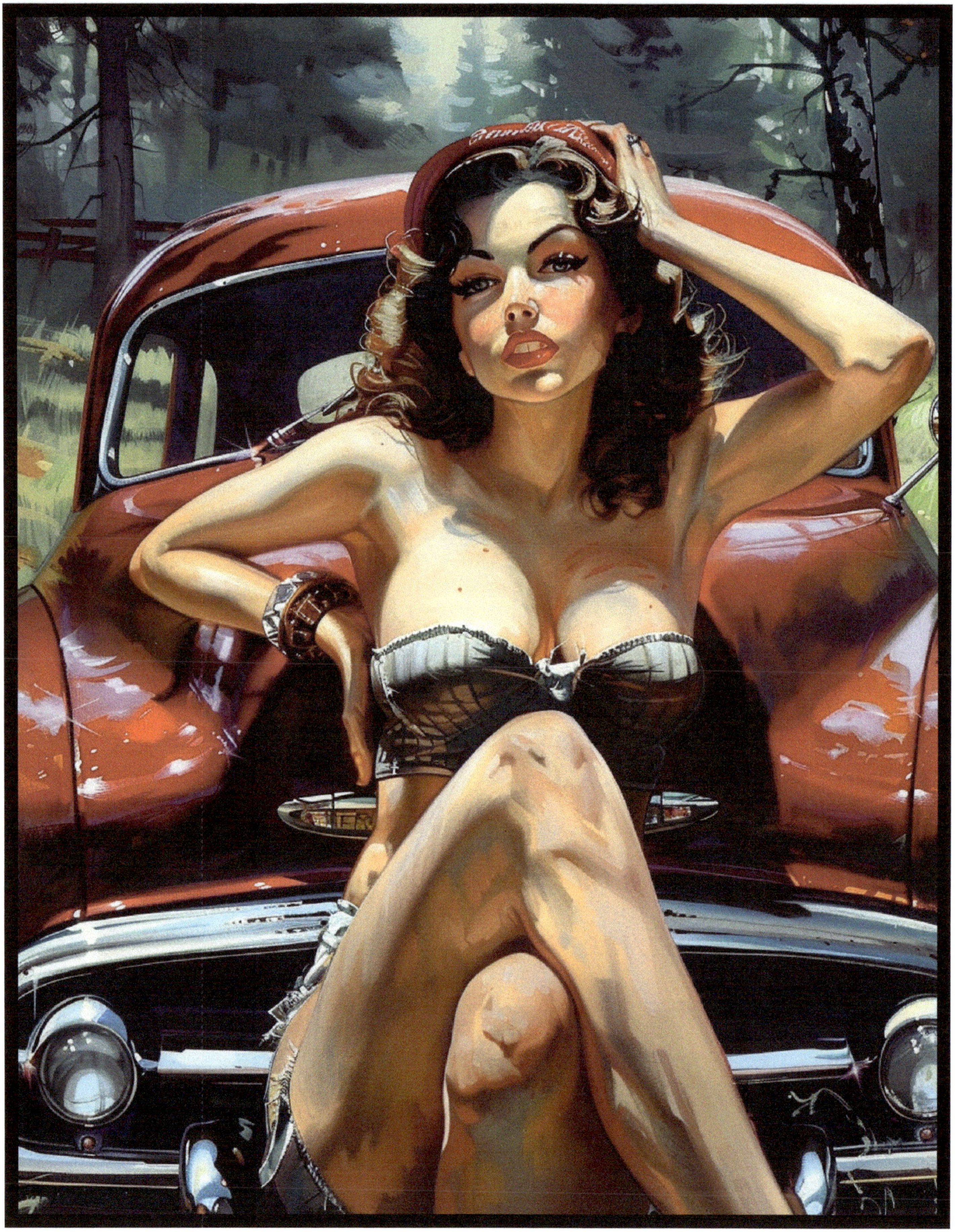

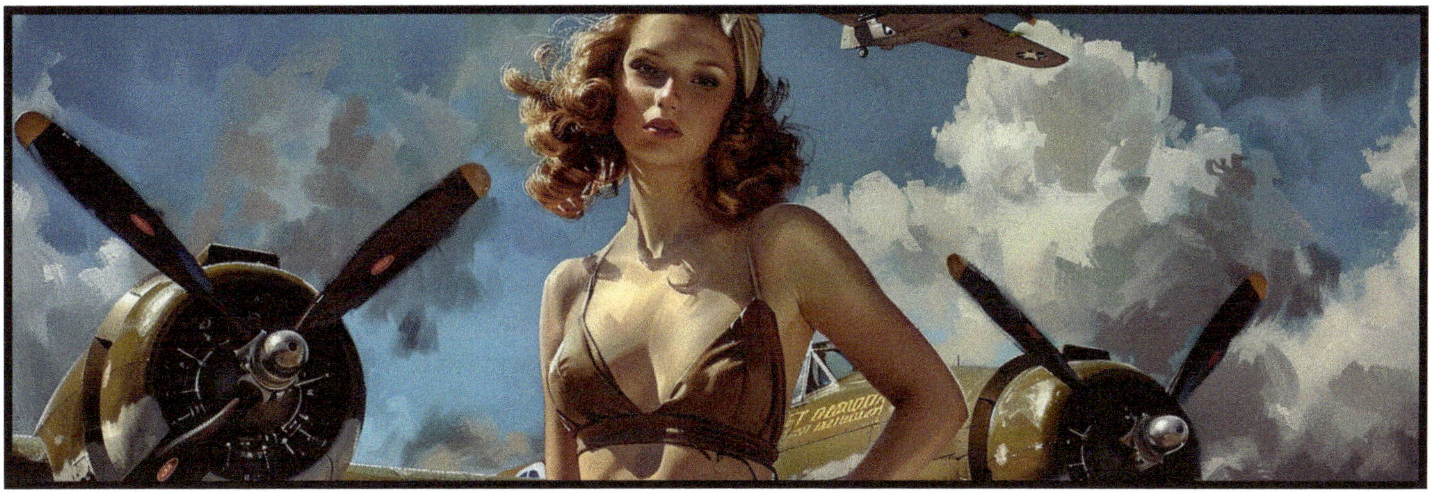

WORLD WAR II AND PIN-UP GIRLS

World War II was a pivotal period for pin-up art, cementing its place in popular culture and significantly expanding its influence. During this time, pin-up girls became more than just images of beauty; they served as vital tools for boosting morale among soldiers and symbolized hope, resilience, and the ideals of the American way of life.

As the United States entered World War II in 1941, the need to maintain high morale among the troops became paramount. Pin-up girls played a crucial role in this effort. These images were often carried by soldiers, hung in barracks, and painted on the noses of aircraft. The pin-up girls of this era were more than mere decorations; they were symbols of what soldiers were fighting for—home, comfort, and the American ideals of freedom and happiness.

One of the most iconic pin-up images of the war was Betty Grable's famous pose in a white swimsuit, looking over her shoulder. This photograph became one of the most popular pin-ups among American soldiers and is often cited as the quintessential image of wartime pin-ups. Grable's wholesome yet alluring image provided a sense of normalcy and an emotional connection to life back home, making it a powerful morale booster.

Artists like Alberto Vargas and Gil Elvgren were instrumental in defining the look of the wartime pin-up. Vargas, who worked for Esquire magazine, created the "Vargas Girls," which became hugely popular among servicemen. His illustrations, known for their sophisticated and glamorous style, often featured women in playful and seductive poses, dressed in military-themed outfits or patriotic attire. These images were both a celebration of female beauty and a nod to the soldiers' bravery and patriotism.

Gil Elvgren, another prominent pin-up artist, contributed to the genre with his vibrant and dynamic illustrations. Elvgren's work often depicted women in everyday situations, with a twist of humor and fantasy. His pin-up girls exuded confidence and charm, embodying the spirit of the American woman as resilient and optimistic. Elvgren's images, widely distributed in calendars and advertisements, became synonymous with the pin-up aesthetic of the 1940s.

The widespread use of pin-up images during the war was also facilitated by the US government's recognition of their value as morale-boosting tools. The government distributed pin-up posters and postcards as part of its propaganda efforts, ensuring that these images reached as many soldiers as possible. The Office of War Information even commissioned artists to create pin-up art that could be used in recruitment posters and other wartime materials.

Pin-up girls also appeared in various other forms of media during the war. They were featured in magazines, advertisements, and comic books, further ingraining their presence in American culture. Publications like Yank, a magazine produced for the military, regularly included pin-up sections, making them accessible to soldiers around the world. These images were often accompanied by articles and letters from home, creating a sense of connection and camaraderie among the troops.

The influence of Hollywood continued to play a significant role in the popularity of pin-up girls during World War II. Actresses like Rita Hayworth, Veronica Lake, and Lana Turner became beloved pin-up icons, their images widely circulated among servicemen. These actresses often posed for promotional photos specifically intended for the troops, combining their star power with patriotic themes to inspire and uplift.

The legacy of World War II pin-up girls extends beyond their role in boosting morale. They also contributed to the evolving perceptions of women in society. While the images often emphasized traditional notions of beauty and femininity, they also showcased women in empowering and active roles. The wartime pin-up girl was not just a passive object of desire; she was a symbol of strength, resilience, and optimism in the face of adversity.

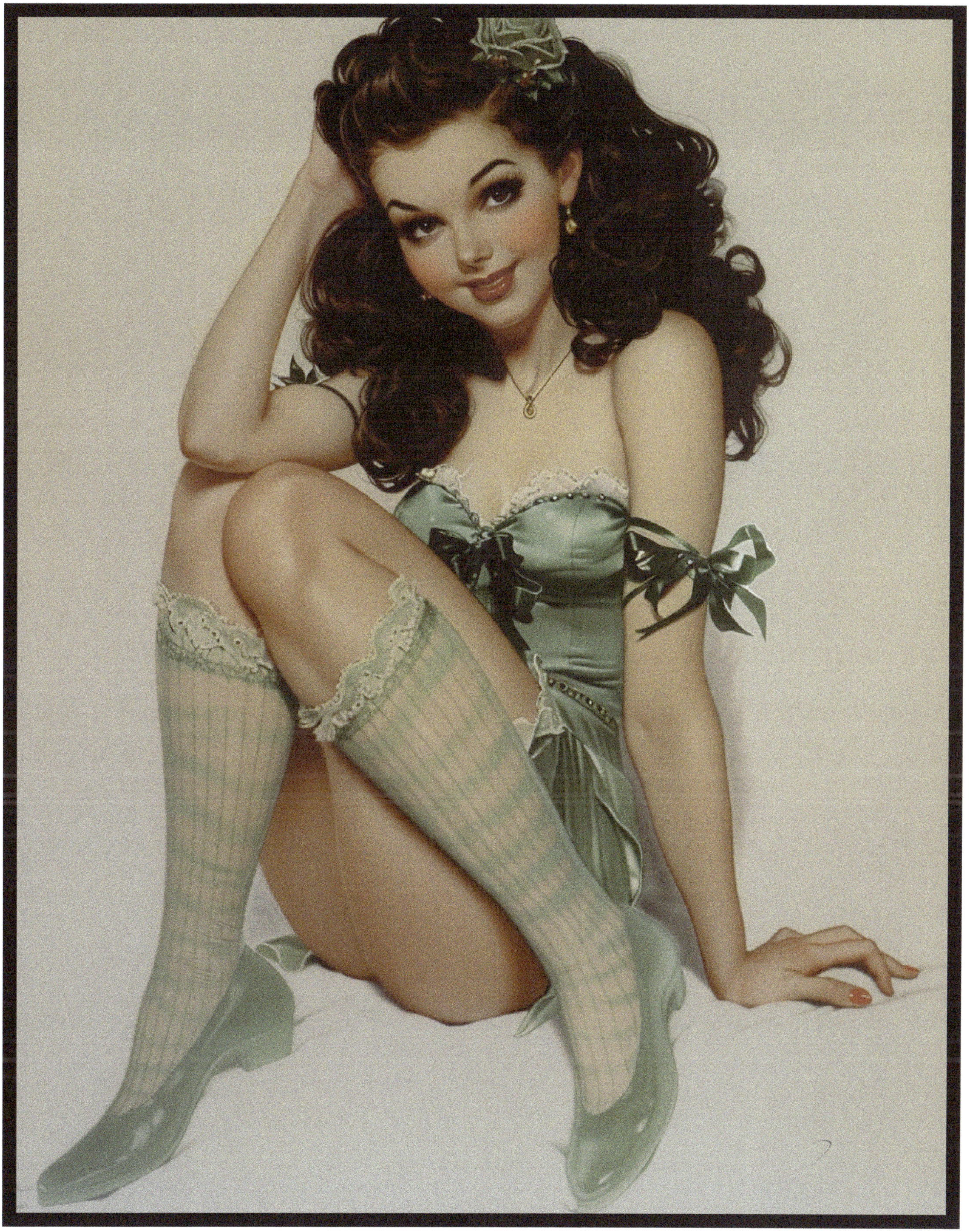

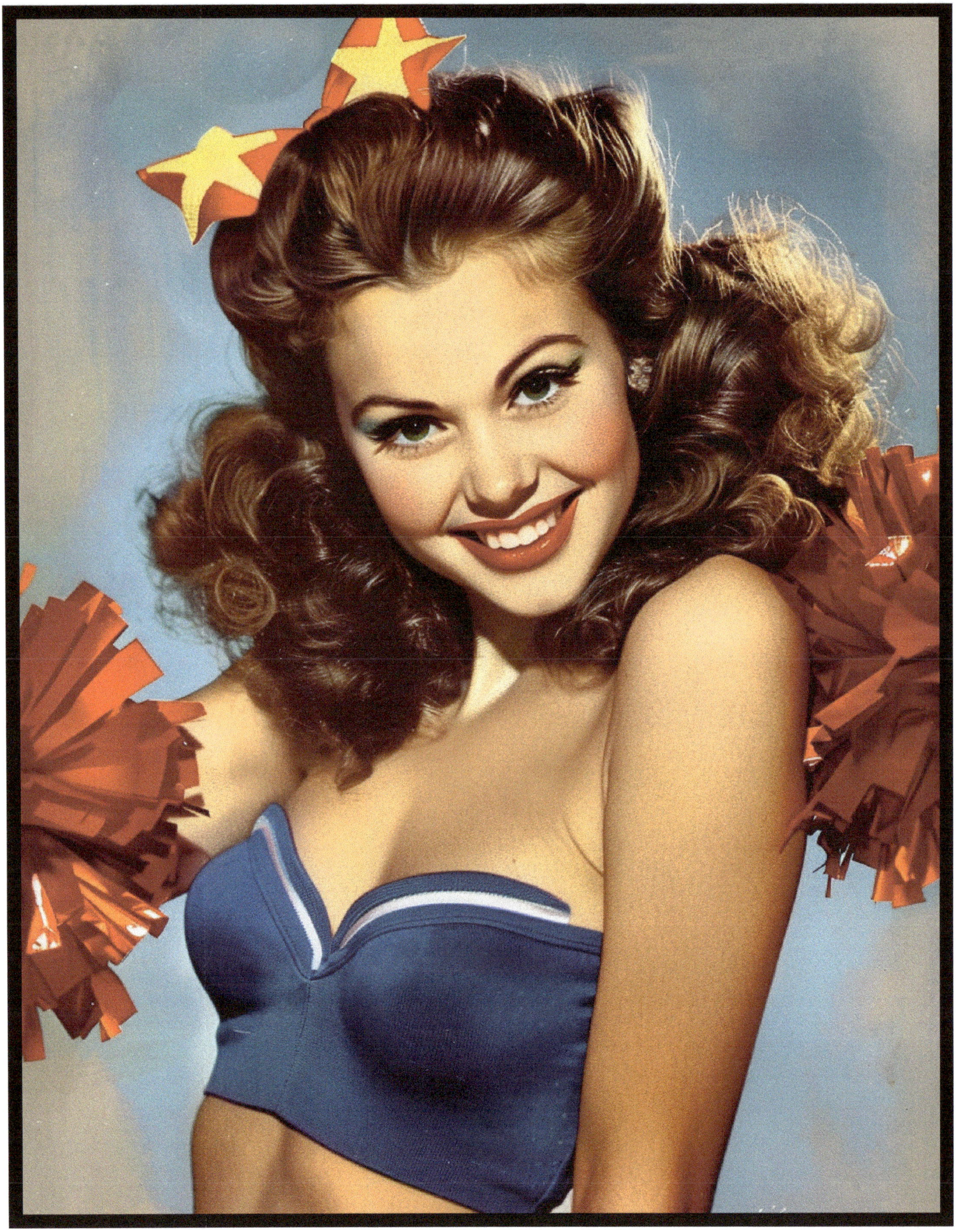

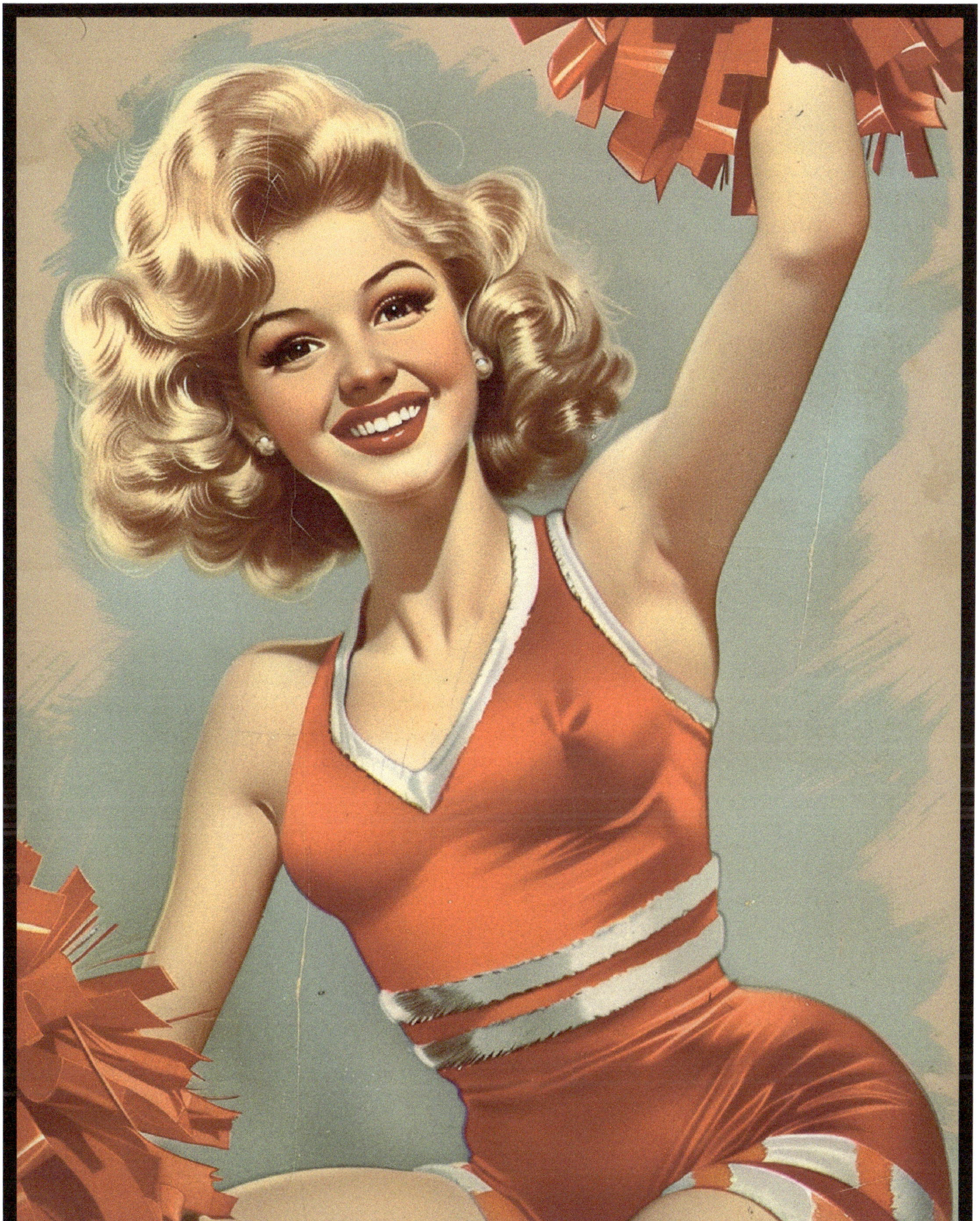

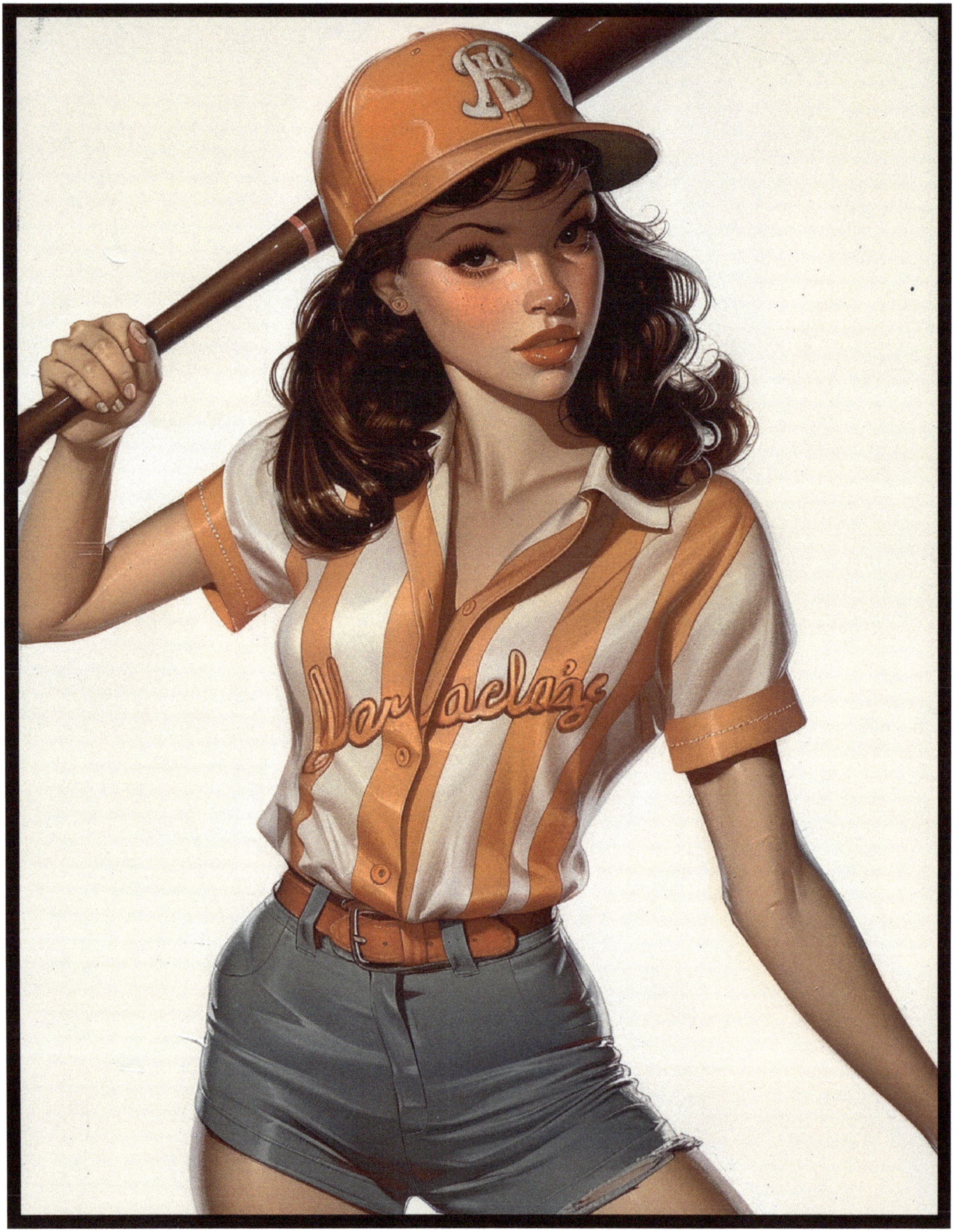

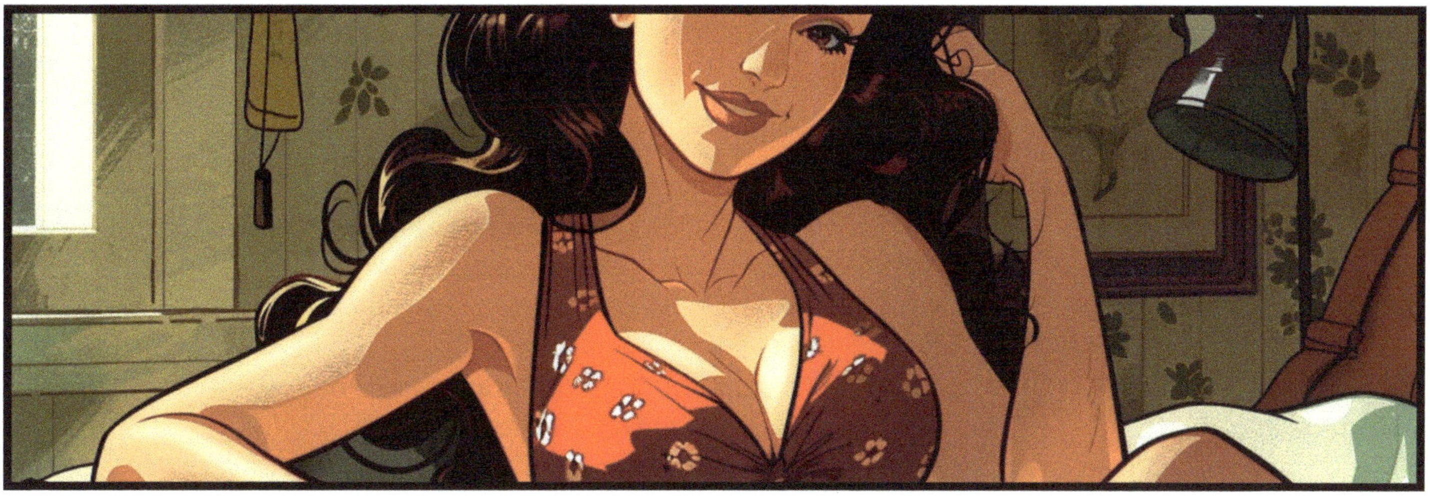

THE BOOM OF PIN-UP: 1950S

The post-war era of the 1950s marked a significant boom in pin-up culture, driven by economic prosperity and cultural shifts that followed World War II. This decade saw the pin-up genre reach new heights of popularity and influence, with the images of glamorous and alluring women becoming an integral part of American life. The pin-up culture of the 1950s was characterized by its integration into mainstream media, advertising, and popular culture, reflecting and shaping the societal norms and values of the time.

This was a time of unprecedented economic growth in the United States. The end of World War II brought about a period of affluence and consumerism, with Americans enjoying higher incomes and greater access to a variety of goods and services. This newfound prosperity fueled a consumer culture that placed a high value on leisure, entertainment, and material comforts. Pin-up art, with its emphasis on beauty and glamour, fit perfectly into this cultural landscape. Advertisers quickly recognized the appeal of pin-up imagery and began to incorporate it into their marketing strategies. Pin-up girls were used to sell a wide range of products, from household appliances to automobiles. Their images adorned calendars, magazine covers, and advertisements, becoming ubiquitous in American homes and public spaces. The use of pin-up art in advertising not only helped to promote products but also reinforced the ideals of femininity and desirability that were central to the consumer culture of the time.

Hollywood continued to play a significant role in the proliferation of pin-up culture during the 1950s. The film industry, buoyed by the economic boom, produced a steady stream of movies that featured glamorous leading ladies. Actresses like Marilyn Monroe, Jayne Mansfield, and Bettie Page became iconic figures, their images often doubling as pin-up art. Marilyn Monroe, in particular, epitomized the

1950s pin-up ideal with her blend of innocence and sensuality. Her famous calendar shots and magazine covers cemented her status as a pin-up legend. The Hollywood star system created a symbiotic relationship between movies and pin-up culture. Promotional photographs of actresses were widely distributed, and these images often served as pin-ups for fans. The allure of these actresses, combined with their on-screen personas, made them perfect embodiments of the pin-up aesthetic. Their widespread popularity helped to further integrate pin-up imagery into the fabric of American popular culture.

The 1950s pin-up culture also reflected broader cultural trends and shifts in societal attitudes towards gender and sexuality. The decade was marked by a return to traditional gender roles, with an emphasis on domesticity and the nuclear family. Pin-up art of this period often portrayed women in roles that aligned with these ideals, showcasing them as both glamorous and nurturing figures. The images reinforced the notion that women could be both desirable and devoted homemakers, embodying the dual expectations of beauty and domesticity. However, the 1950s were also a time of underlying tensions and contradictions. While pin-up art celebrated traditional femininity, it also pushed the boundaries of acceptable public displays of sexuality. The images often walked a fine line between innocence and eroticism, reflecting the complexities of the post-war cultural landscape. This duality is perhaps best exemplified by Bettie Page, whose pin-up photographs ranged from wholesome to risqué, challenging conventional norms and paving the way for more explicit forms of sexual expression in popular culture.

The boom of pin-up culture in the 1950s left a lasting legacy that continues to influence art, fashion, and media today. The pin-up images of this era captured the ideals and aspirations of a generation, offering a blend of fantasy and reality that resonated deeply with the public. The visual style and themes established during this decade have become enduring elements of the pin-up genre, inspiring countless artists and enthusiasts in the years that followed. In conclusion, the post-war era of the 1950s was a golden age for pin-up culture, marked by economic prosperity, the influence of Hollywood, and the integration of pin-up imagery into mainstream media and advertising. The decade's pin-up art reflected and shaped the cultural values of the time, celebrating beauty, glamour, and the ideals of traditional femininity while also hinting at deeper societal changes. The impact of 1950s pin-up culture remains evident today, as pin-up art continues to be celebrated for its enduring charm and cultural significance.

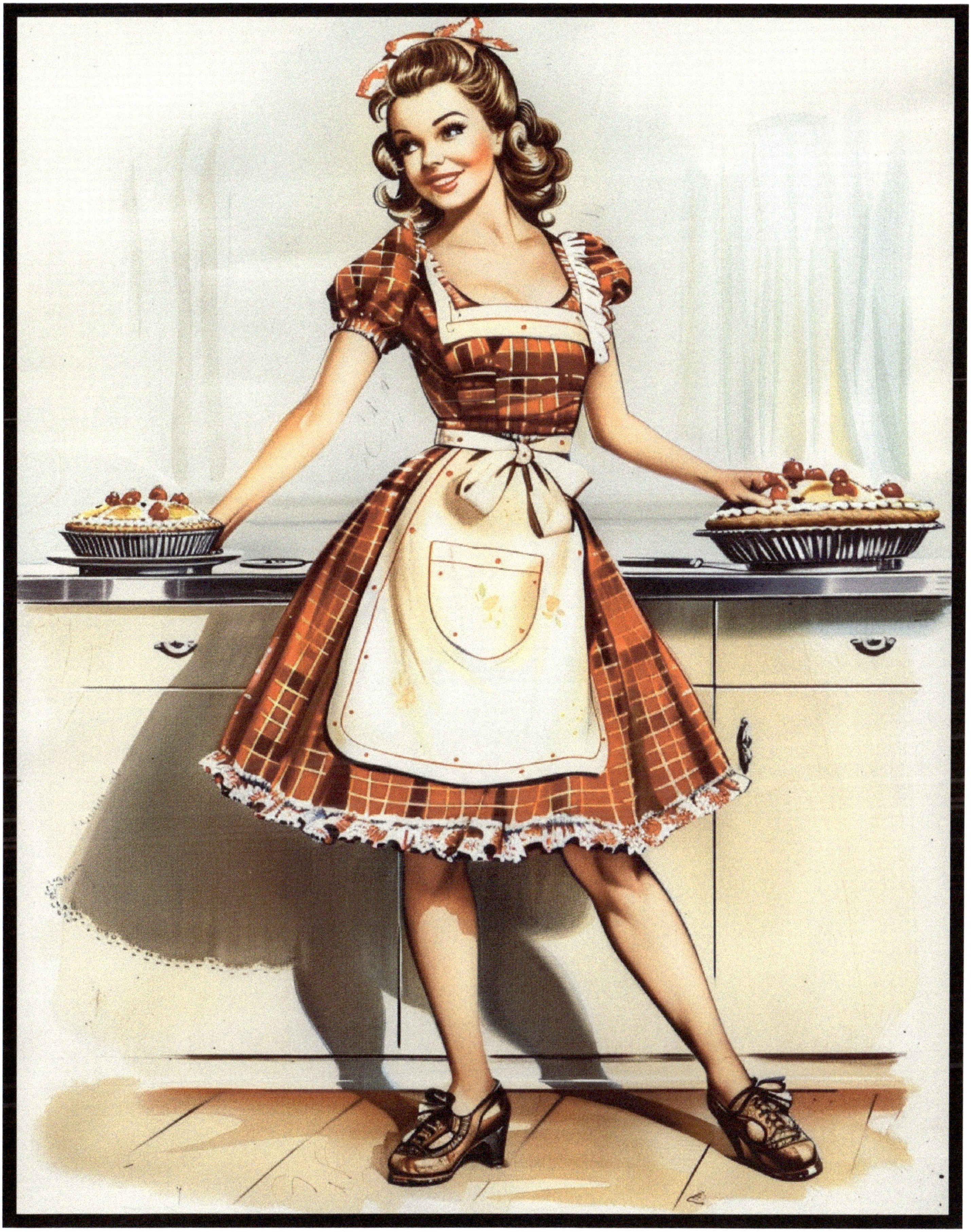

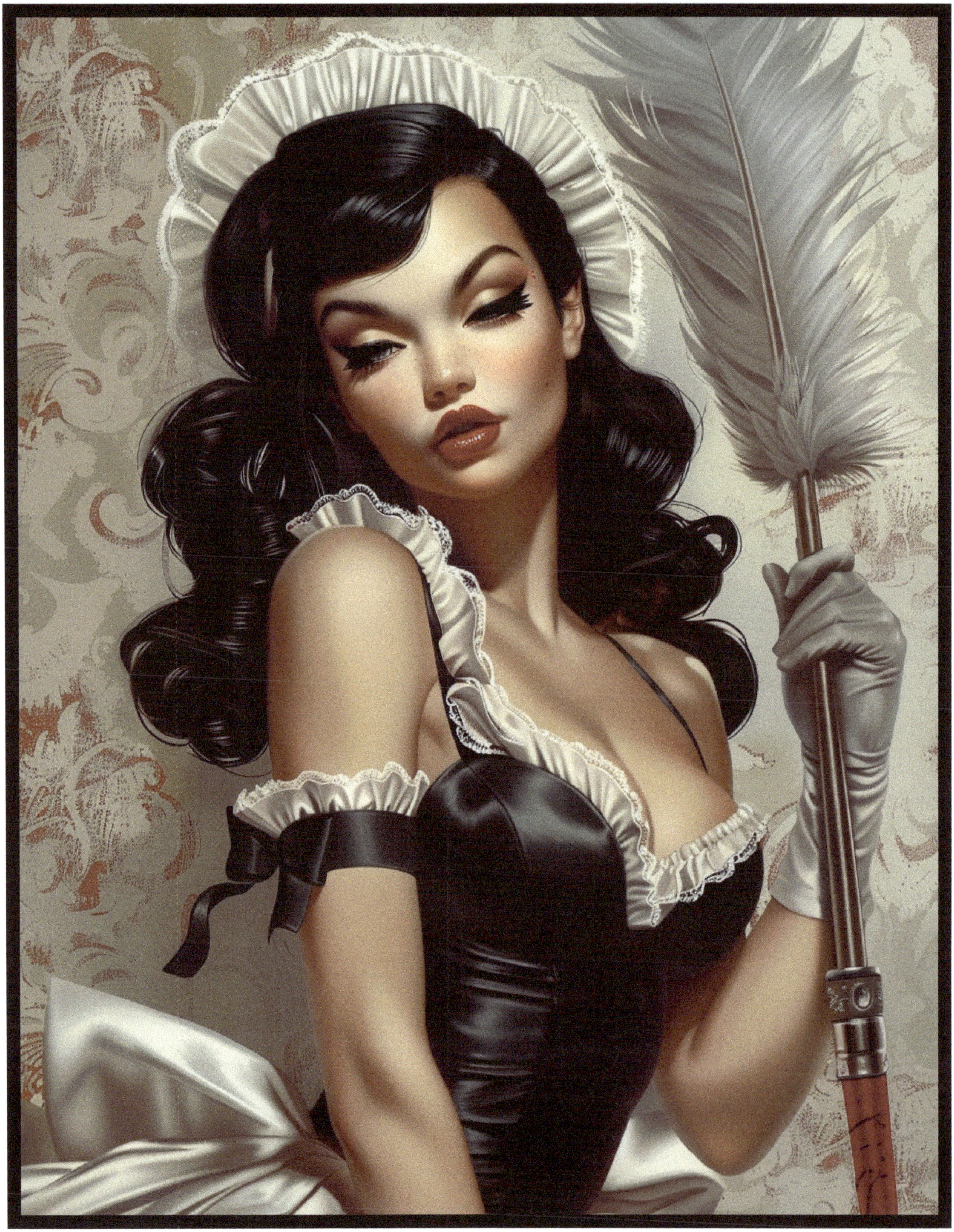

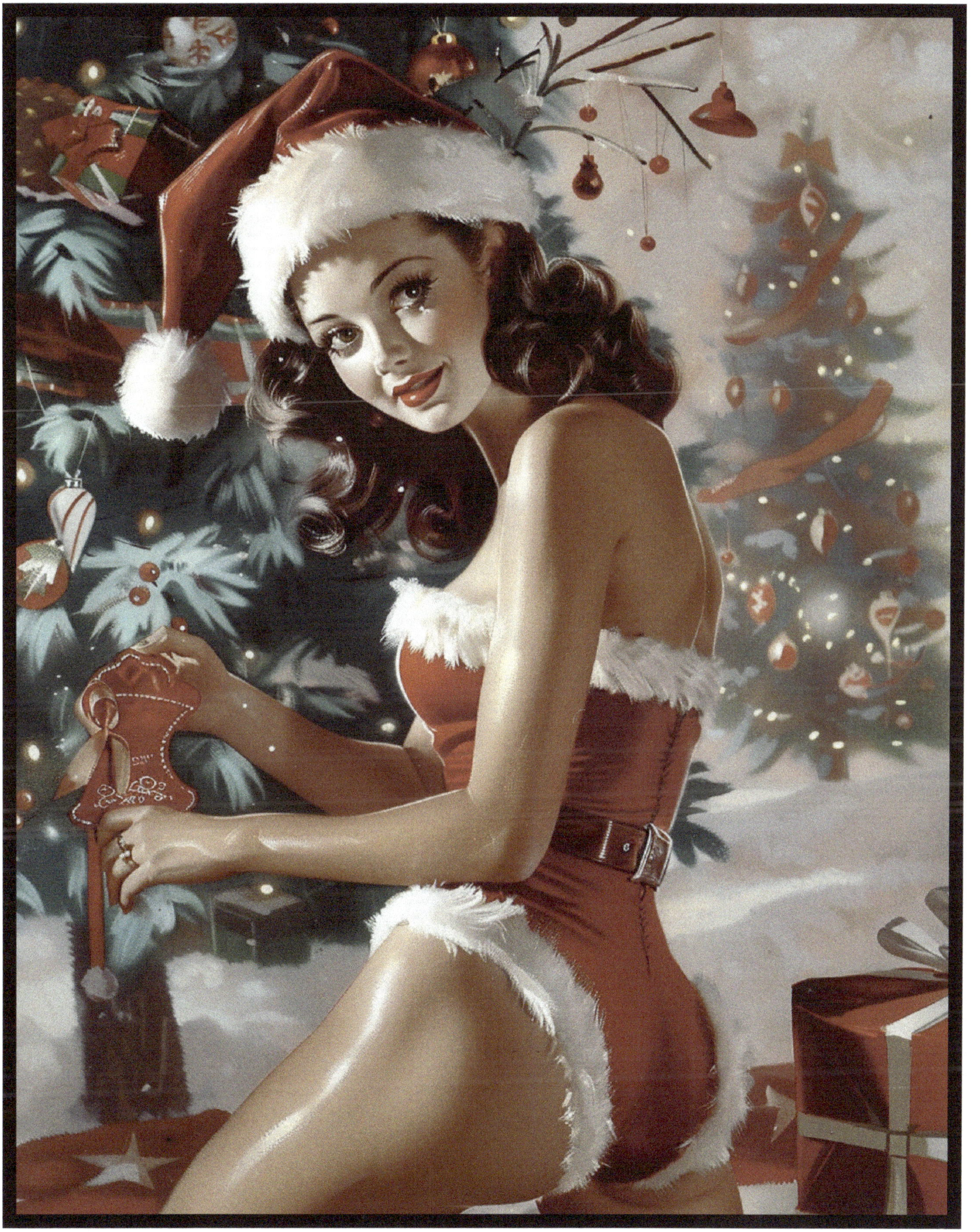

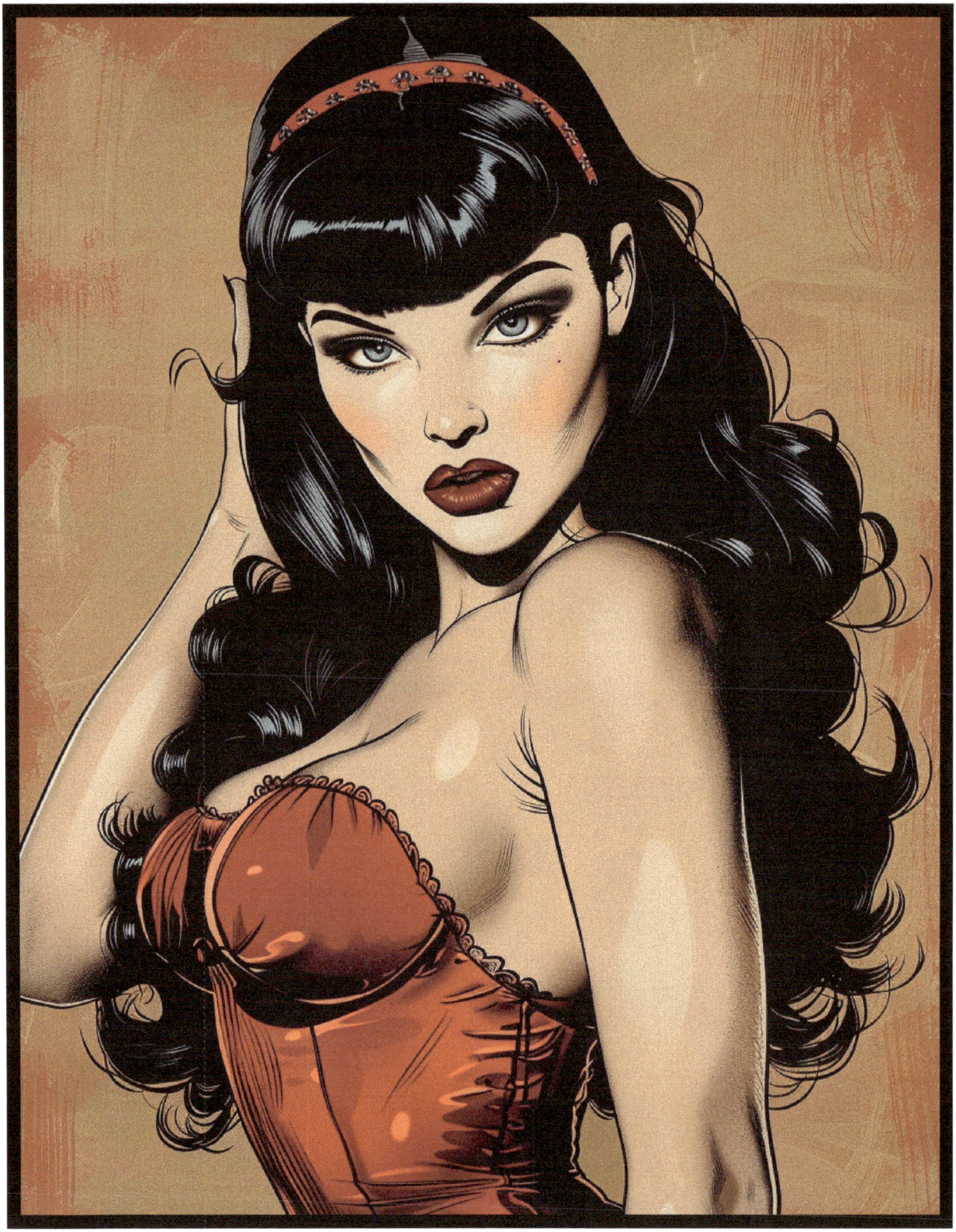

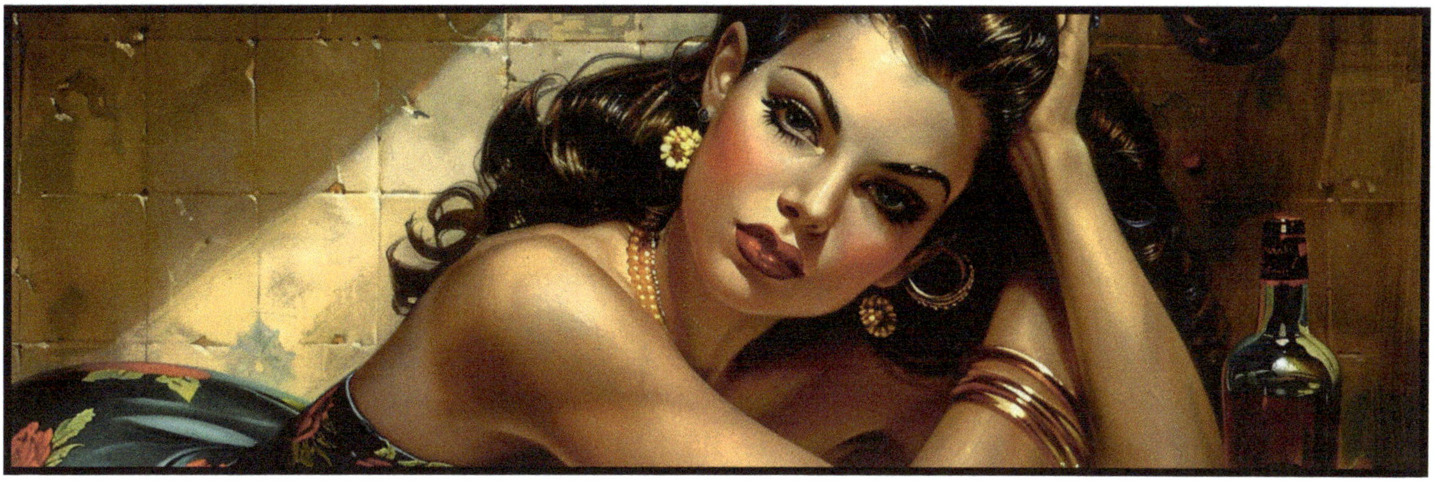

PIN-UPS IN MEDIA AND ADVERTISING

The integration of pin-up art into media and advertising during the 1950s marked a significant expansion of the genre's influence and visibility. This era saw pin-up imagery permeating various aspects of everyday life, from magazine covers to commercial advertisements, reflecting and shaping contemporary cultural norms and consumer behavior.

One of the most prominent platforms for pin-up art during the 1950s was the magazine industry. Publications like "Esquire," "Life," and "Playboy" regularly featured pin-up girls on their covers and within their pages. These magazines reached a wide audience, bringing pin-up imagery into millions of homes and making it a staple of American popular culture. "Esquire" magazine played a particularly important role in the popularization of pin-up art. The magazine featured illustrations by renowned artists such as Alberto Vargas and George Petty, whose works became synonymous with the pin-up genre. The "Vargas Girls" and "Petty Girls" were characterized by their sophisticated, alluring poses and glamorous styling, capturing the imagination of readers and setting high standards for beauty and elegance. "Playboy," first published in 1953, also contributed significantly to the proliferation of pin-up art. Founder Hugh Hefner recognized the commercial appeal of combining quality journalism with provocative images of beautiful women. Playboy's centerfolds and cover models quickly became iconic, with Marilyn Monroe gracing the cover of the first issue. The magazine's blend of intellectual content and sensual imagery helped to legitimize and popularize pin-up art in a new and influential format.

The 1950s were a golden age for advertising, and pin-up art played a key role in many marketing campaigns. Advertisers capitalized on the widespread appeal of pin-up girls to sell a wide variety of products, from automobiles to household appliances. Their images adorned calendars, magazine covers, and advertisements, becoming ubiquitous in American homes and public spaces. The use of pin-up art in advertising was not only effective in capturing consumer attention but also in associating products with ideals of beauty, glamour, and modernity. Pin-up girls were often depicted in advertisements as the ideal consumer—stylish, attractive, and effortlessly using the product being marketed. This strategy was particularly effective in targeting male consumers, who were drawn to the allure of the pin-up girl, as well as female consumers, who aspired to emulate the glamorous lifestyle depicted in the ads. Automobile advertisements frequently featured pin-up girls posing next to sleek new cars, reinforcing the connection between desirability and modern technology. Similarly, household products like refrigerators, washing machines, and vacuum cleaners were advertised using images of beautiful women demonstrating their ease of use and efficiency. These advertisements not only sold products but also promoted the ideal of the perfect homemaker, reflecting and reinforcing the cultural norms of the time.

Calendars were another popular medium for pin-up art during the 1950s. Many companies produced calendars featuring pin-up girls as promotional items, distributing them to customers and clients as a way to keep their brand visible throughout the year. These calendars often showcased the work of prominent pin-up artists, ensuring high-quality and visually appealing images. The annual calendar featuring Gil Elvgren's pin-up girls became particularly famous. Elvgren's illustrations were known for their vibrant colors, playful scenarios, and expressive characters. His work depicted women in a variety of humorous and sometimes precarious situations, adding an element of fun and fantasy to the everyday. These calendars were highly sought after and became collectible items, further cementing the popularity of pin-up art.

The pervasive use of pin-up art in media and advertising during the 1950s had a profound impact on American culture. These images helped to shape societal standards of beauty and femininity, promoting ideals of glamour, sophistication, and desirability. At the same time, they contributed to the commercialization of female imagery, where women's beauty was often used as a tool to sell products and ideas. Pin-up art's integration into media and advertising also reflected broader cultural trends, including the celebration of consumerism and the idealization of the American Dream. The images of glamorous women enjoying modern conveniences and luxuries resonated with the public's aspirations for prosperity and success in the post-war era.

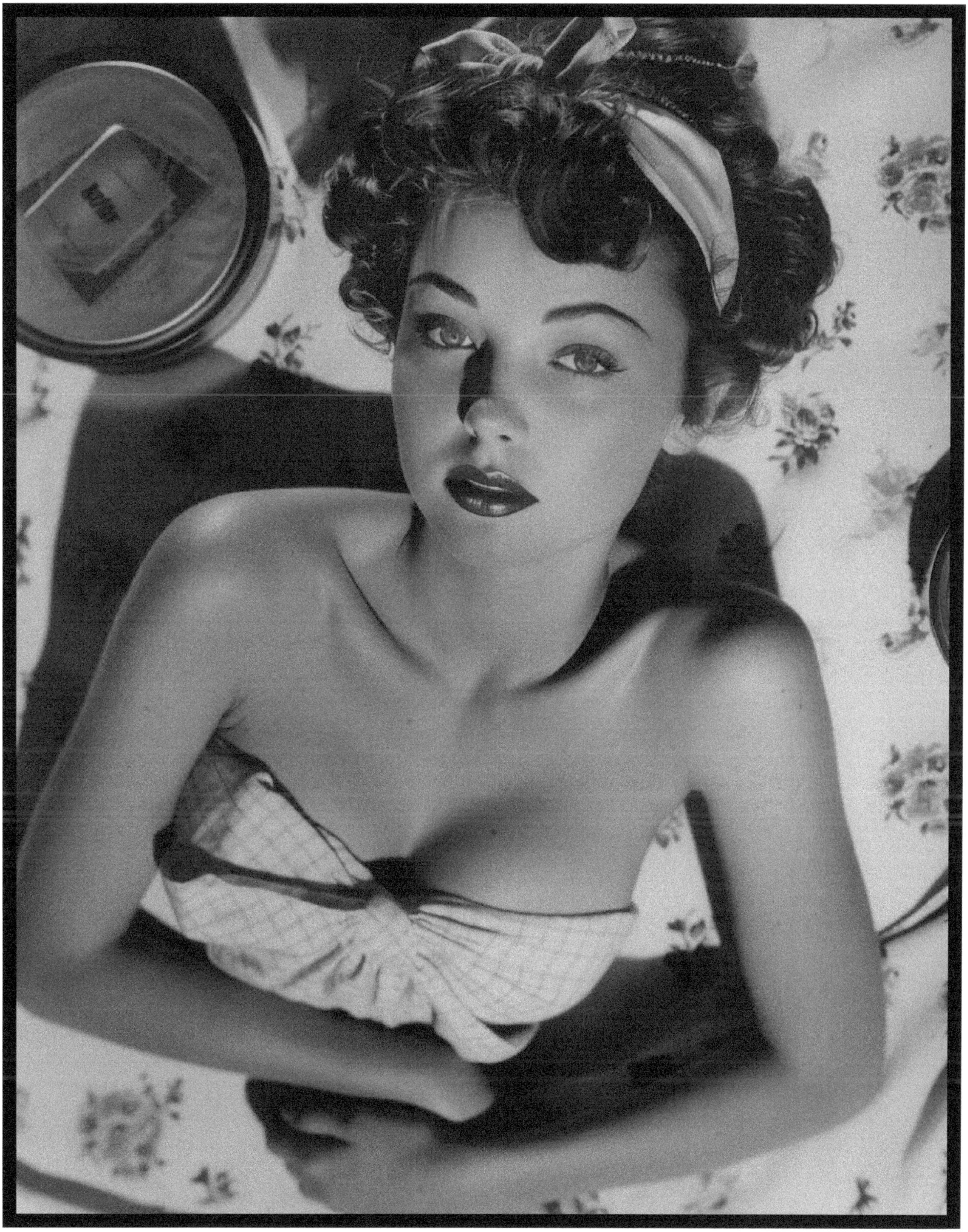

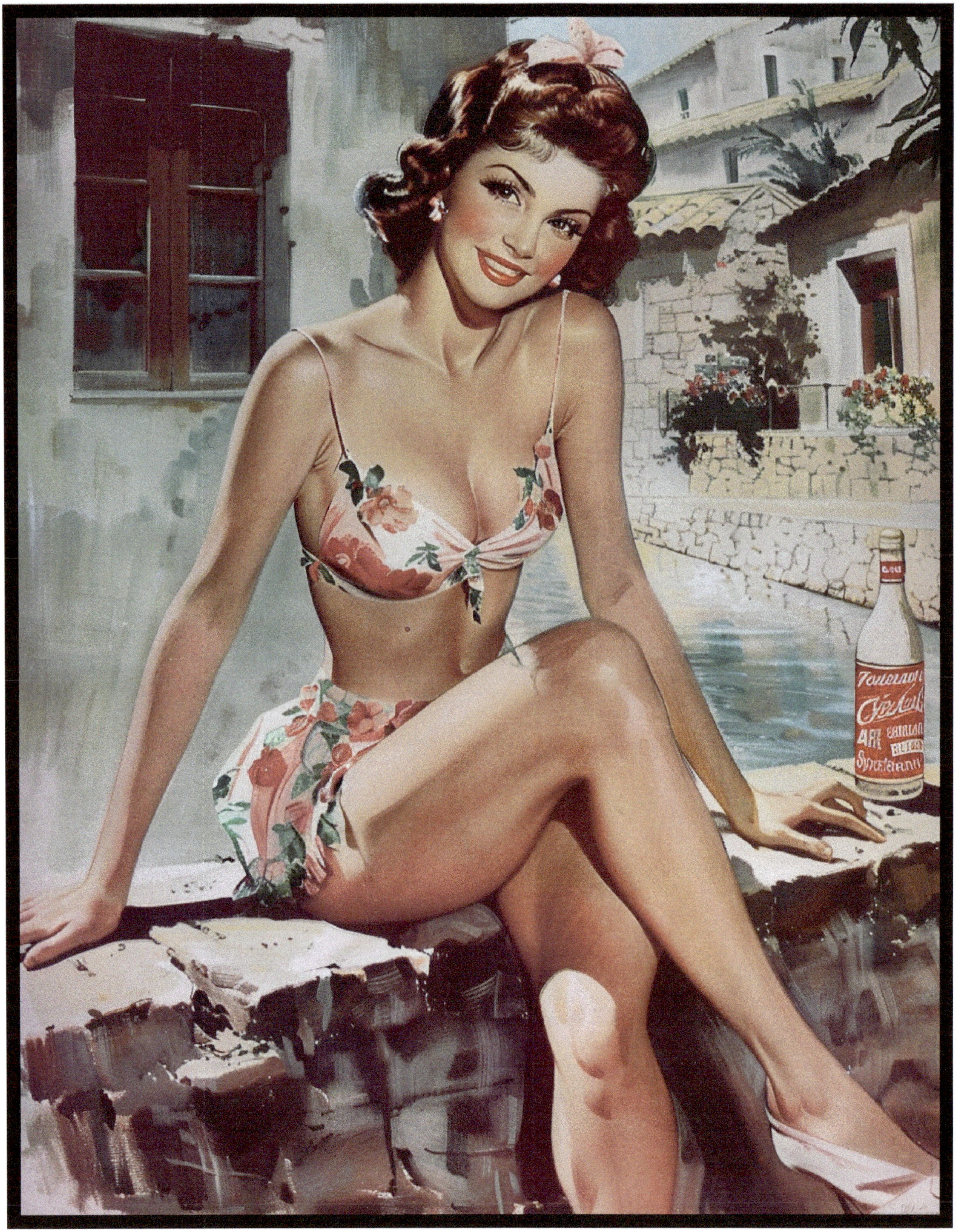

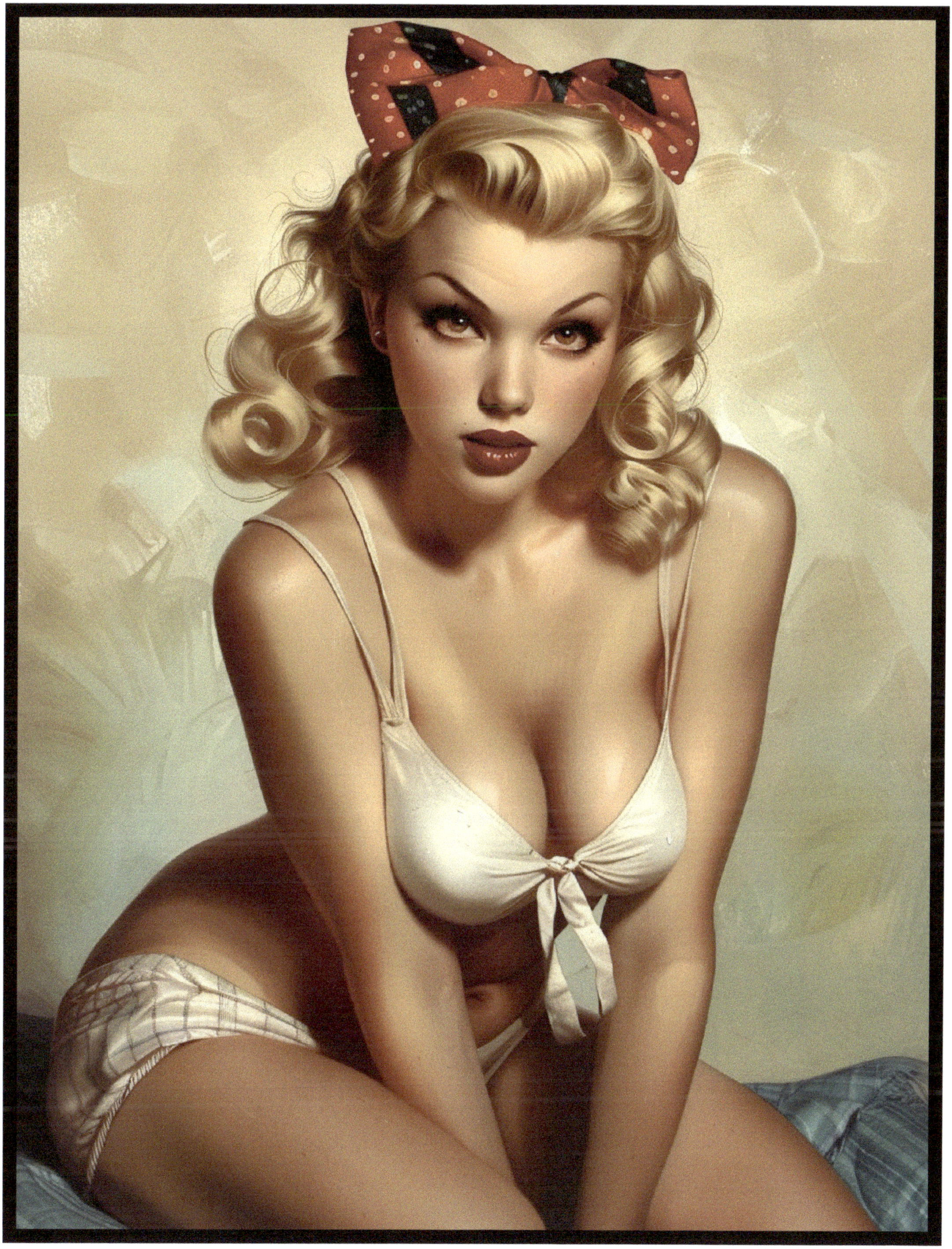

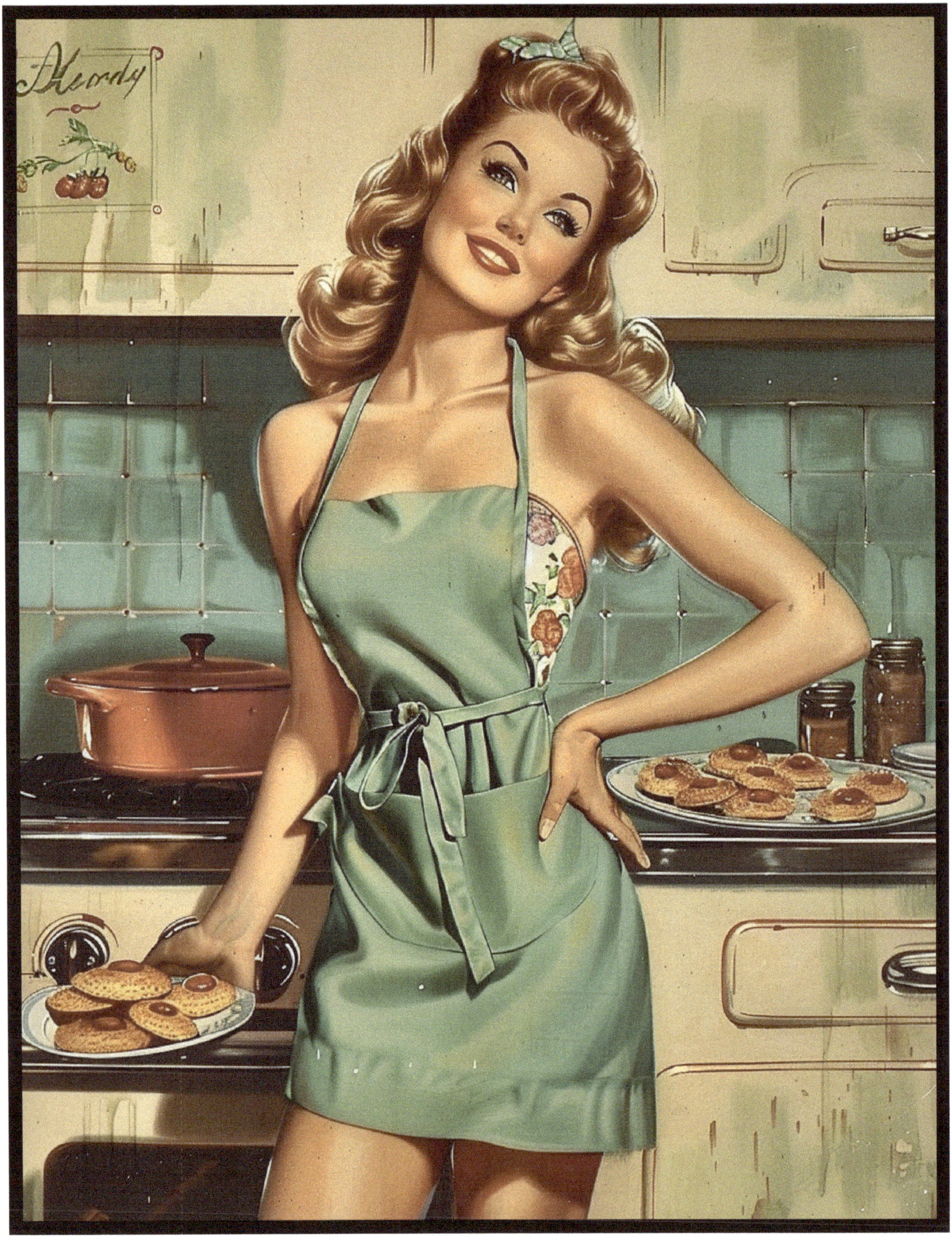

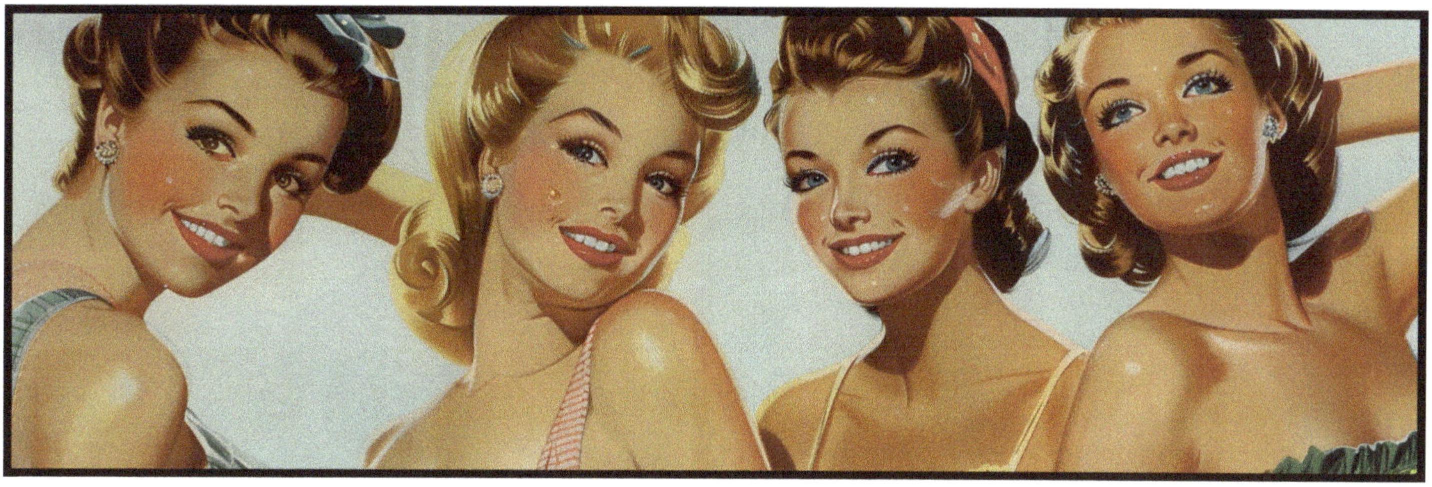

CULTURAL IMPACT AND SHIFTS

The cultural impact of pin-up art during the 1950s was profound, reflecting and influencing the era's social norms, values, and attitudes towards gender and sexuality. The widespread popularity of pin-up imagery in media and advertising played a crucial role in shaping the cultural landscape of the time, embedding ideals of beauty, femininity, and consumerism into the fabric of American life.

Pin-up art in the 1950s was emblematic of the era's return to traditional gender roles following World War II. The end of the war brought about a renewed emphasis on domesticity and the nuclear family, with women encouraged to embrace their roles as wives, mothers, and homemakers. Pin-up images often depicted women in domestic settings, exuding both glamour and competence as they engaged in household activities. This portrayal reinforced the notion that a woman's primary sphere was the home, aligning with societal expectations of the time.

At the same time, pin-up art celebrated a heightened sense of femininity and sexuality. The images were characterized by their playful and seductive poses, showcasing women as confident and alluring figures. This emphasis on sexual appeal was a departure from the more conservative portrayals of women in previous decades, reflecting a broader cultural shift towards more open expressions of sexuality. The pin-up girl became a symbol of desirable femininity, embodying the ideals of beauty, charm, and seduction.

The influence of pin-up art extended beyond its aesthetic appeal, shaping consumer behavior and advertising strategies. Advertisers capitalized on the allure of pin-up girls to sell a wide range of products, from household appliances to fashion items. The association of beauty and glamour with consumer goods helped to drive the burgeoning consumer culture of the 1950s. Pin-up imagery in advertisements suggested that using these products could help women achieve the same level of attractiveness and sophistication as the models depicted. This marketing strategy not only boosted sales but also reinforced the cultural association between consumption and femininity

Despite its celebration of traditional femininity, pin-up art also contained elements of subversion and complexity. While the images often emphasized conventional beauty standards, they also showcased women as confident and self-assured, capable of commanding attention and admiration. This duality reflected the tensions and contradictions of the post-war cultural landscape, where societal norms were both reaffirmed and subtly challenged.

The 1950s were also a time of underlying social and cultural shifts that would later give rise to more significant changes in attitudes towards gender and sexuality. The pin-up art of this era, with its emphasis on glamour and sensuality, laid the groundwork for the more explicit and diverse representations of female sexuality that would emerge in the following decades. The playful and sometimes provocative nature of pin-up images hinted at a growing acceptance of female sexual expression, paving the way for the sexual revolution of the 1960s and 1970s.

The legacy of 1950s pin-up culture continues to resonate today, influencing contemporary art, fashion, and media. The visual style and themes established during this era have become enduring elements of the pin-up genre, inspiring new generations of artists and enthusiasts. Modern interpretations of pin-up art often embrace a broader range of body types and identities, reflecting contemporary values of diversity and inclusivity while still celebrating the glamour and allure that defined the original genre.

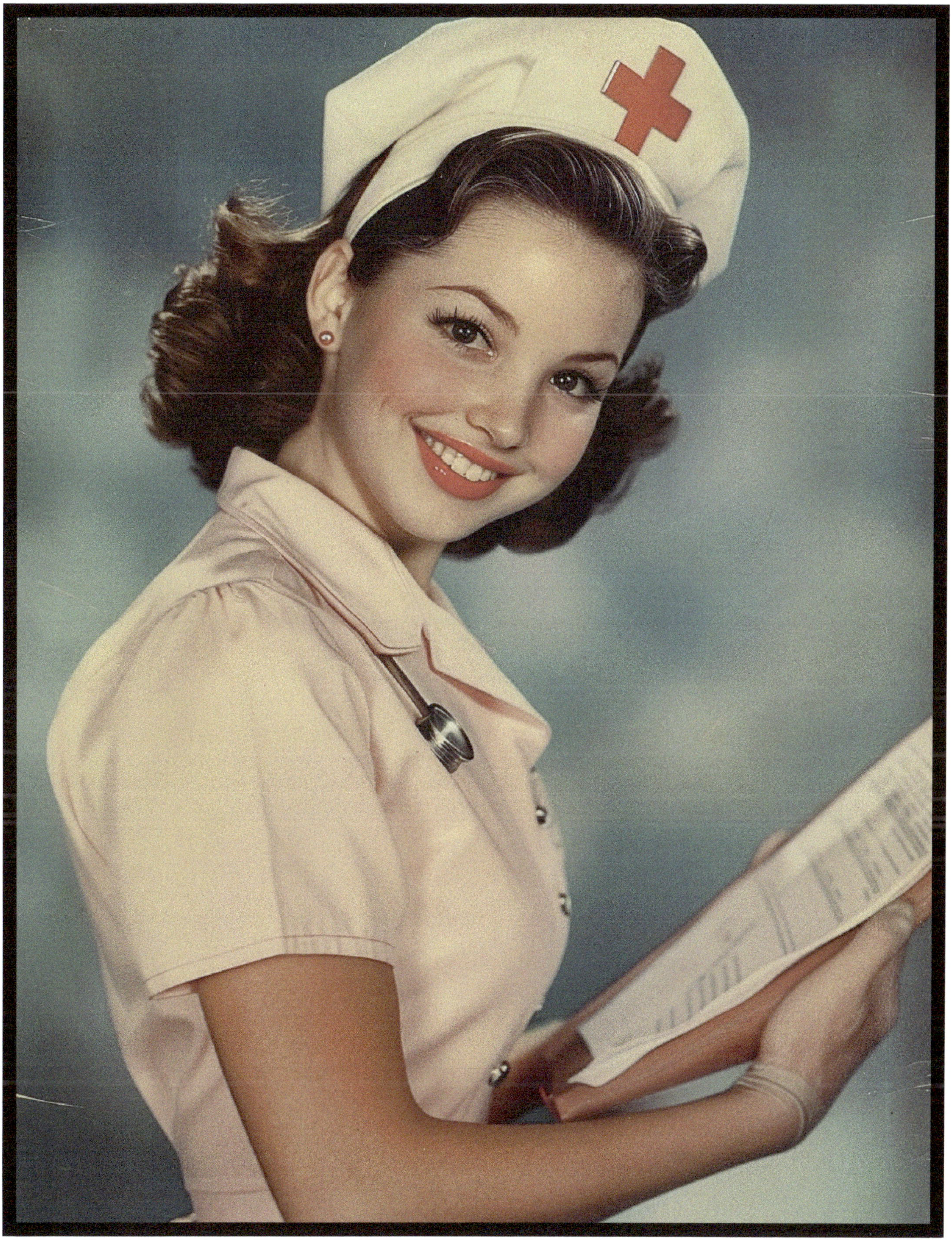

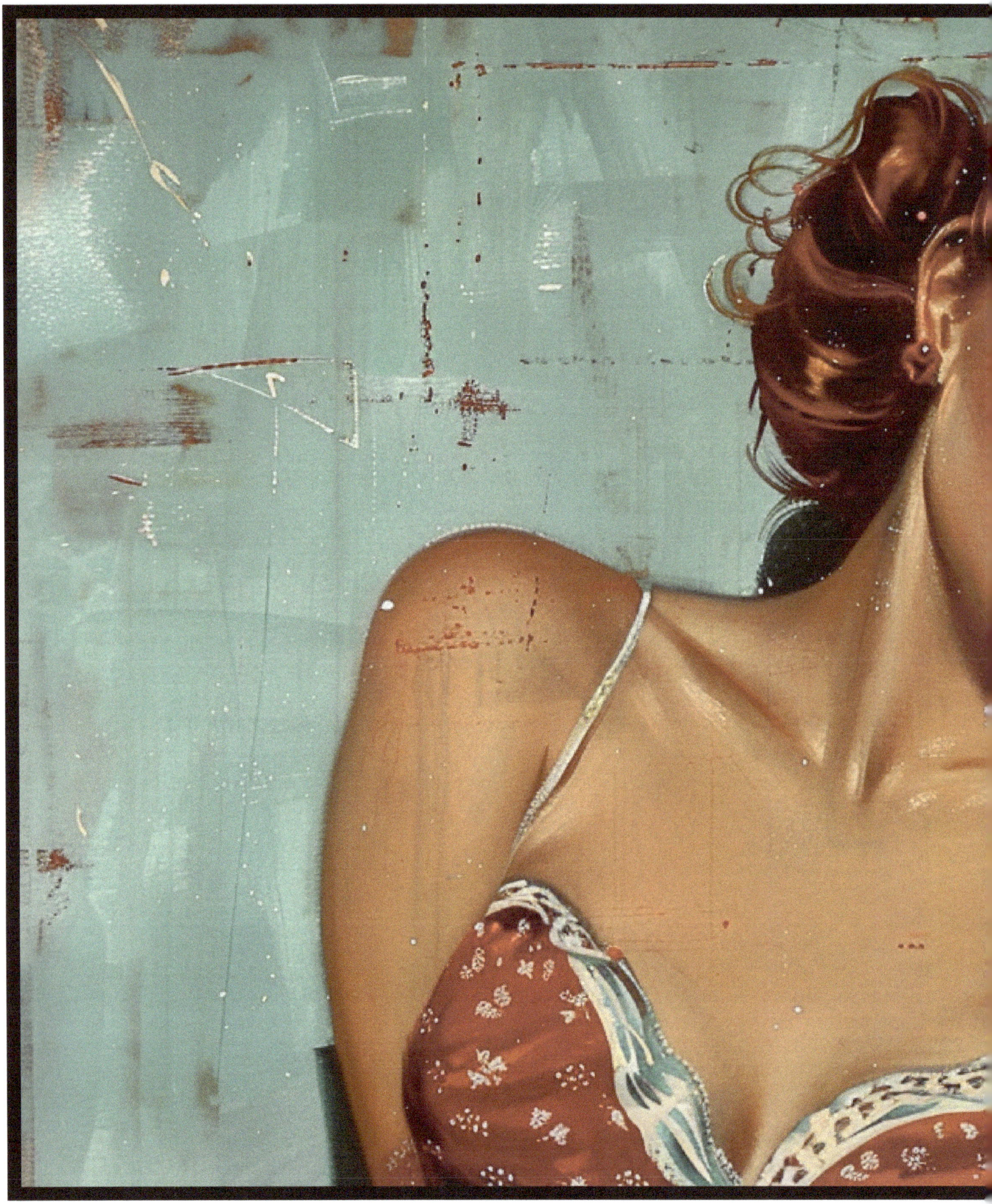

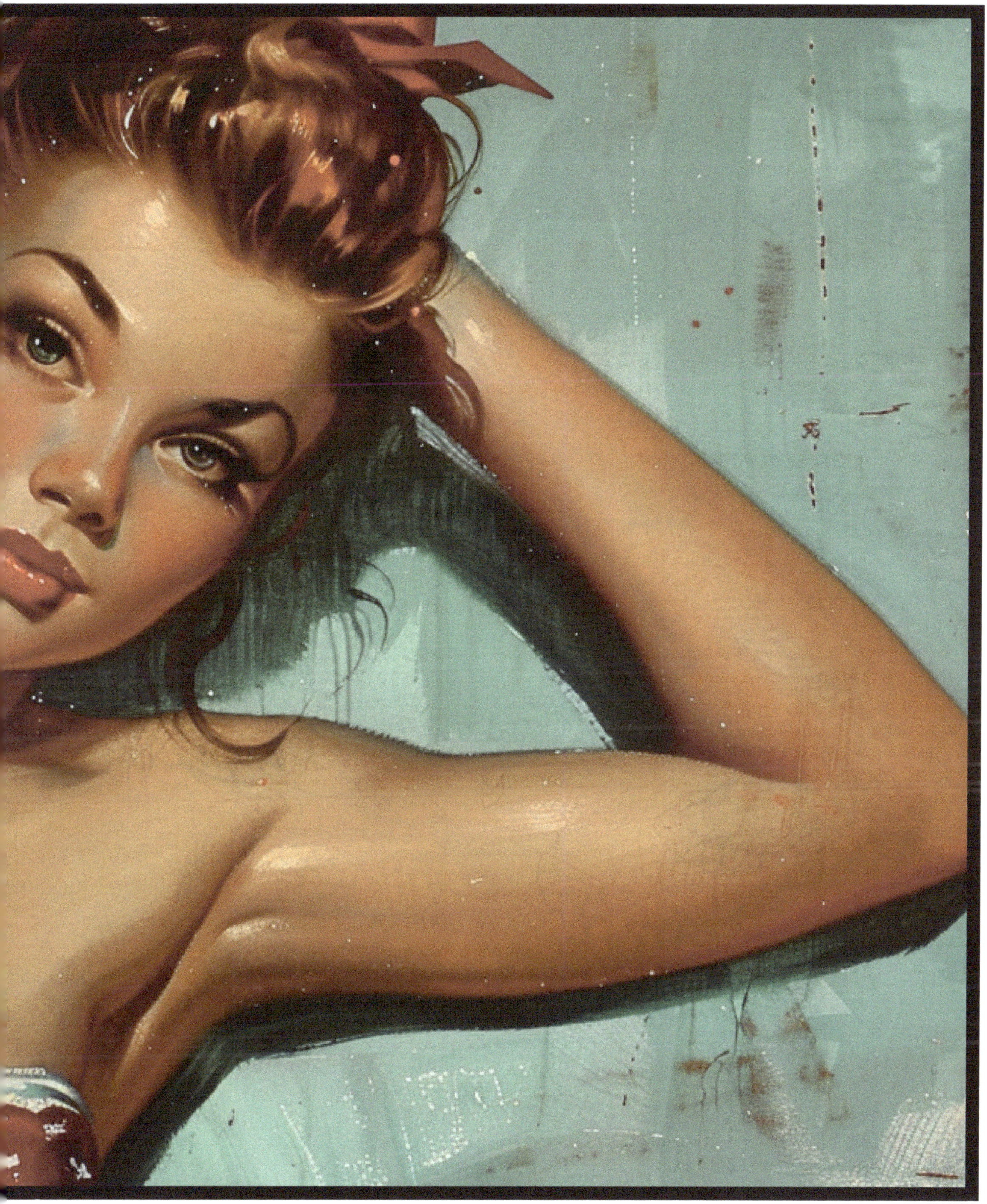

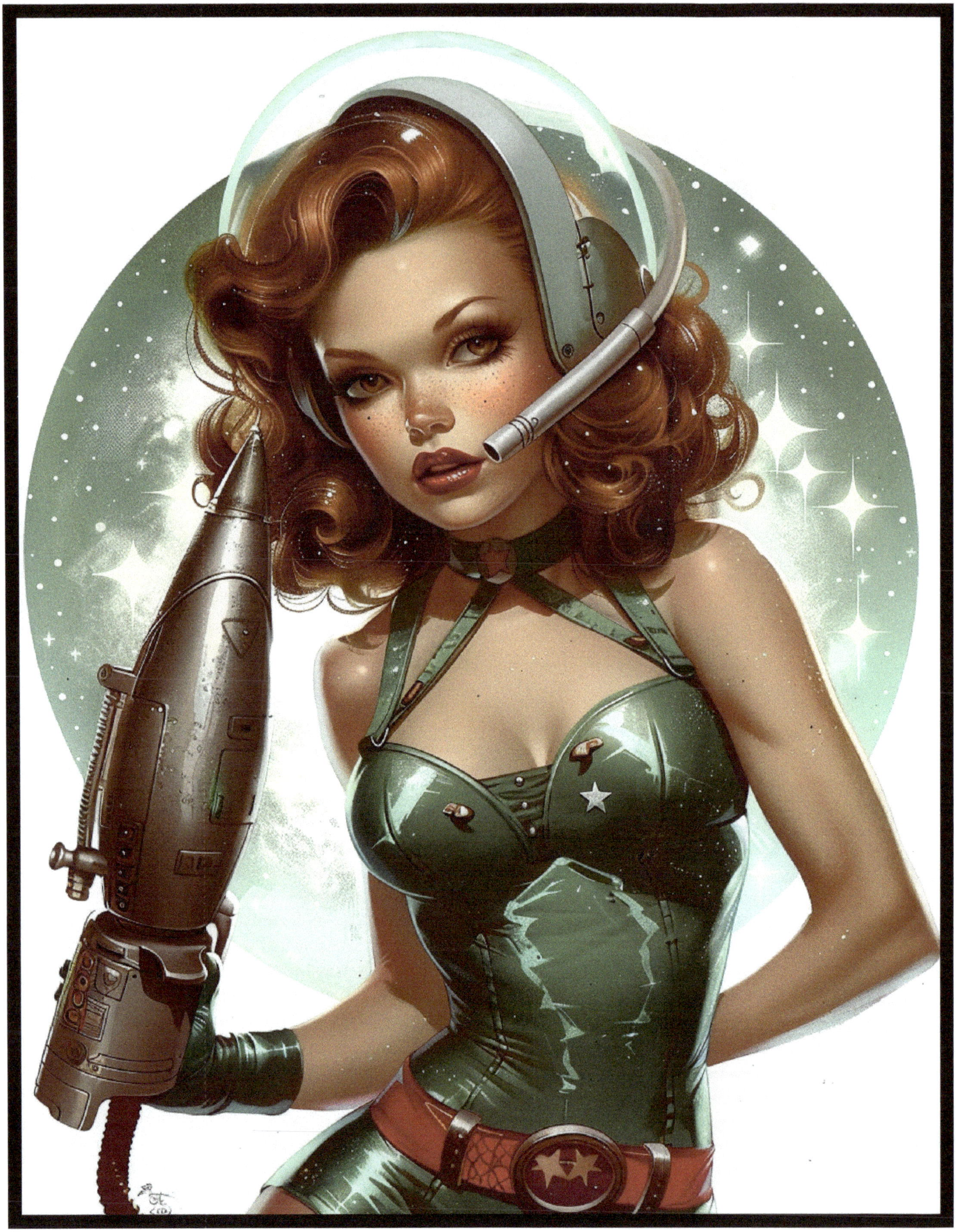

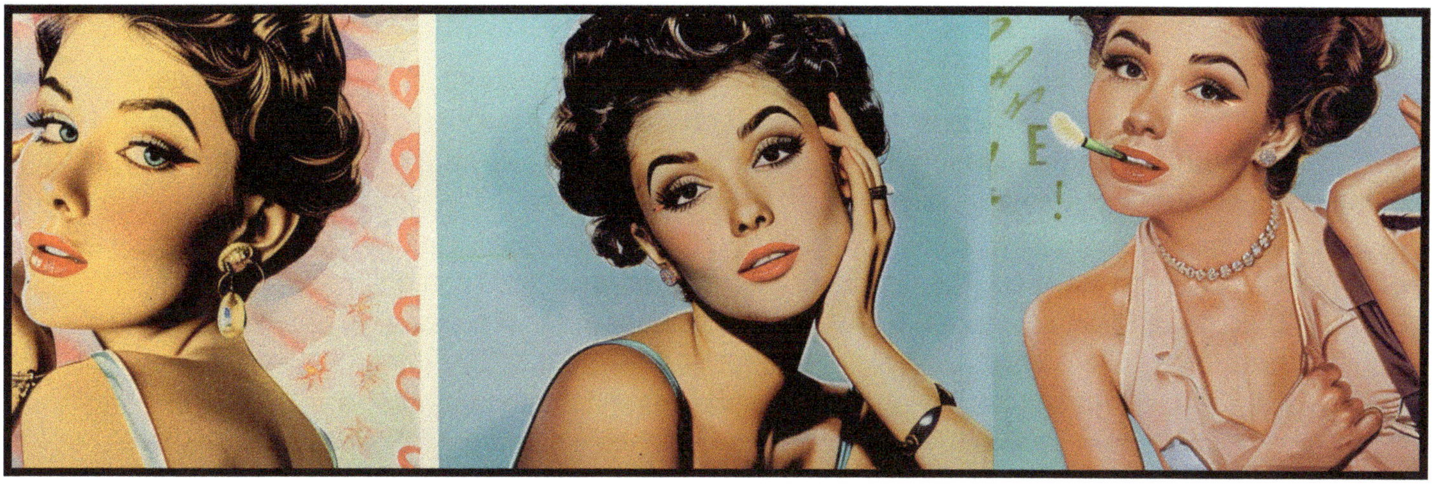

THE EVOLUTION: 1960-1980

The period from the 1960s to the 1980s saw significant transformations in pin-up art, reflecting broader cultural, social, and technological changes. During these decades, pin-up imagery evolved from the traditional illustrations and photographs of the mid-20th century to embrace new styles, mediums, and themes. This era marked a shift towards more diverse and complex representations of women, influenced by the counterculture movement, the sexual revolution, and advancements in media and technology.

In the 1960s, the cultural landscape of the United States and much of the Western world was undergoing profound changes. The counterculture movement, characterized by a rejection of traditional values and norms, brought about a new openness towards issues of sexuality and gender. This period saw the emergence of more explicit and provocative forms of pin-up art, as artists and photographers began to explore themes of sexual liberation and empowerment.

One of the most significant figures of this era was Bettie Page, whose work bridged the gap between the traditional pin-up art of the 1950s and the more daring imagery of the 1960s. Although her career peaked in the 1950s, Page's influence persisted into the following decade, as her images became symbols of sexual freedom and rebellion. Her photographs, which often featured bondage and fetish themes, challenged conventional norms and pushed the boundaries of what was considered acceptable in mainstream media.

The 1960s also saw the rise of Playboy magazine as a major cultural force. Founded in the early 1950s, Playboy gained prominence in the 1960s, with its blend of high-quality journalism, fiction, and provocative photography. The magazine's centerfolds featured nude or semi-nude models, known as Playmates, who became iconic figures in their own right. Playboy's sophisticated and sexually explicit imagery reflected the era's evolving attitudes towards sexuality and contributed to the mainstream acceptance of pin-up art as a legitimate form of entertainment and expression.

As the 1970s dawned, the sexual revolution continued to reshape societal norms. This decade was marked by a greater acceptance of sexual expression and experimentation, which was reflected in the pin-up art of the time. Magazines like Penthouse and Hustler emerged as competitors to Playboy, offering even more explicit content and pushing the boundaries of erotic imagery. These publications featured pin-up models in increasingly daring poses, emphasizing a rawer and more unfiltered portrayal of sexuality.

The influence of rock 'n' roll and the emerging punk rock movement also left its mark on pin-up art during the 1970s. Album covers, posters, and promotional materials often featured pin-up-style imagery that blended elements of glamour, rebellion, and edginess. Artists like Olivia De Berardinis gained recognition for their work, which combined traditional pin-up aesthetics with contemporary themes and a modern sensibility. De Berardinis' illustrations, characterized by their vibrant colors and dynamic compositions, became emblematic of the evolving pin-up genre.

The 1980s brought about further changes, driven by advancements in technology and shifts in cultural trends. The advent of video technology and the rise of cable television introduced new platforms for pin-up imagery. Music videos, television shows, and advertisements began to incorporate pin-up elements, reaching wider audiences and further embedding the genre into popular culture.

The fashion industry also played a significant role in the evolution of pin-up art during the 1980s. The emergence of supermodels like Cindy Crawford and Elle Macpherson, who frequently appeared in glamorous and seductive poses for fashion magazines and advertisements, echoed the pin-up tradition. These models, with their striking looks and confident personas, became modern-day pin-up icons, bridging the gap between fashion and erotic art.

Throughout the 1960s, 1970s, and 1980s, pin-up art continued to adapt and evolve, reflecting the changing attitudes and values of society. The genre embraced new styles, mediums, and themes, moving beyond the traditional illustrations and photographs of the mid-20th century. This period marked a shift towards more diverse and complex representations of women, influenced by the counterculture movement, the sexual revolution, and advancements in media and technology.

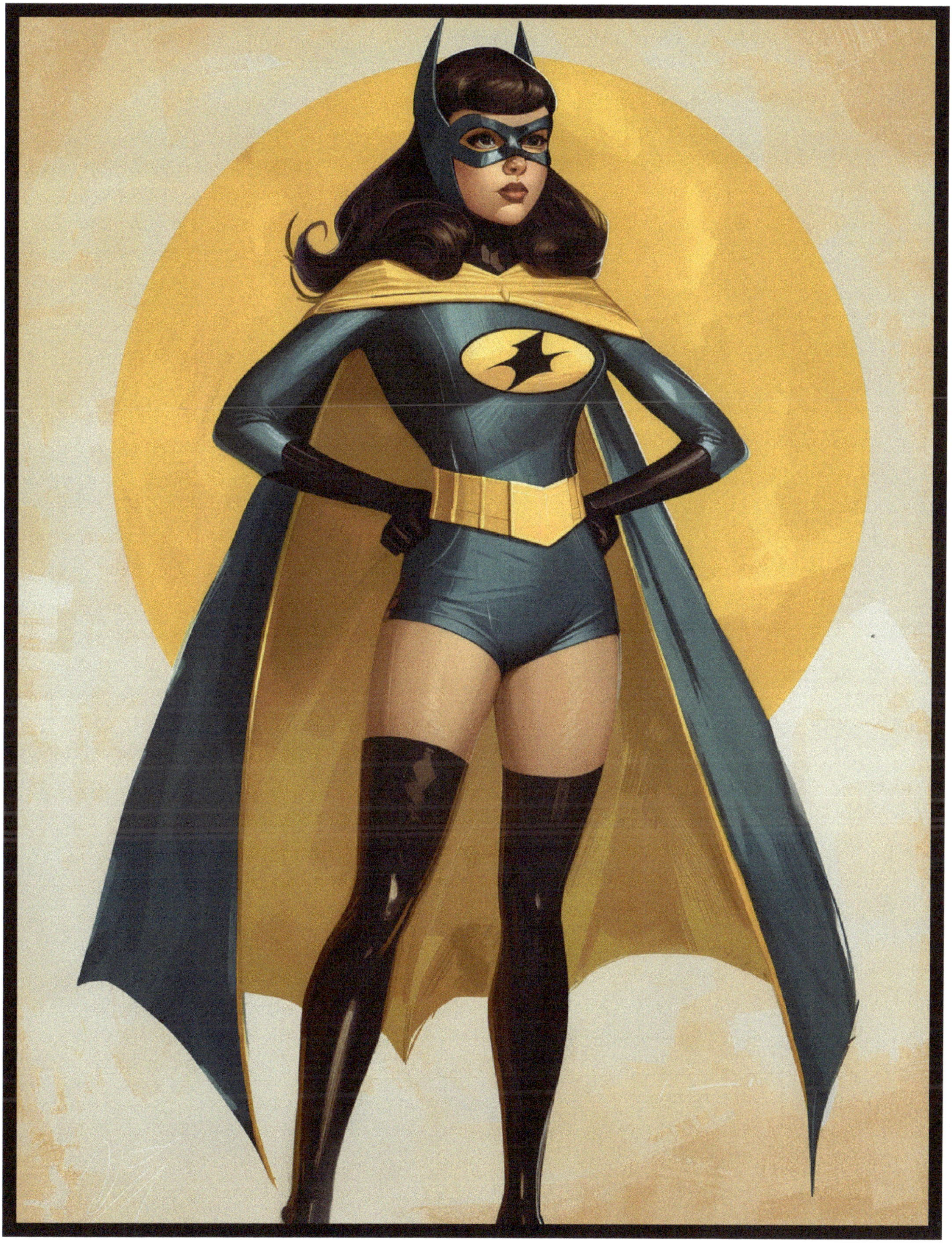

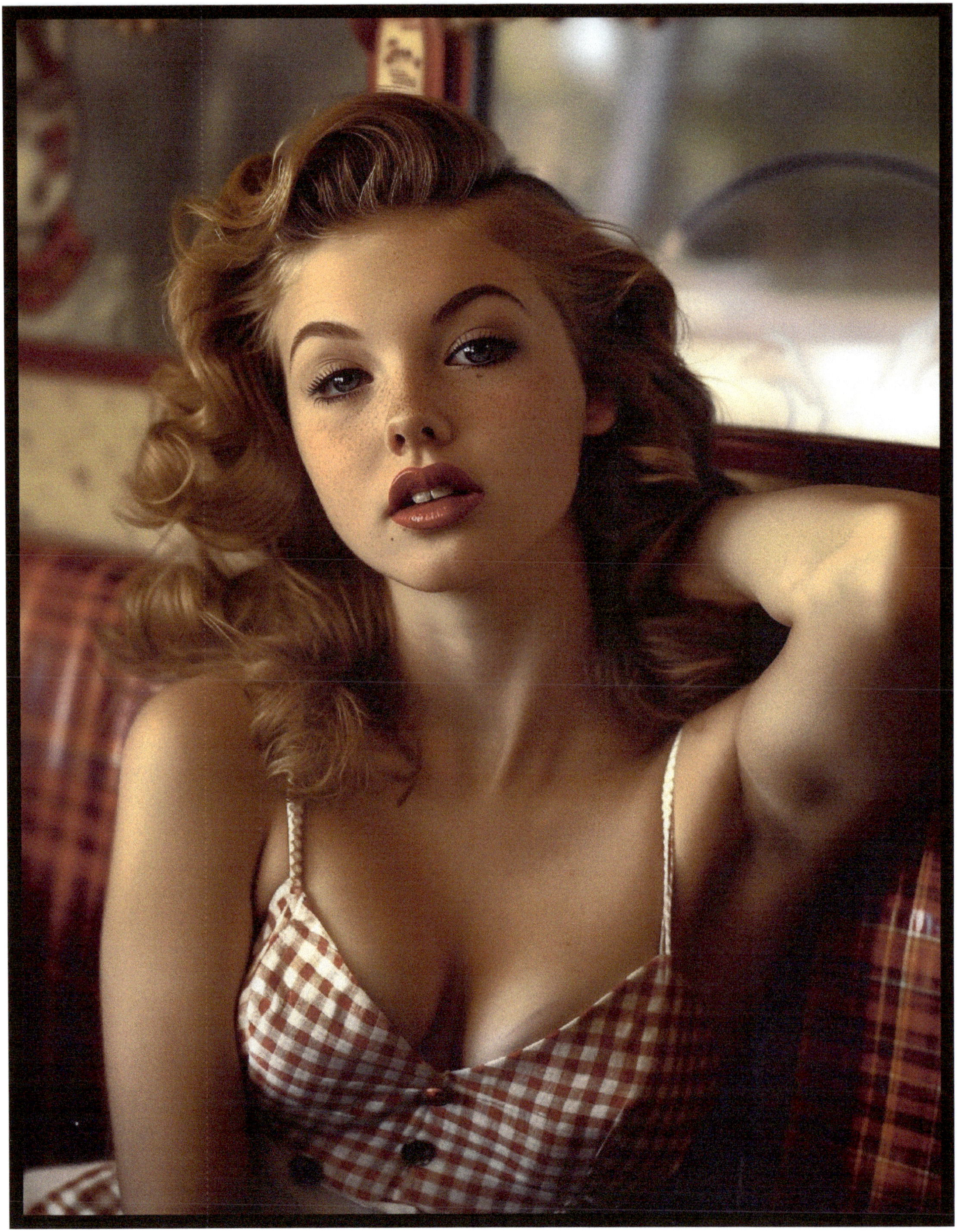

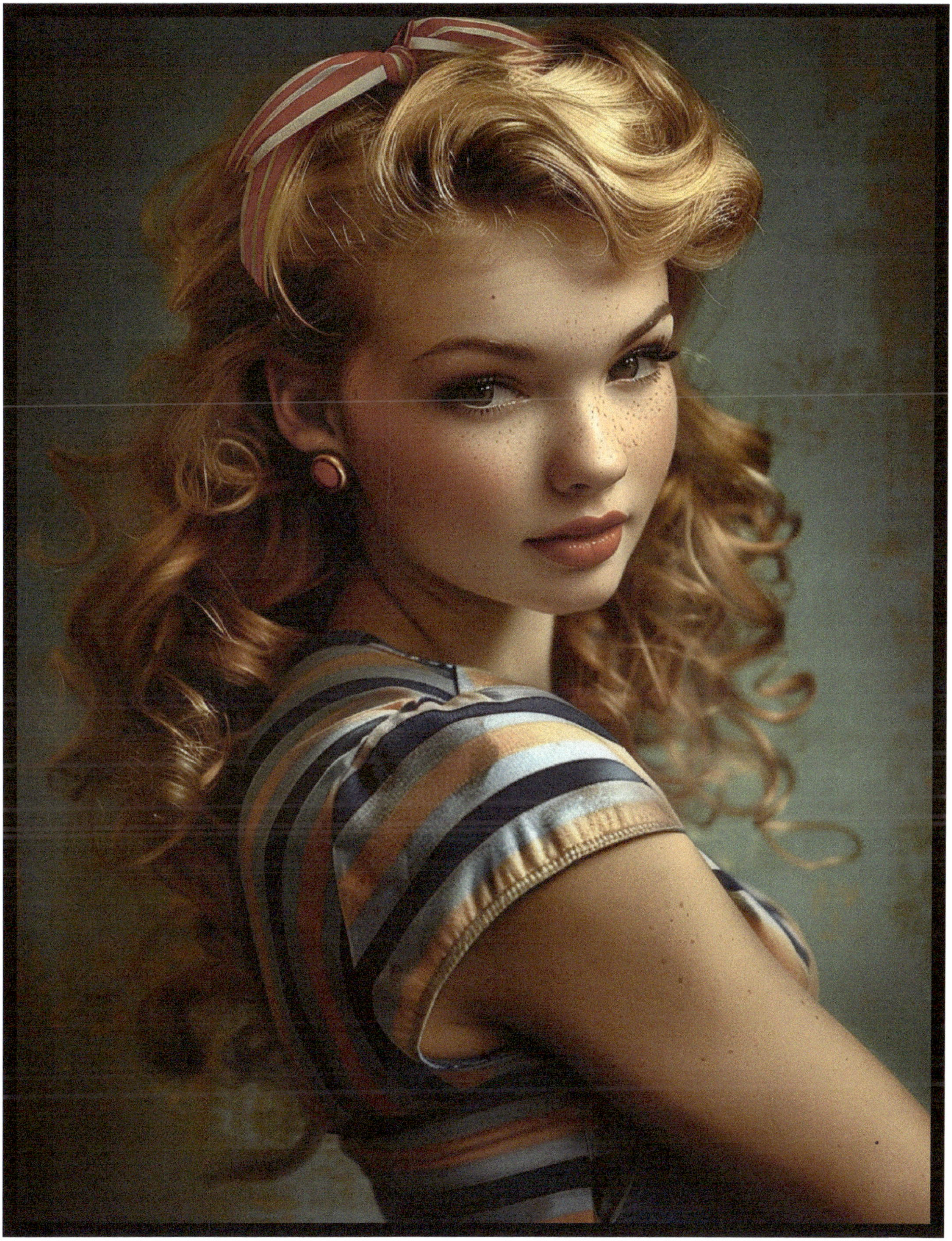

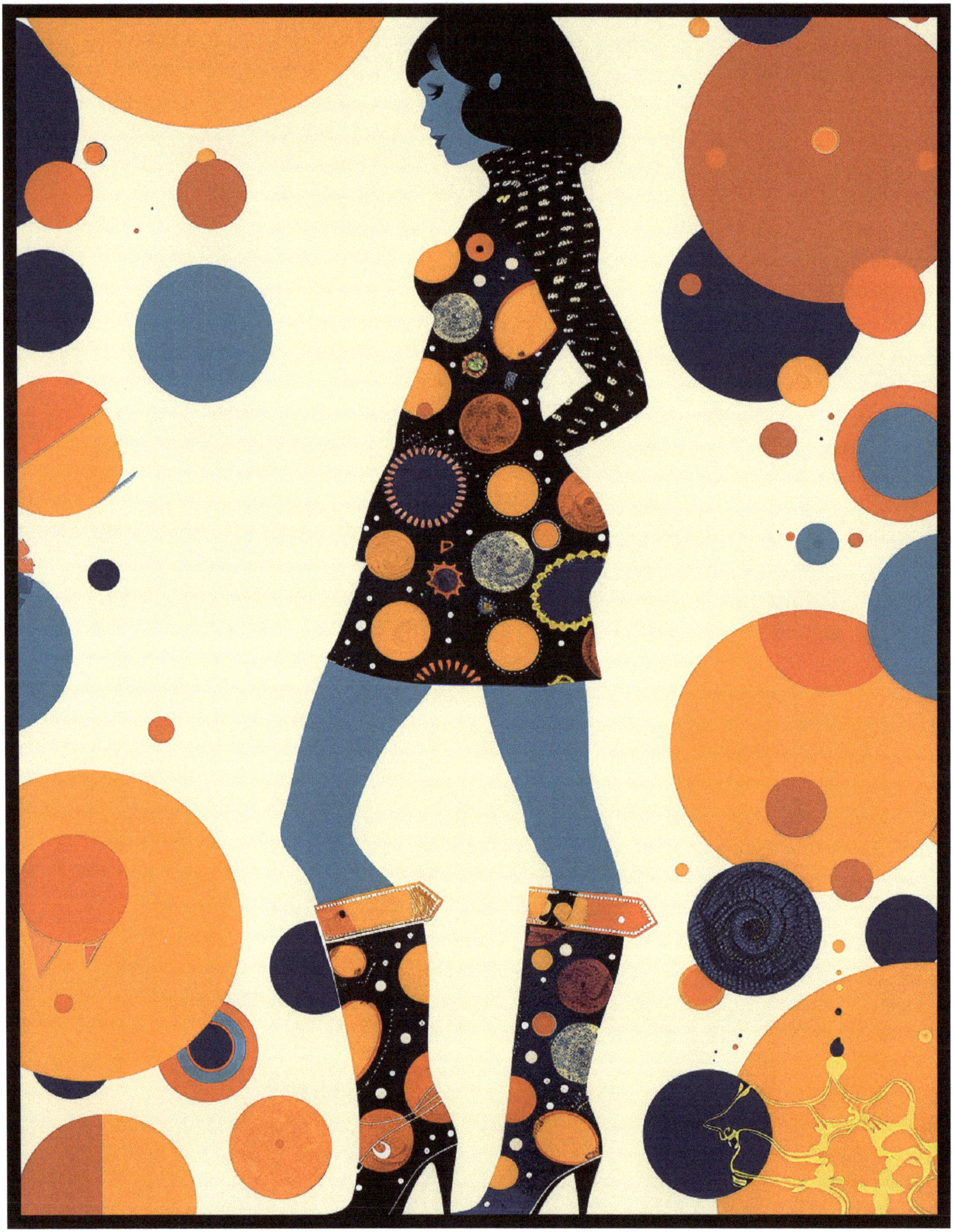

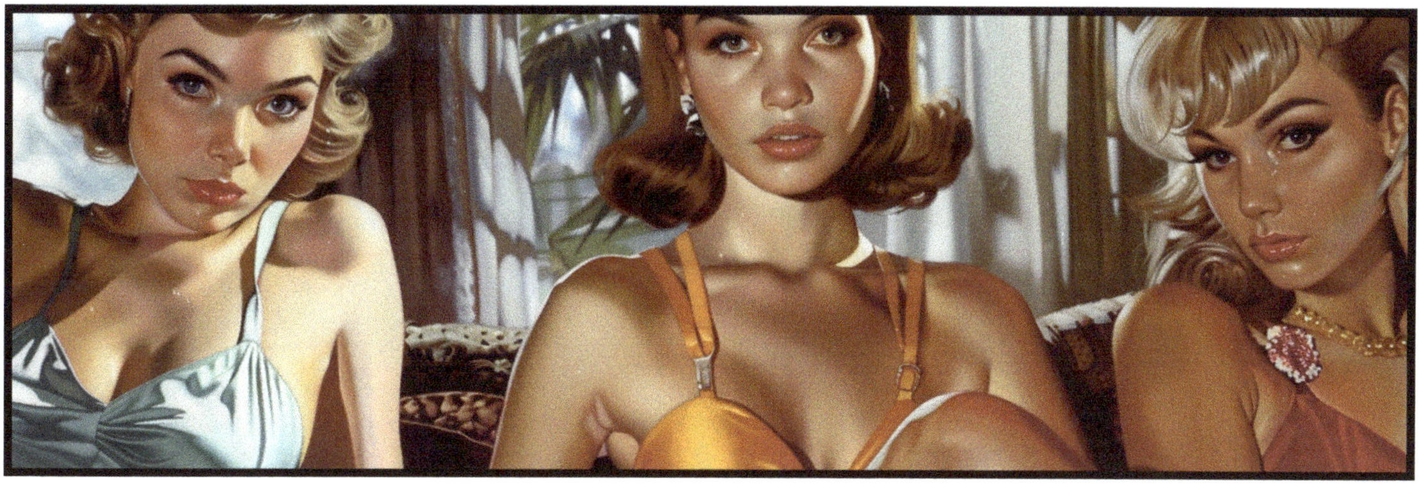

PIN-UP AND COUNTERCULTURE

During the counterculture movement, pin-up art began to incorporate more explicit and provocative themes, moving away from the playful innocence of the 1950s. This shift was a response to the era's more open attitudes towards sexuality and a desire to challenge conventional norms. Bettie Page's earlier work, featuring bondage and fetish imagery, continued to influence the genre, symbolizing sexual liberation and countercultural rebellion.

The rise of publications like Penthouse and Hustler further pushed the boundaries of erotic imagery, reflecting the counterculture's rejection of censorship. These magazines featured pin-up models in daring poses, offering a rawer portrayal of sexuality and emphasizing the movement's embrace of sexual openness.

The influence of rock 'n' roll and punk rock also impacted pin-up art during this time. Album covers, posters, and promotional materials often blended elements of glamour and rebellion, aligning with the counterculture's alternative lifestyles and anti-establishment attitudes. Artists like Robert Crumb and Olivia De Berardinis played key roles in this evolution. Crumb's underground comix featured exaggerated and provocative depictions of women, capturing the counterculture's challenge to societal norms, while De Berardinis brought a refined, artistic approach to pin-up illustration.

The counterculture era's impact on pin-up art extended into film and television, where pin-up-style characters and themes reached wider audiences. Films like "Barbarella" and television shows incorporated sex appeal with humor and adventure, reflecting changing attitudes towards female sexuality and the growing acceptance of explicit content in mainstream entertainment.

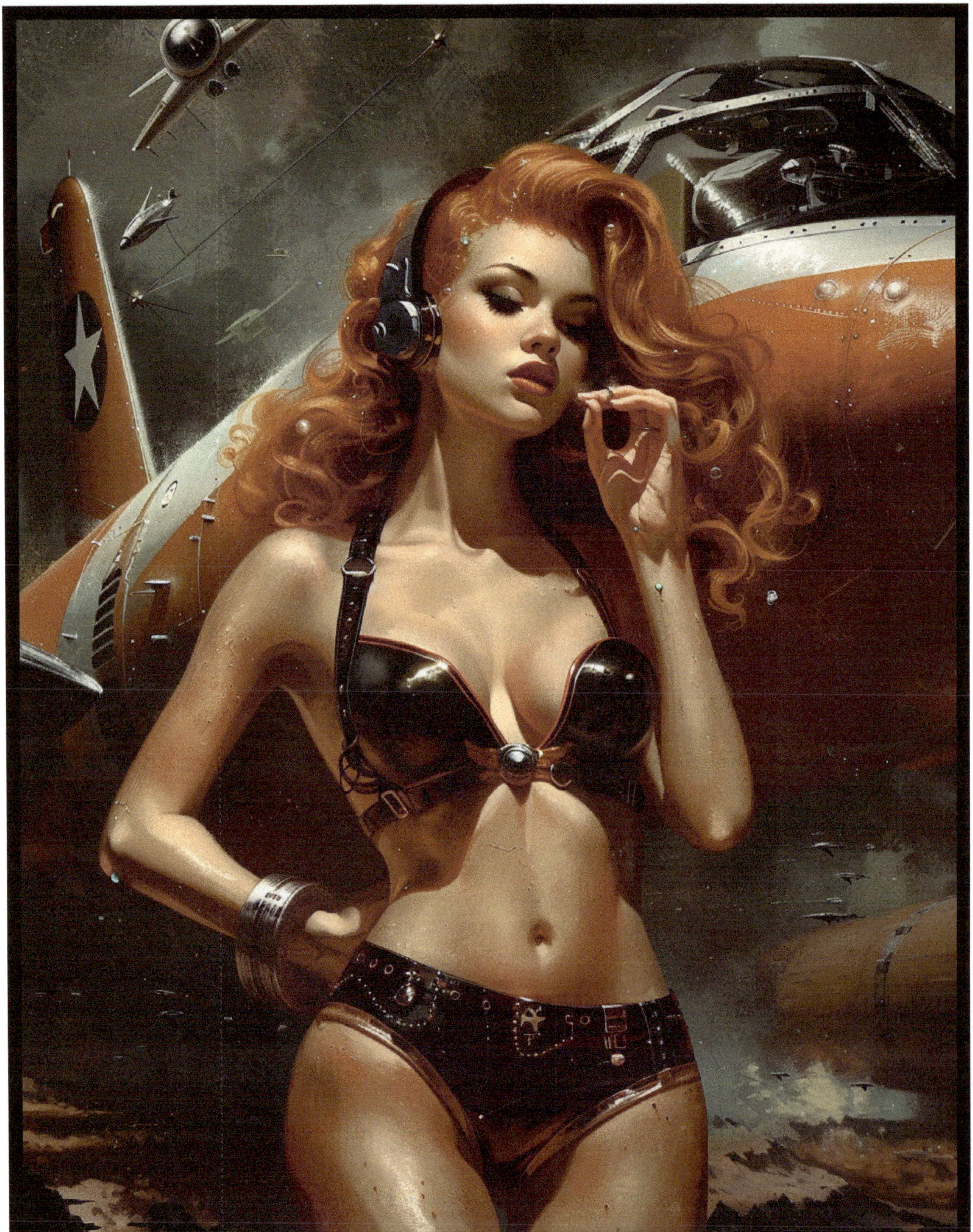

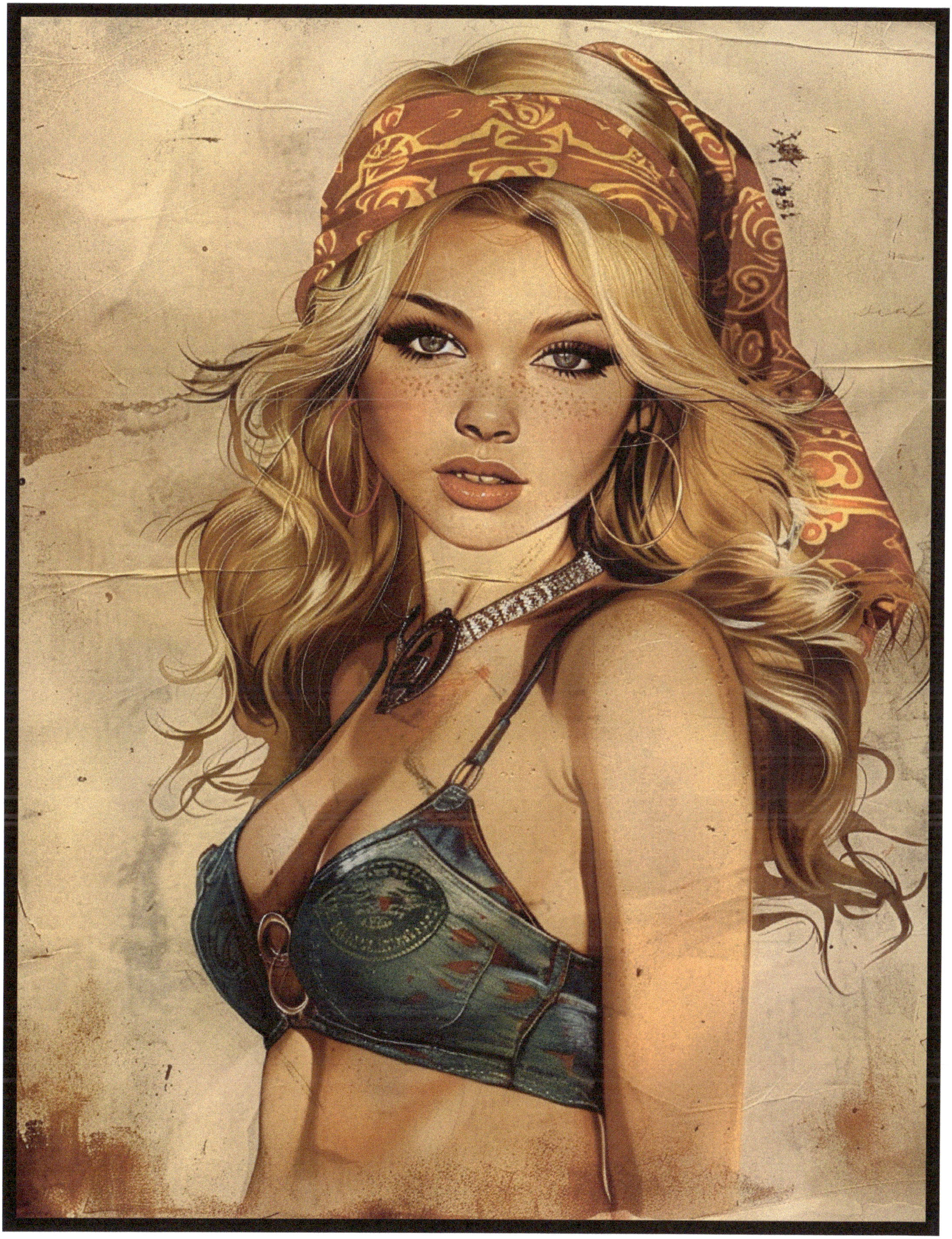

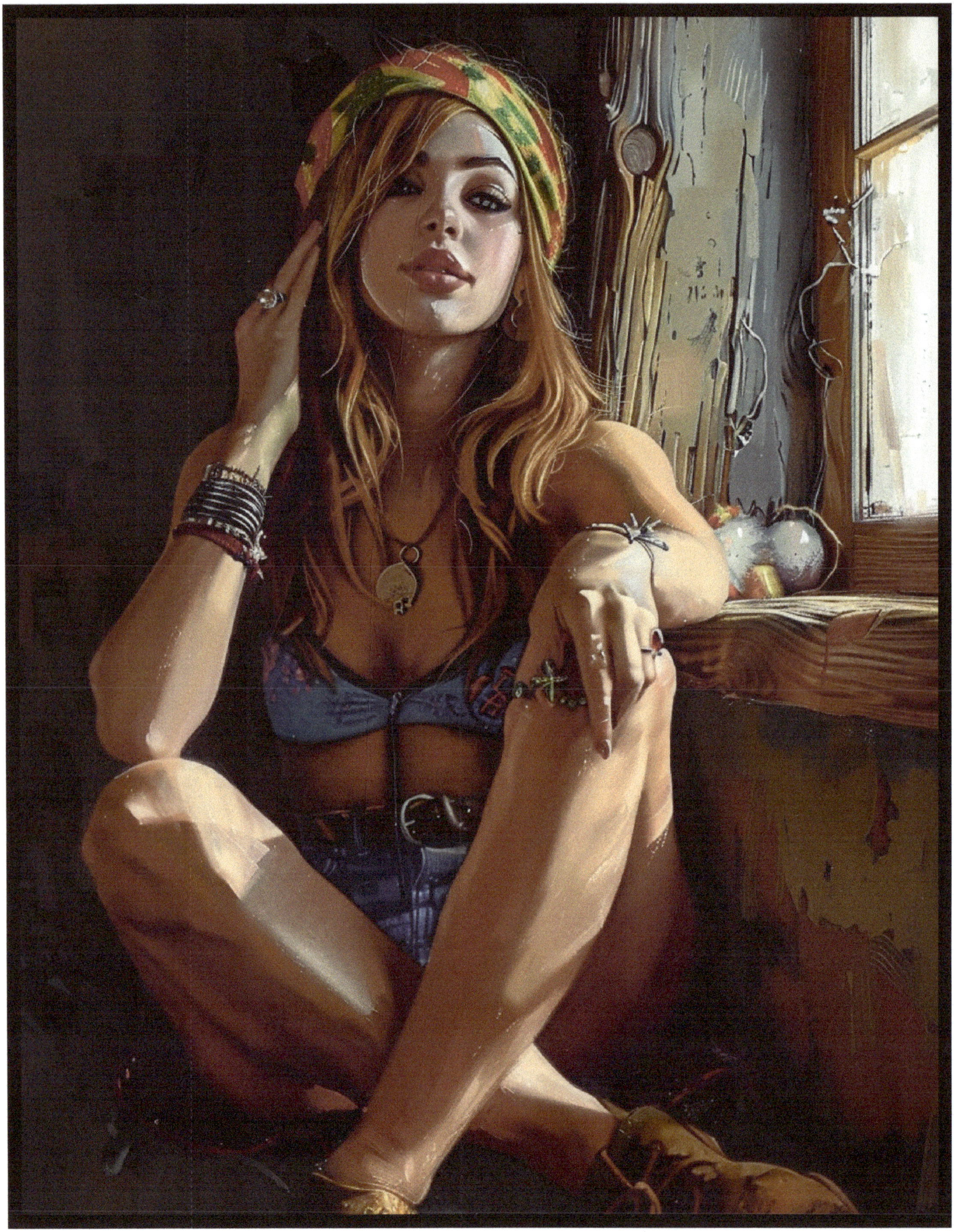

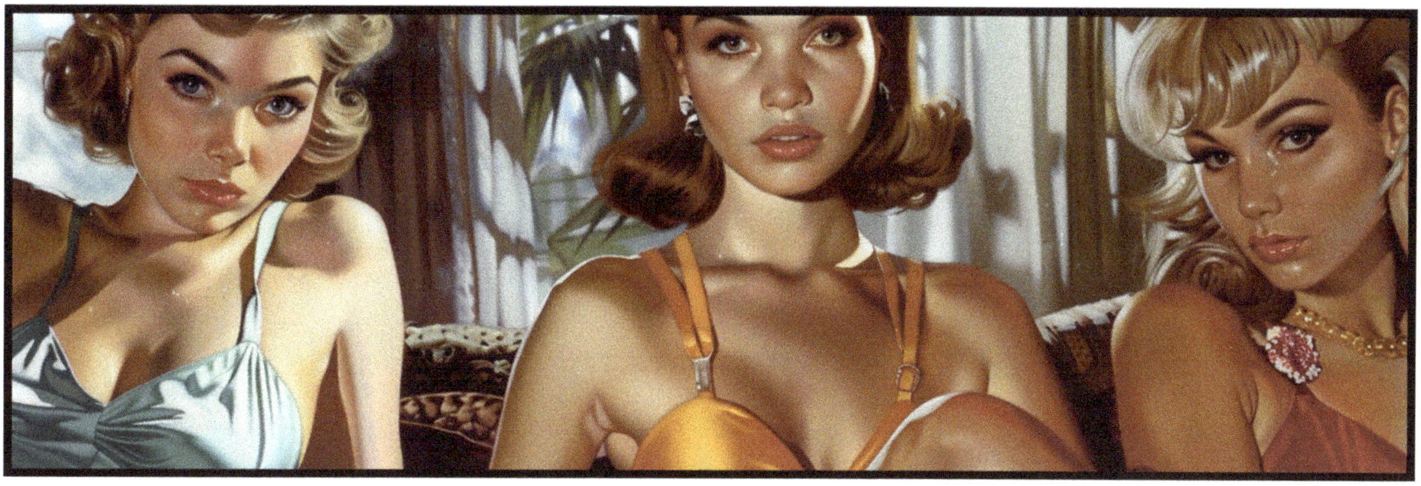

SEXUAL REVOLUTION

The Sexual Revolution challenged the conservative norms of the previous decades, advocating for open discussions about sex and a broader acceptance of sexual diversity. This cultural shift was driven by various factors, including the rise of feminist movements, the availability of birth control, and a general questioning of traditional authority. In this context, pin-up art began to explore themes that were previously considered taboo.

Artists and publications responded to the changing times by producing more daring and provocative images. The new wave of pin-up art was characterized by its explicitness and willingness to push boundaries. The illustrations and photographs of this era depicted women in a variety of erotic and sensual poses, celebrating their sexual autonomy and breaking away from the more restrained portrayals of the past.

The feminist movement played a crucial role in reshaping the narrative around pin-up art. While earlier pin-ups often reinforced traditional gender roles, the new wave of imagery sought to empower women by portraying them as active participants in their own sexuality. This shift was evident in the work of artists who embraced the feminist ethos, creating images that celebrated women's strength, independence, and sexual agency.

The influence of the Sexual Revolution also extended to the portrayal of men in pin-up art. The era saw the emergence of images that celebrated male beauty and sexuality, challenging the traditional gender dynamics that had long dominated the genre. This inclusivity reflected a broader cultural acceptance of diverse sexual identities and orientations, aligning with the revolution's goals of equality and liberation.

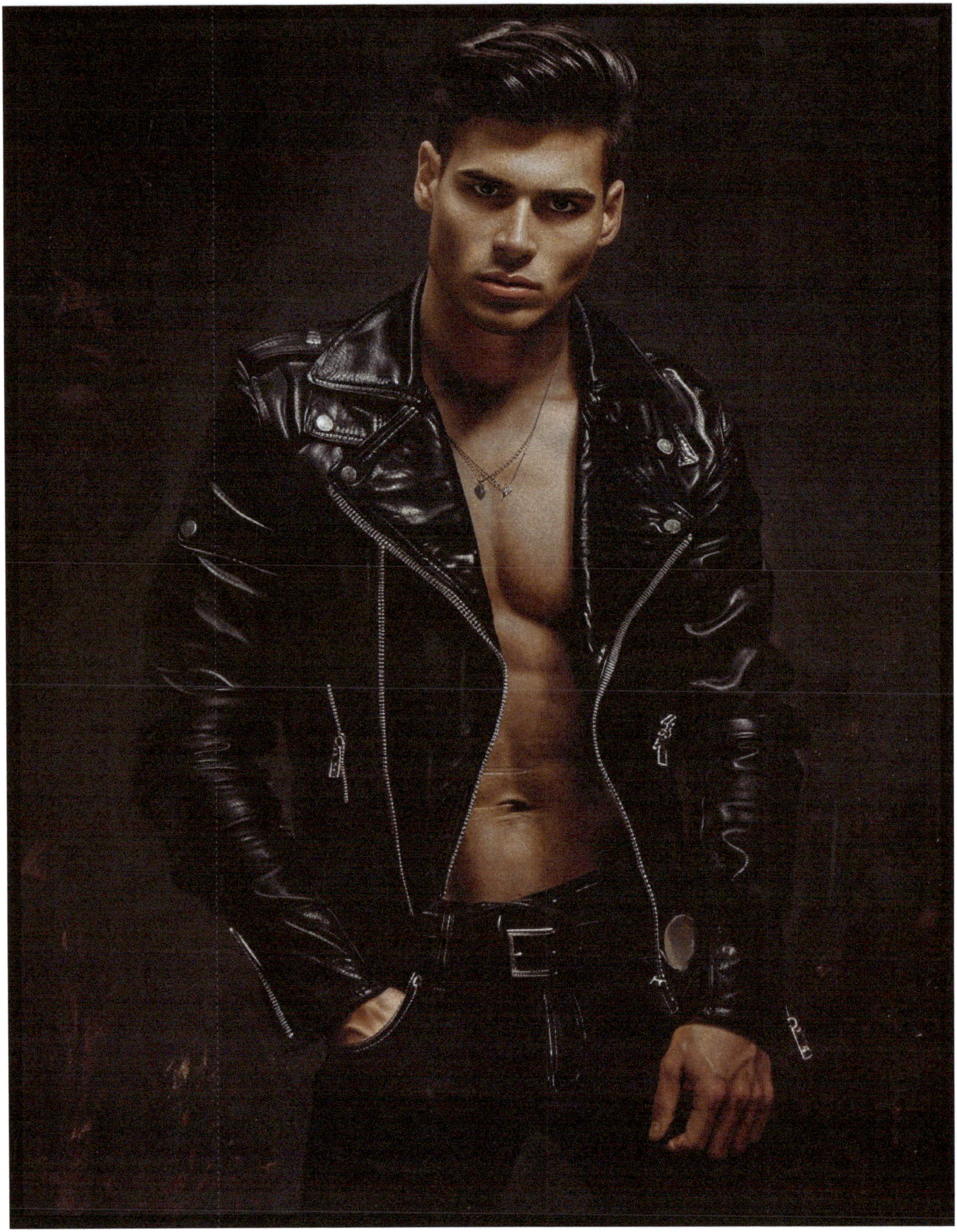

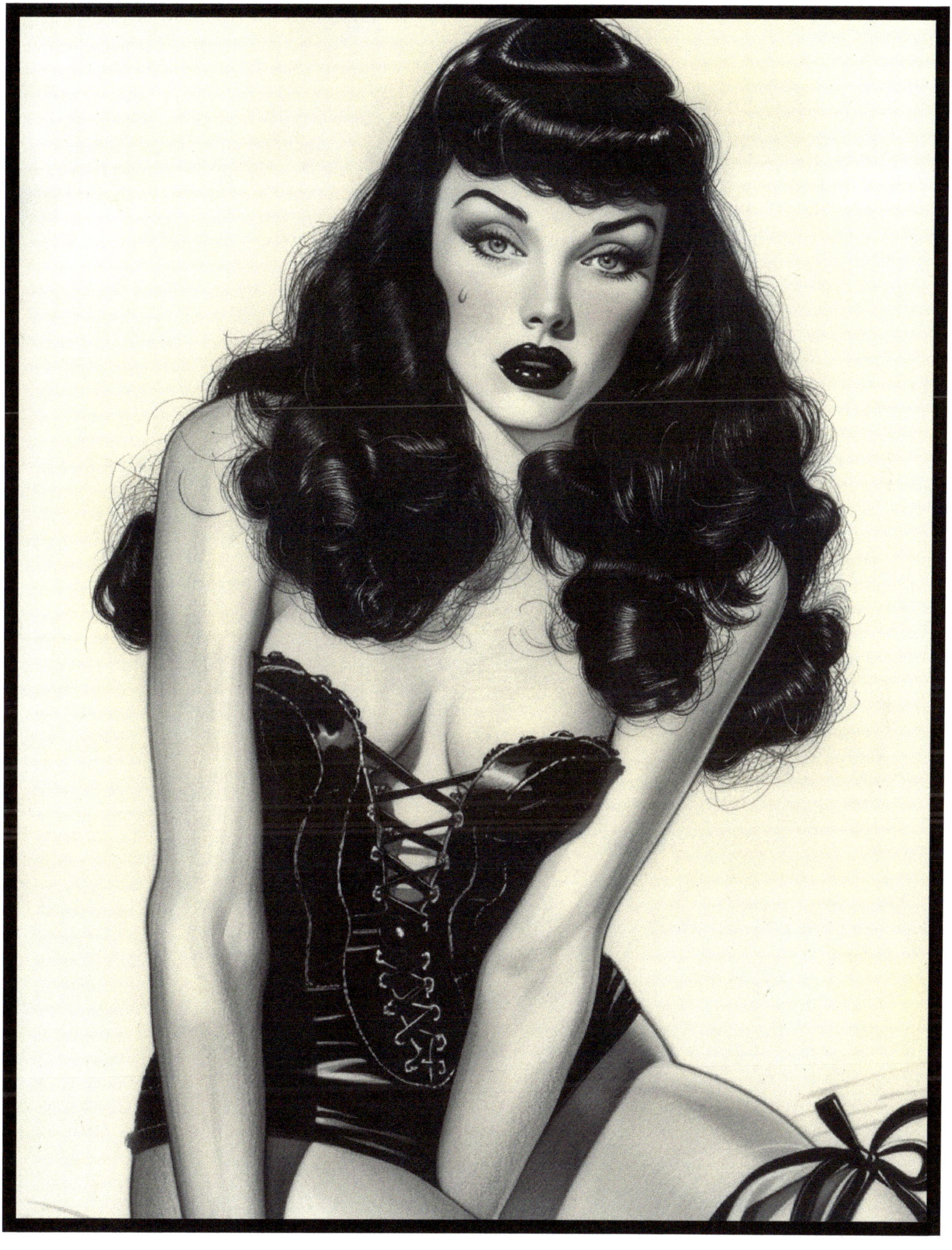

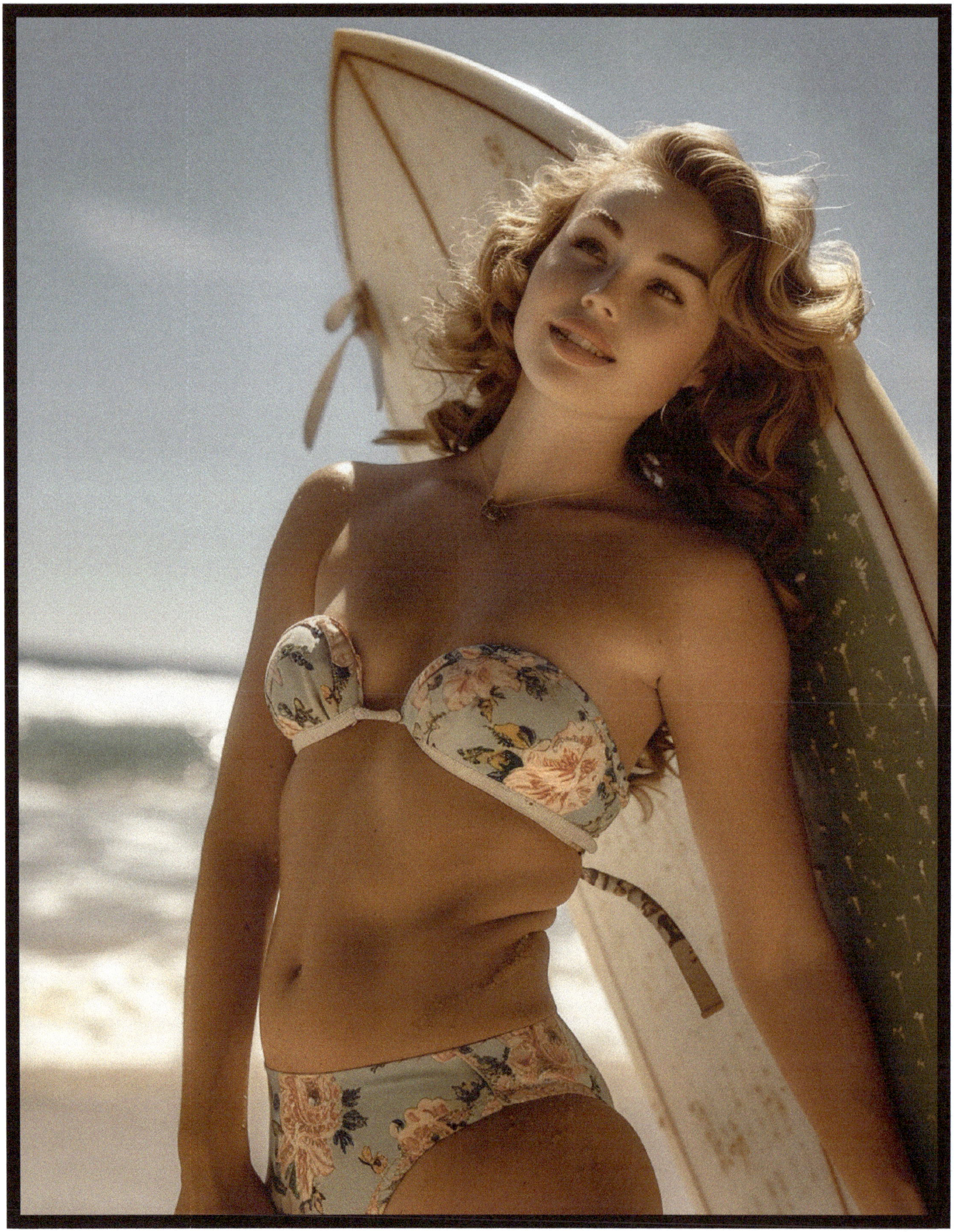

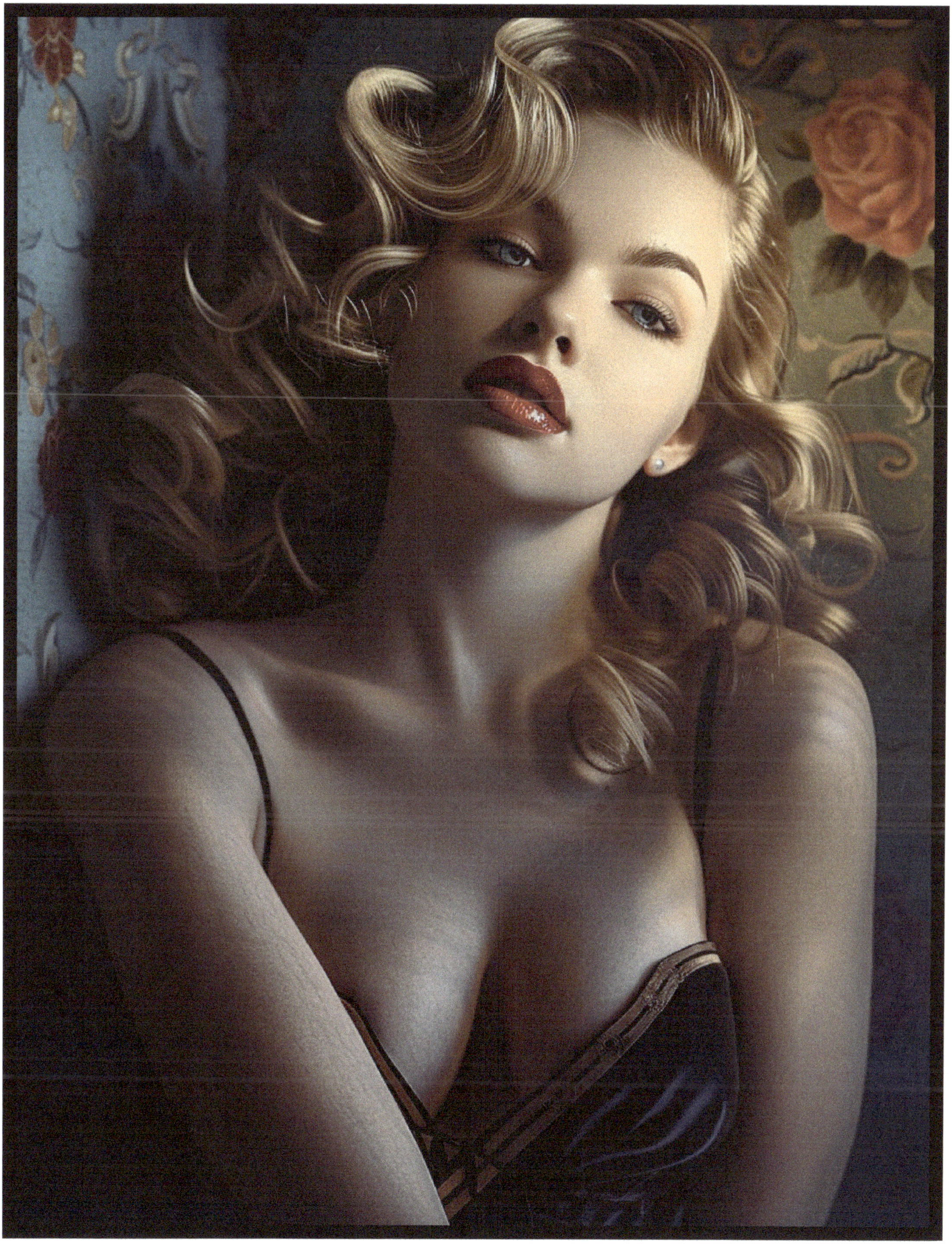

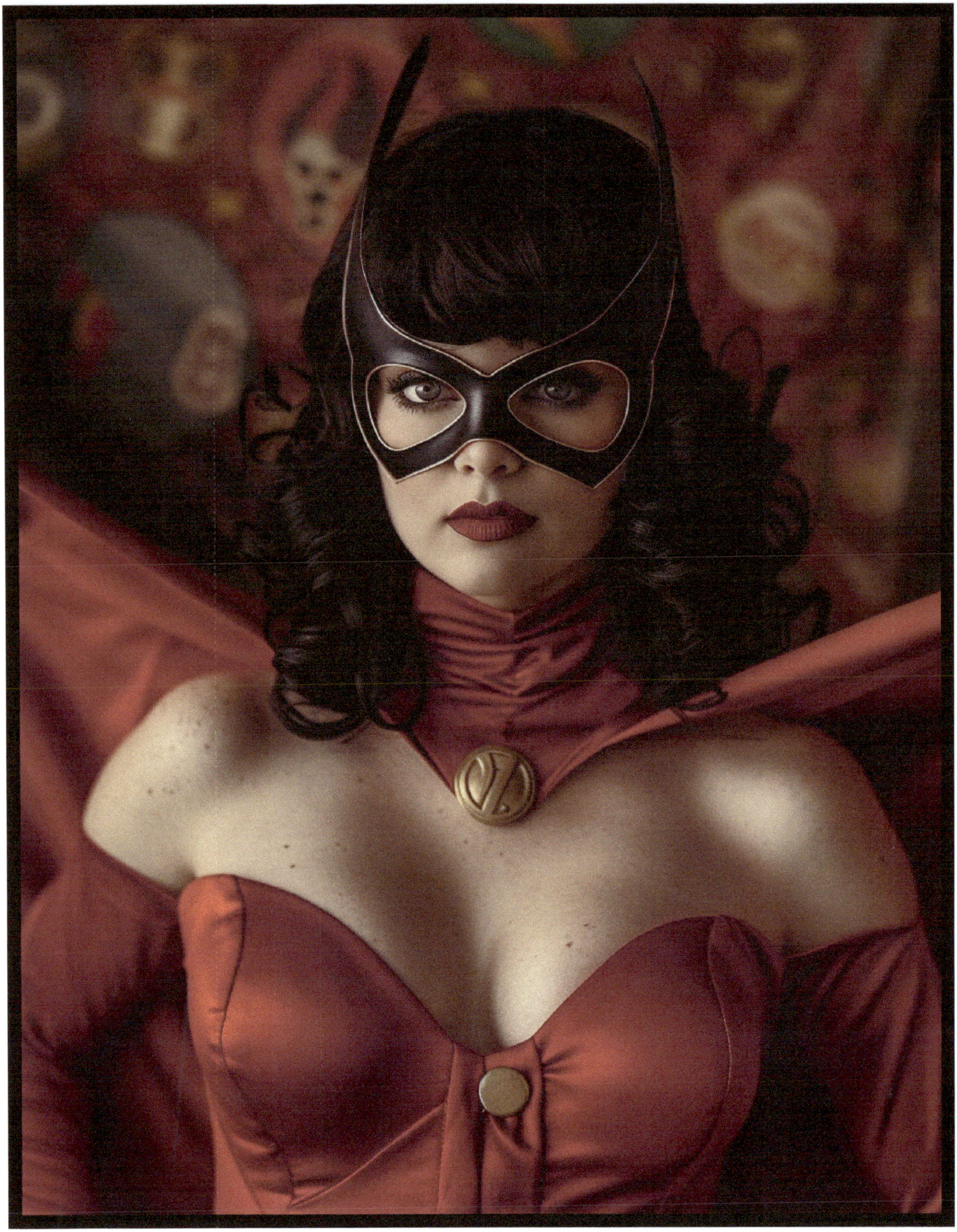

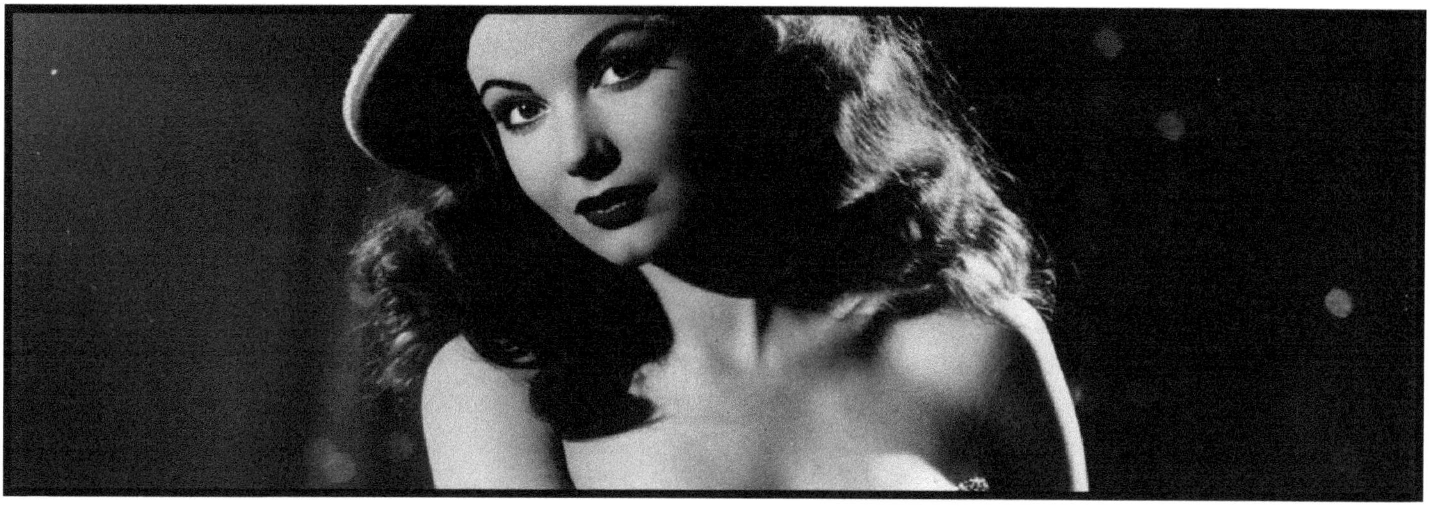

TRANSITION TO PHOTOGRAPHY

The transition from illustrated pin-ups to photographic representations marked a significant evolution in the genre, beginning prominently with the rise of Playboy magazine in the 1950s and extending into the subsequent decades. This shift not only changed the medium of pin-up art but also broadened its cultural impact and reach.

Playboy, founded by Hugh Hefner in 1953, was instrumental in this transition. While it initially included illustrated pin-ups, the magazine quickly became known for its high-quality photographic centerfolds. The first issue famously featured Marilyn Monroe in a nude calendar shoot, setting a precedent for the blend of sophistication and eroticism that would define the magazine. Playboy's use of photography allowed for a more realistic and immediate depiction of beauty, capturing the nuances of the human form that illustrations could not.

The shift to photography brought a new level of realism and intimacy to pin-up art. Photographs could capture the texture of skin, the play of light and shadow, and the unique expressions and personalities of the models. This realism made the images more relatable and tangible to the audience, enhancing their appeal. The use of professional photographers and sophisticated lighting techniques helped to create images that were both artistic and alluring.

Beyond Playboy, other publications and media followed suit, embracing photographic pin-ups as a standard. Magazines like Penthouse and Hustler pushed the boundaries further, with more explicit content that catered to a growing demand for uncensored depictions of sexuality. These magazines often featured full-color spreads and elaborate photo shoots that highlighted the models' allure in increasingly provocative ways.

The transition to photography also expanded the venues in which pin-up art could be found. Calendars, posters, and postcards featuring photographic pin-ups became popular, bringing these images into everyday spaces. The realism of photography allowed these images to blend seamlessly into various aspects of popular culture, from advertising to music album covers.

The advent of color photography further enhanced the impact of photographic pin-ups. Color images brought a vibrancy and immediacy that black-and-white photographs lacked. The rich hues and lifelike representation of color photography made the images even more captivating and engaging. This technological advancement coincided with the broader cultural trends of the 1960s and 1970s, which celebrated bold, vibrant aesthetics.

Photography also allowed for greater diversity in the depiction of pin-up models. The realism of the medium meant that a wider range of body types, skin tones, and facial features could be represented more authentically. This inclusivity reflected the changing societal attitudes towards beauty and representation, aligning with the broader cultural movements advocating for diversity and acceptance.

The influence of photographic pin-ups extended beyond print media into television and film. Shows and movies began to incorporate pin-up-style photography in their promotional materials, further blurring the lines between different forms of media. The visual language of pin-up art, with its emphasis on glamour and sensuality, became a staple in the marketing of various entertainment products.

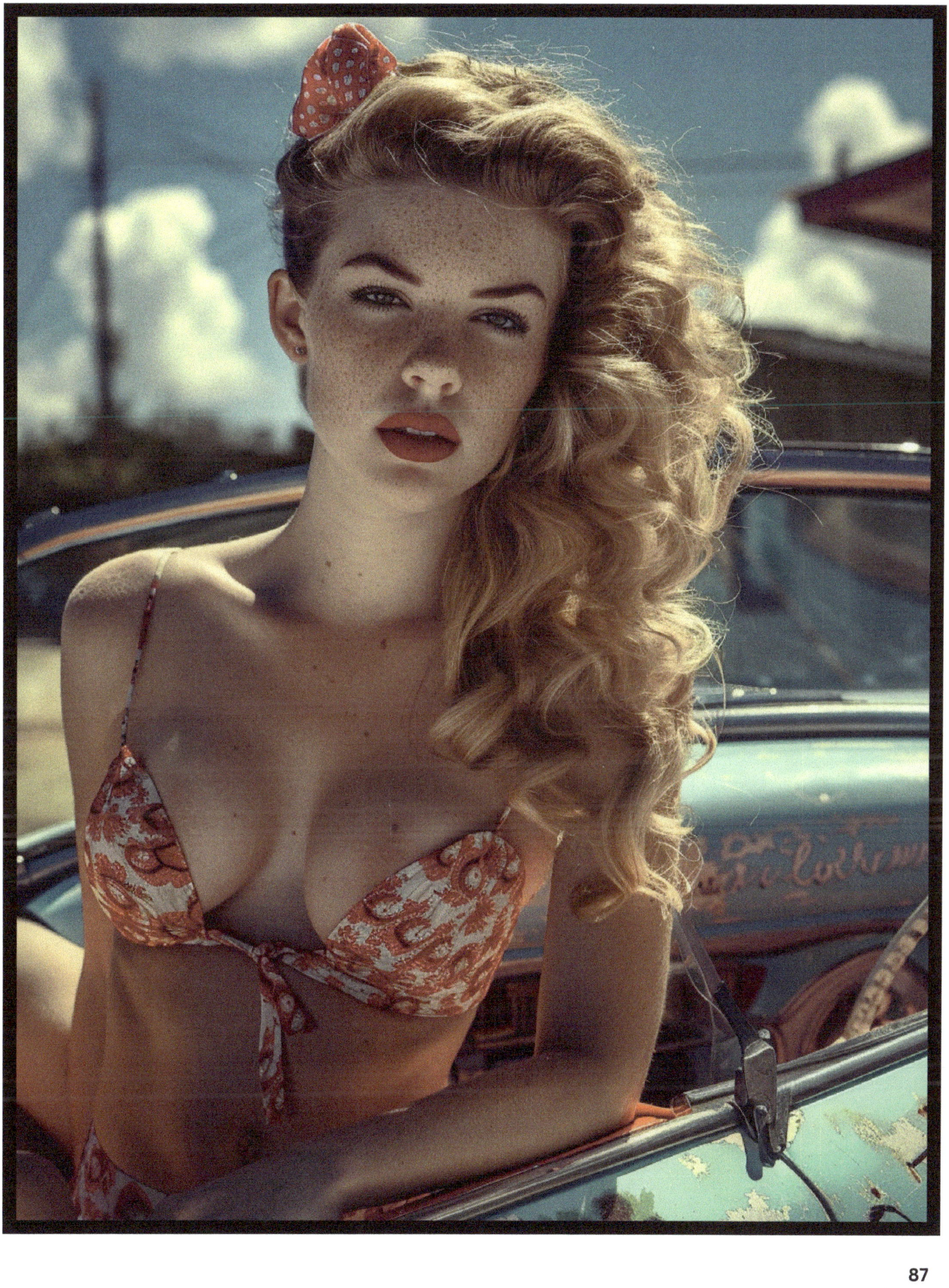

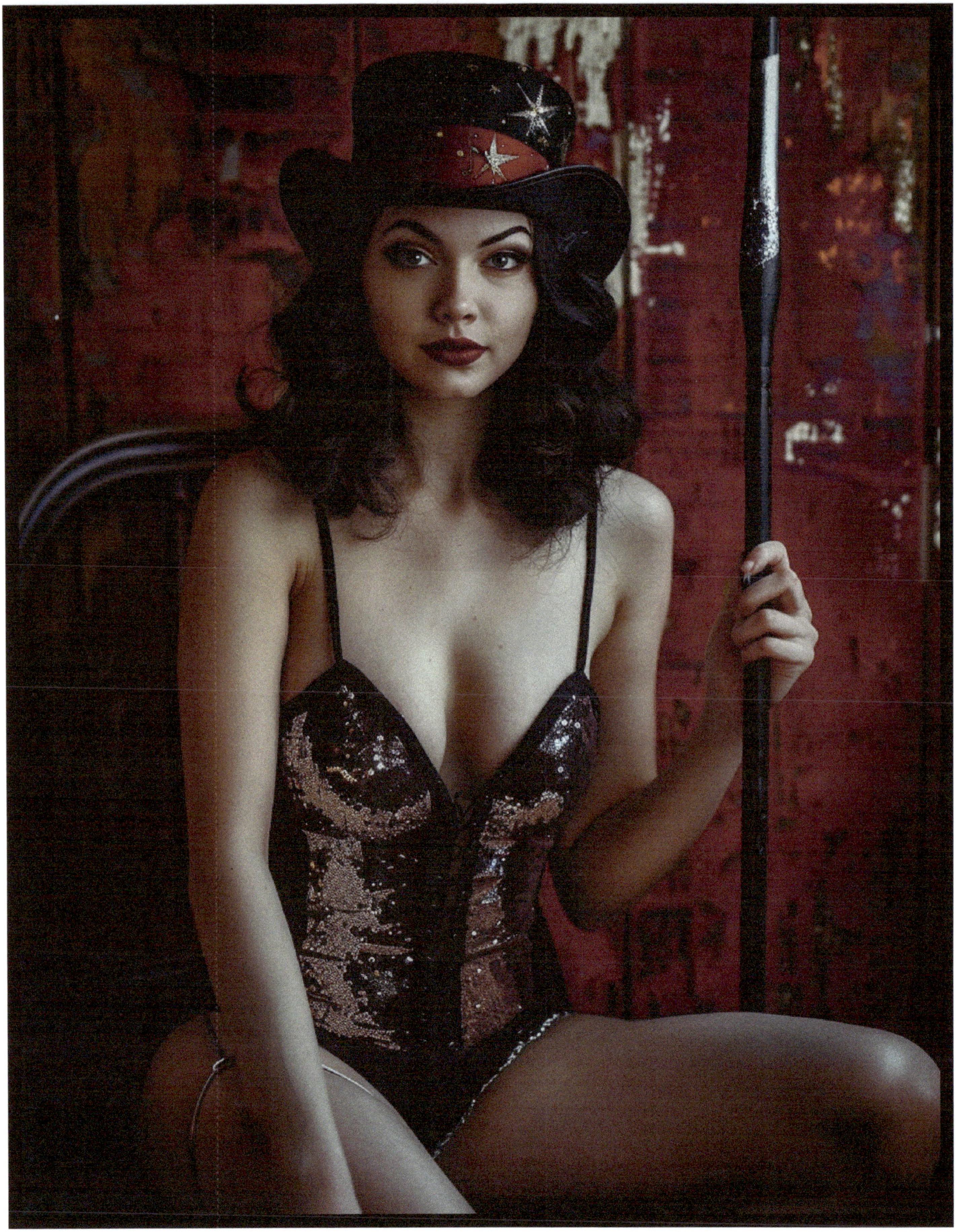

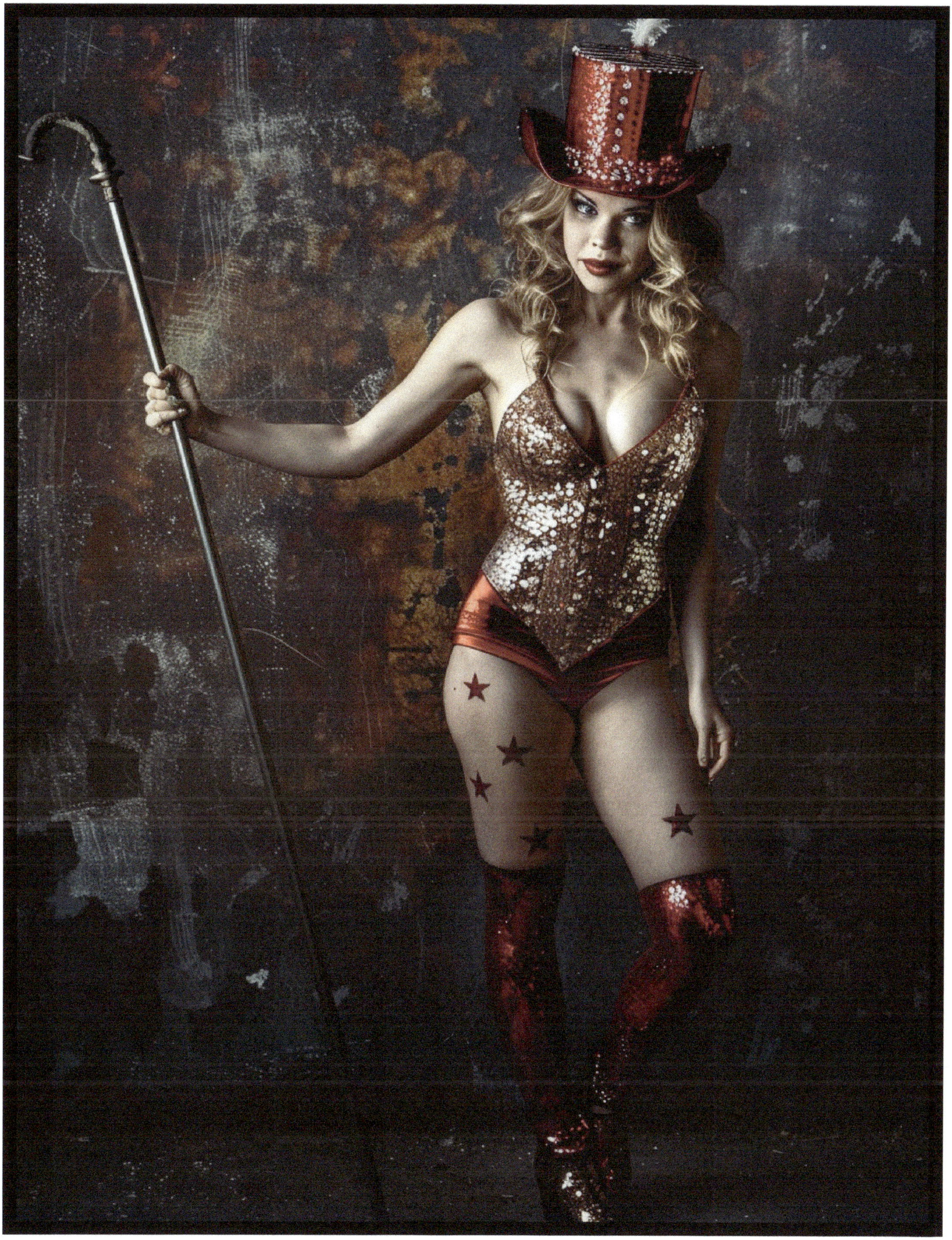

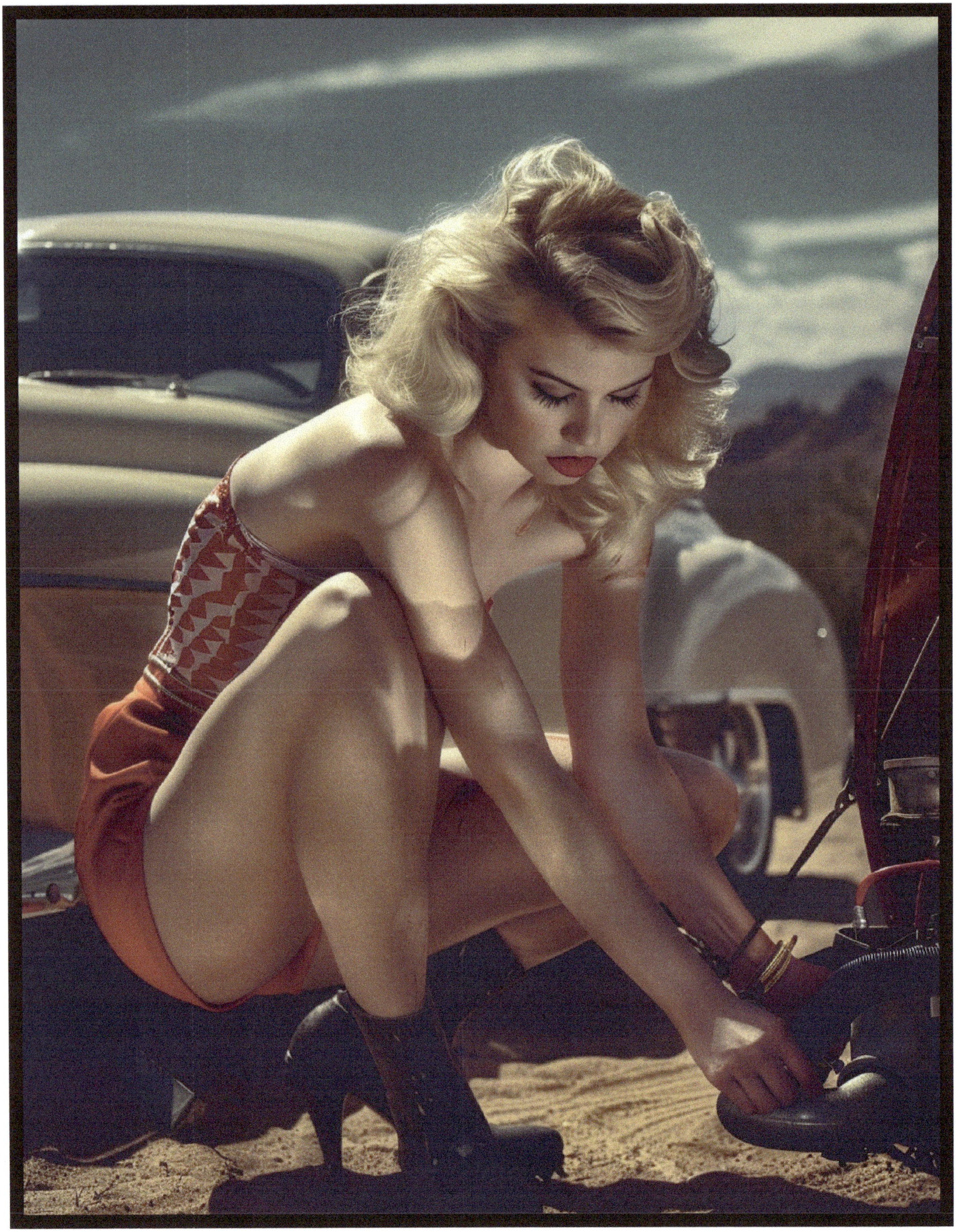

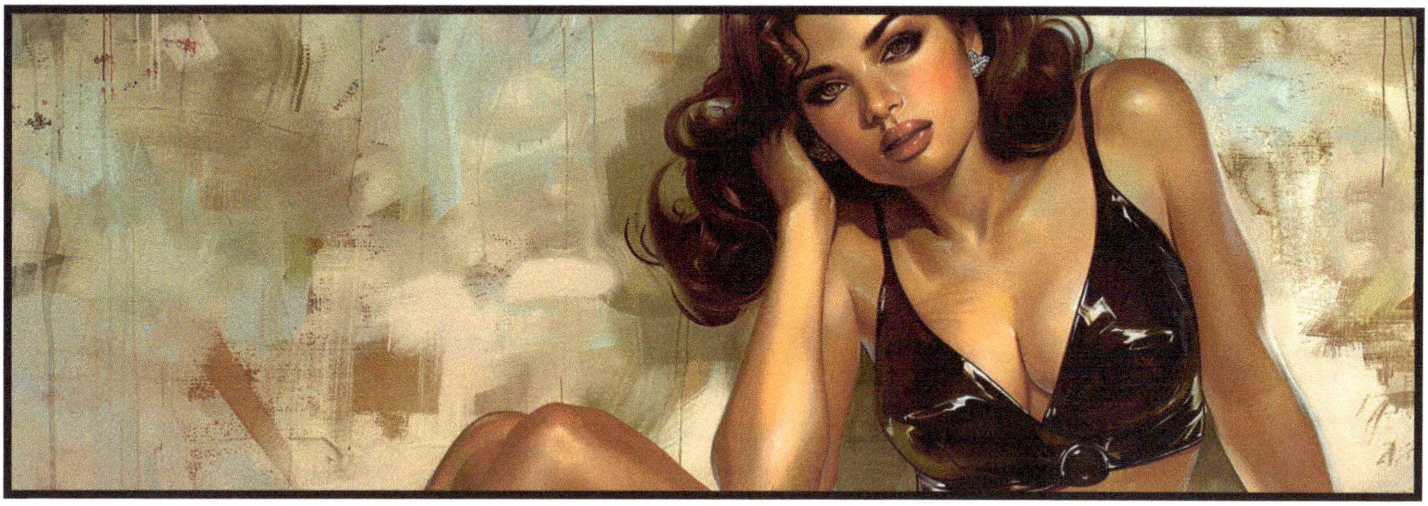

1990S-PRESENT: NEO PIN-UP

From the 1990s to the present, pin-up art has experienced a revival and transformation known as the Neo Pin-Up Movement. This contemporary evolution reflects changing societal values, technological advancements, and a renewed interest in vintage aesthetics, all while pushing the boundaries of the traditional pin-up genre.

The Neo Pin-Up Movement is characterized by a fusion of classic pin-up elements with modern sensibilities. Artists and photographers began revisiting the styles and themes of mid-20th century pin-ups, infusing them with contemporary fashion, diverse representations, and innovative techniques. This revival is partly driven by a nostalgic appreciation for the past, coupled with a desire to reinterpret and modernize the genre.

One of the significant aspects of the Neo Pin-Up Movement is its emphasis on inclusivity and diversity. Unlike the more homogeneous portrayals of beauty in earlier decades, contemporary pin-up art celebrates a wide range of body types, ethnicities, and gender identities. This inclusivity reflects broader cultural shifts towards acceptance and representation, making pin-up art more accessible and relevant to a diverse audience.

Technological advancements, particularly the rise of digital photography and social media, have played a crucial role in the Neo Pin-Up Movement. Digital tools have made it easier for artists to create and share their work with a global audience. Platforms like Instagram and Pinterest have become hubs for pin-up enthusiasts, fostering communities and providing a space for new artists to gain exposure. The accessibility of digital photography has democratized the creation of pin-up art, allowing amateur and professional photographers alike to contribute to the genre's evolution.

The fashion industry has also embraced the Neo Pin-Up Movement, with designers drawing inspiration from vintage styles to create contemporary pin-up fashion. High-waisted skirts, victory rolls, and retro swimsuits have made a comeback, blending nostalgic charm with modern trends. This fashion revival has been popularized by celebrities and influencers who adopt pin-up aesthetics, further integrating the style into mainstream culture.

Tattoos have become a significant element of the Neo Pin-Up Movement, with many pin-up enthusiasts incorporating vintage-inspired designs into their body art. Tattoo artists have developed a distinct style that combines traditional pin-up imagery with modern tattoo techniques, creating a unique fusion that celebrates both art forms. This trend reflects the movement's broader embrace of individuality and personal expression.

The Neo Pin-Up Movement has also expanded into various media, including film, music, and literature. Movies and music videos often feature pin-up-inspired visuals, while contemporary literature explores the cultural and historical significance of pin-up art. These multi-media representations help to keep the genre dynamic and relevant, ensuring that pin-up art continues to evolve and resonate with new generations.

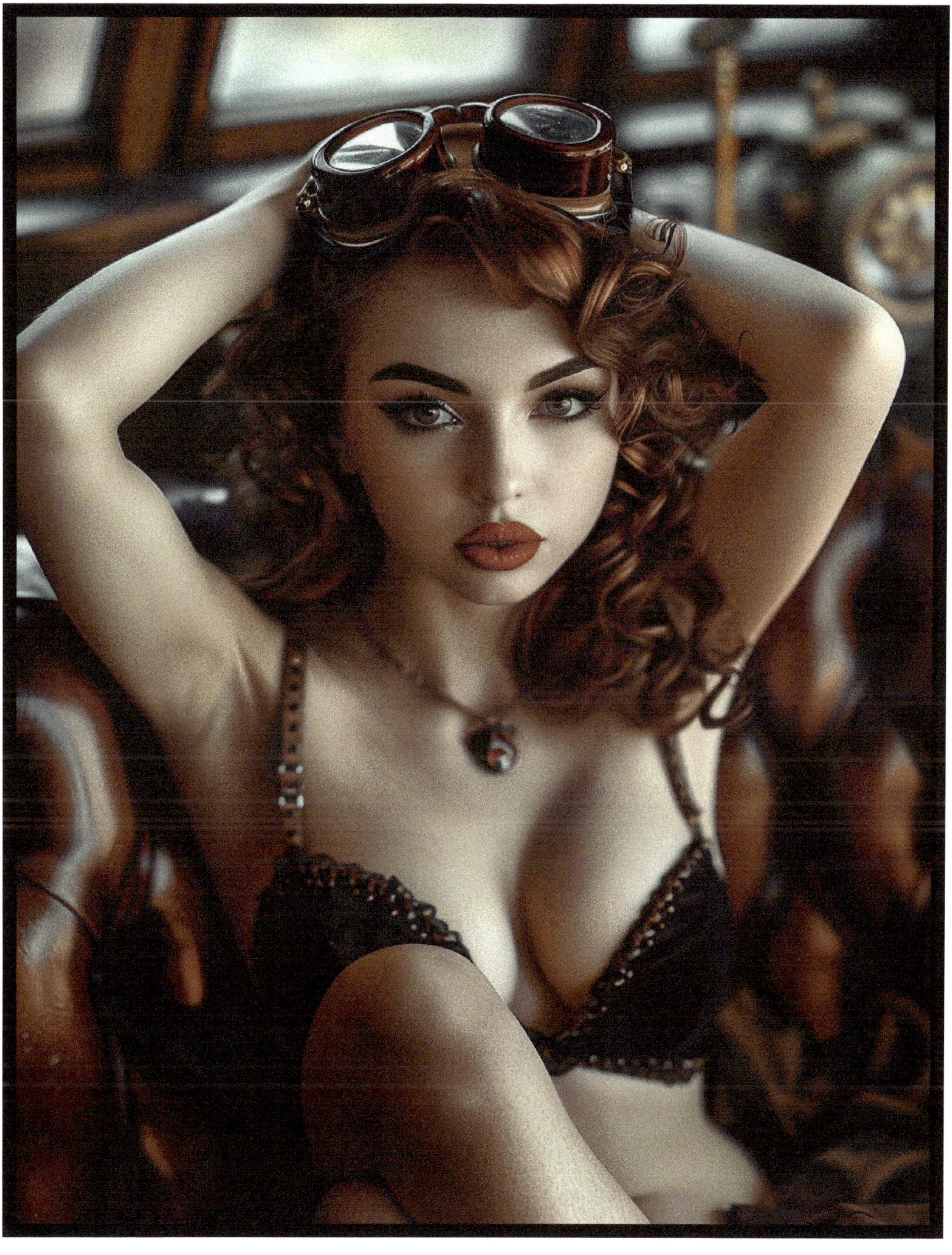

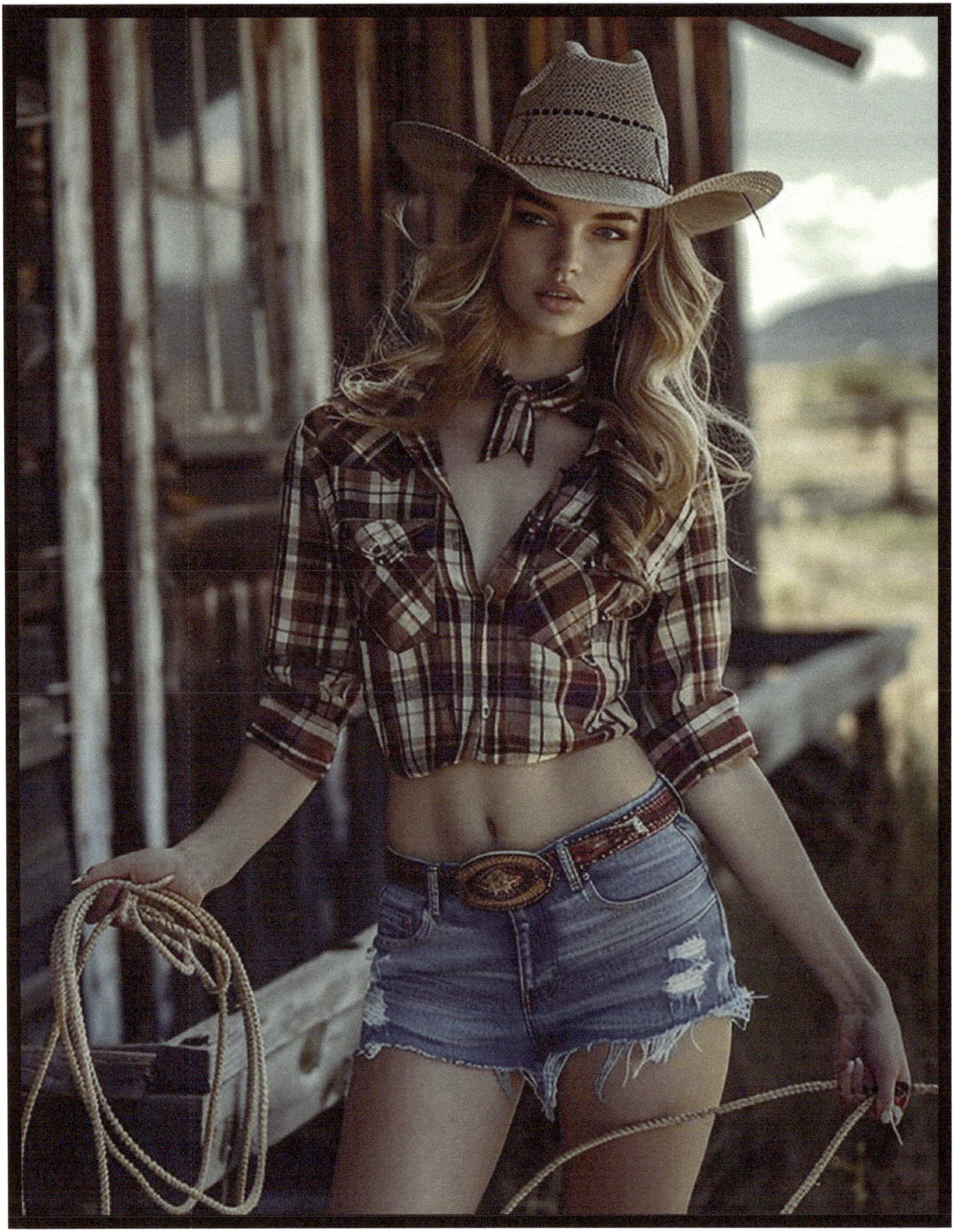

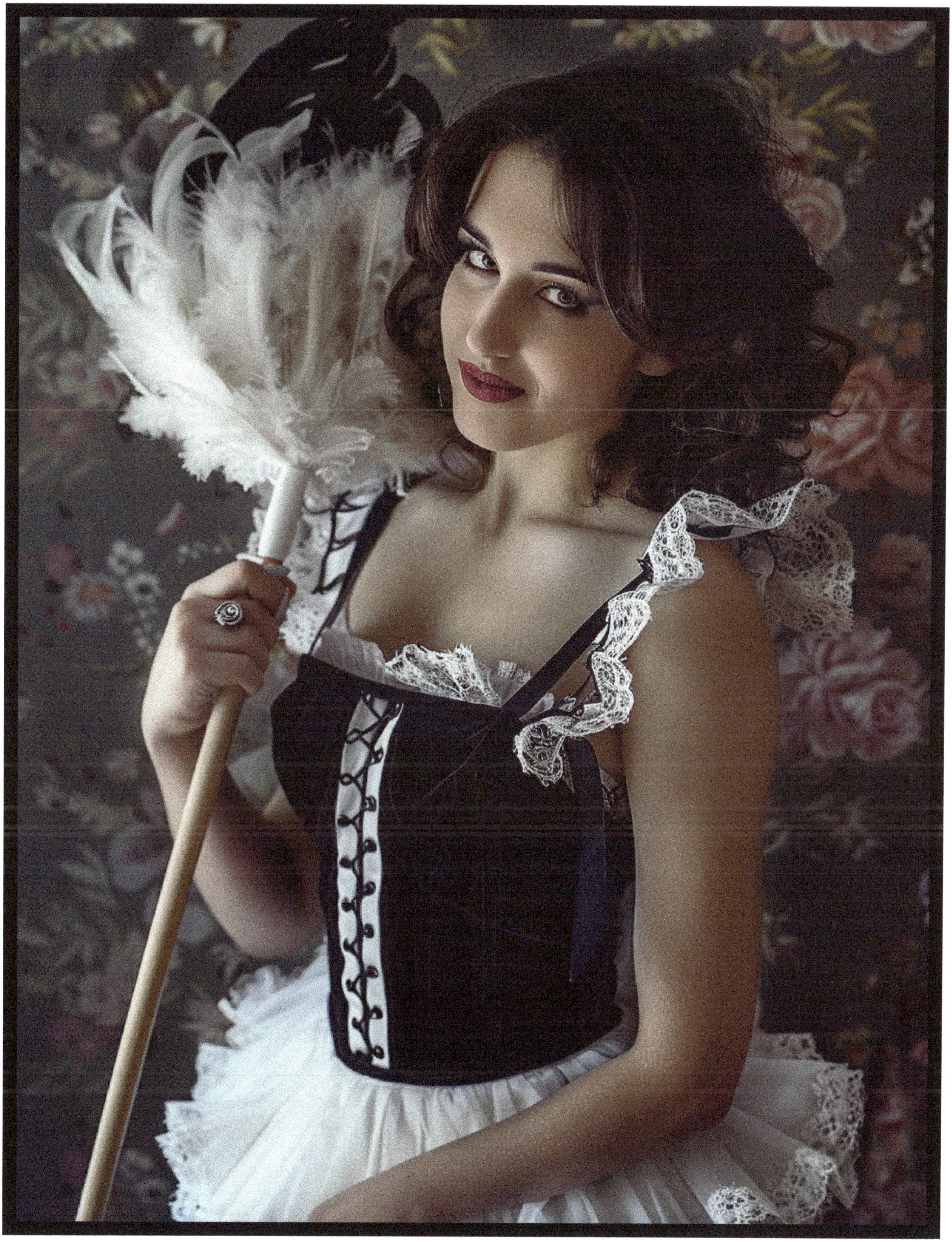

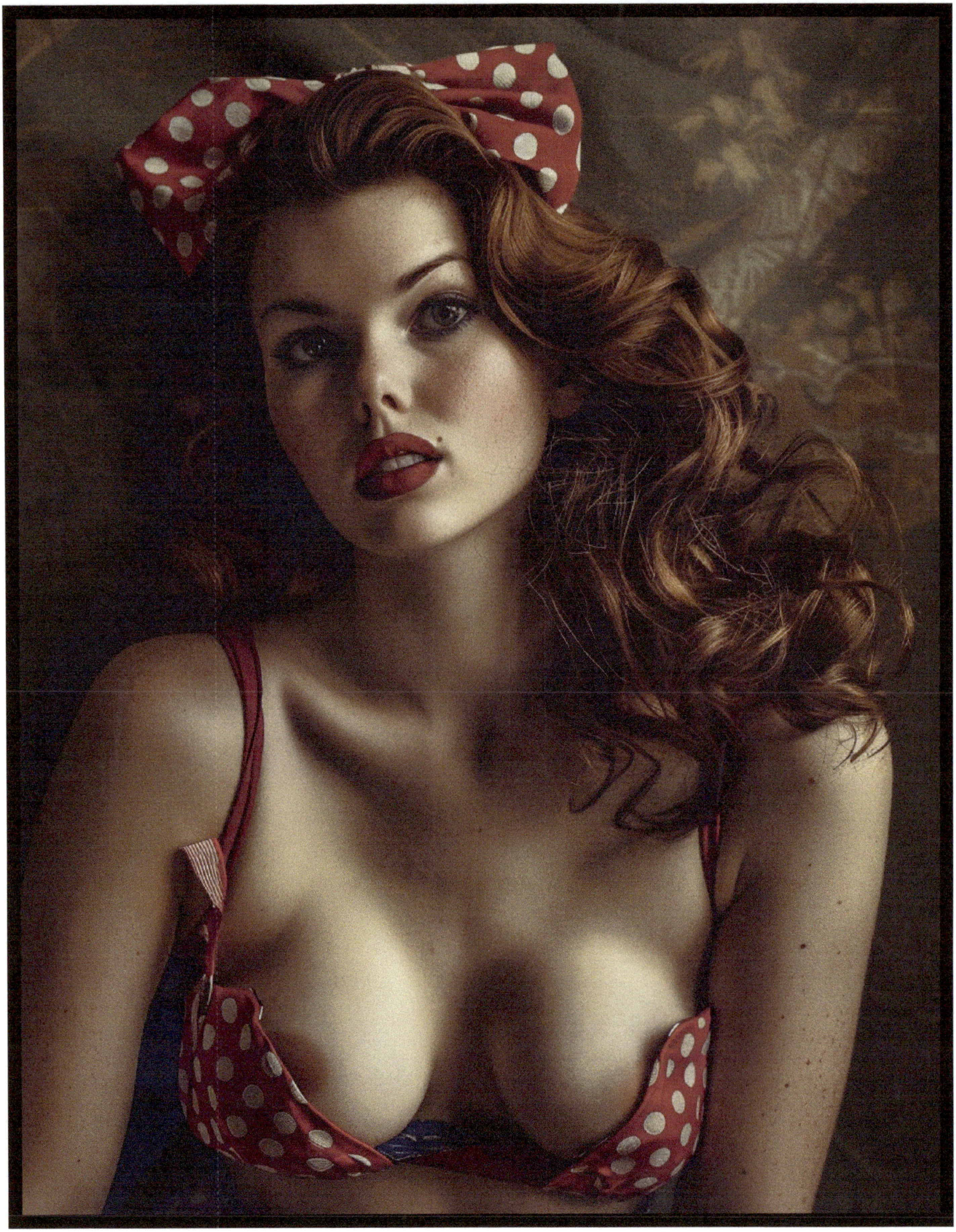

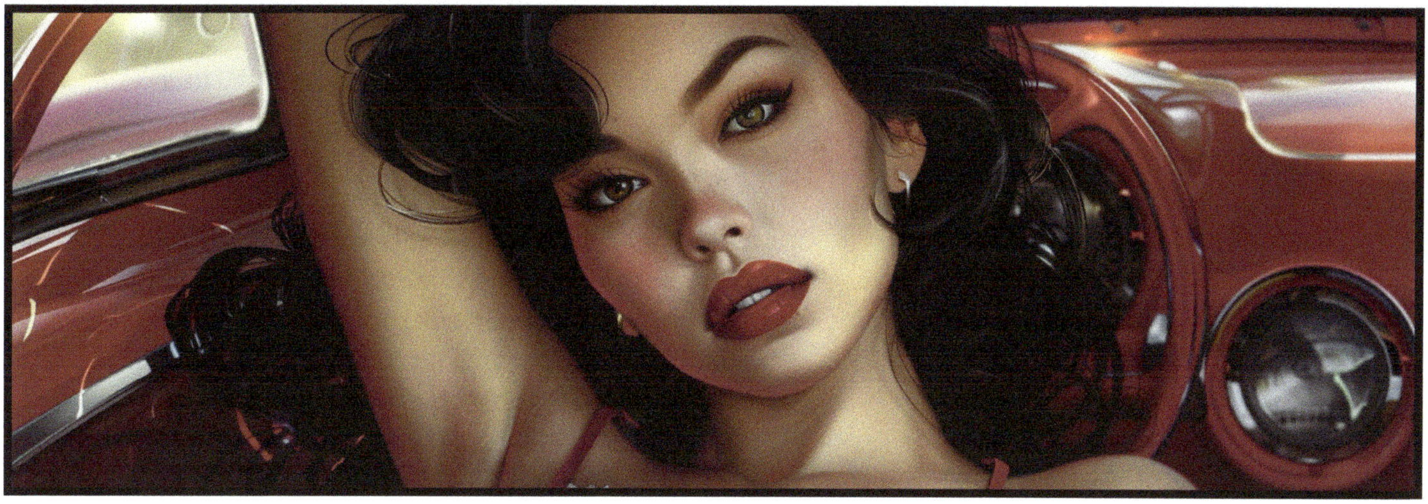

DIGITAL ART AND NEW MEDIA

he advent of digital art and new media has revolutionized the pin-up genre, introducing new possibilities for creativity, distribution, and interaction. This technological shift has allowed artists to experiment with innovative techniques and reach wider audiences, transforming how pin-up art is created and consumed in the digital age.

Digital art tools such as graphic design software, drawing tablets, and 3D modeling programs have provided artists with unprecedented flexibility and precision. Programs like Adobe Photoshop, Illustrator, and Procreate enable detailed and complex compositions that were difficult to achieve with traditional media. Artists can easily manipulate colors, textures, and lighting, resulting in high-quality, polished pin-up images that retain the charm of classic styles while exploring new aesthetics.

The rise of social media platforms like Instagram, DeviantArt, and Pinterest has dramatically expanded the audience for pin-up art. These platforms allow artists to share their work instantly with a global community, receive feedback, and build a following. The interactive nature of social media fosters a sense of community among pin-up enthusiasts and provides artists with valuable exposure. Hashtags and dedicated groups help connect like-minded individuals, promoting collaboration and inspiration within the pin-up art community.

Digital art has also enabled the integration of pin-up art into various multimedia projects. Video games, virtual reality (VR), and augmented reality (AR) experiences incorporate pin-up elements, creating immersive environments that engage users in novel ways. For example, video games may feature pin-up-inspired characters or settings, blending nostalgia with modern interactive storytelling. VR and AR technologies allow users to experience pin-up art in a more dynamic and personalized manner, enhancing the connection between the art and its audience.

Online marketplaces like Etsy, Redbubble, and Society6 have further transformed the pin-up art landscape by providing artists with platforms to sell their digital and physical works. These marketplaces offer prints, apparel, accessories, and home decor items featuring pin-up art, making it easier for fans to incorporate their favorite styles into their daily lives. The ability to reach customers directly without the need for traditional galleries or intermediaries has empowered many artists to sustain their careers and grow their brands independently.

Additionally, digital art has facilitated the fusion of pin-up art with other contemporary art forms. Mixed media projects that combine digital illustration with photography, typography, and animation are increasingly popular. This blending of techniques allows for innovative expressions that push the boundaries of traditional pin-up art, creating fresh and exciting visuals that appeal to modern audiences.

Crowdfunding platforms like Patreon and Kickstarter have also played a significant role in supporting pin-up artists. These platforms allow fans to directly support their favorite creators through subscriptions or project-based funding. This financial backing enables artists to focus on their craft, experiment with new ideas, and produce high-quality work without relying solely on traditional commercial avenues.

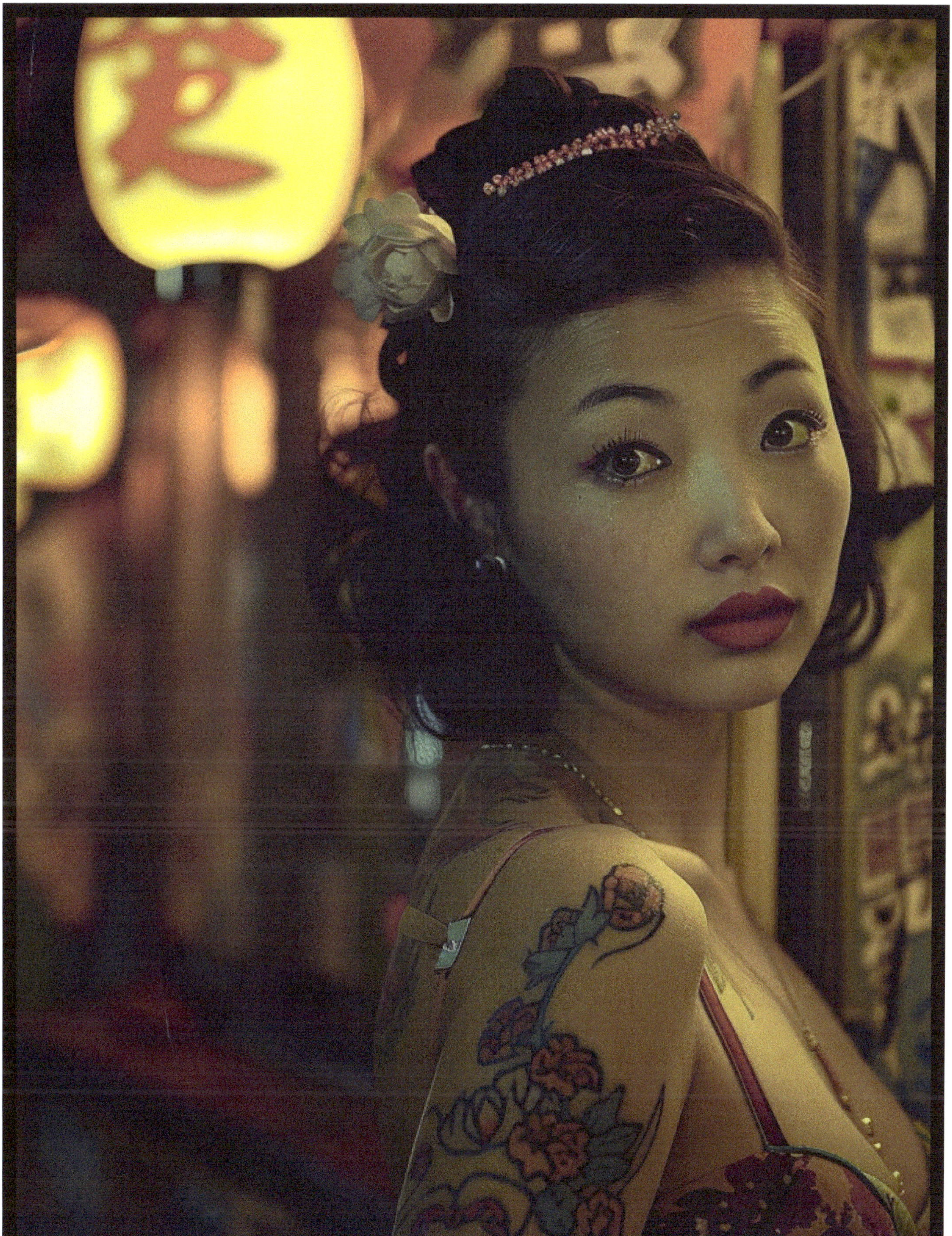

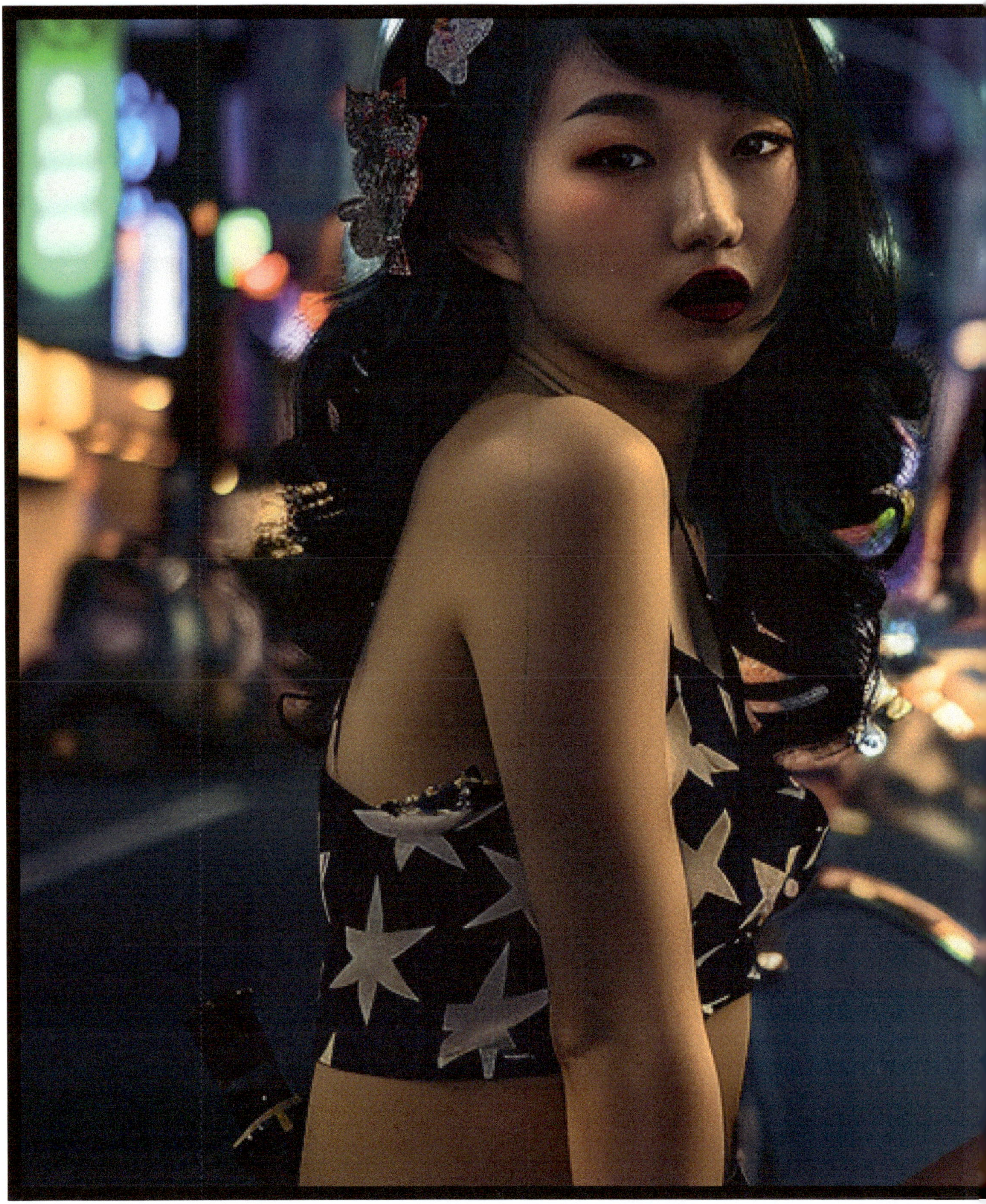

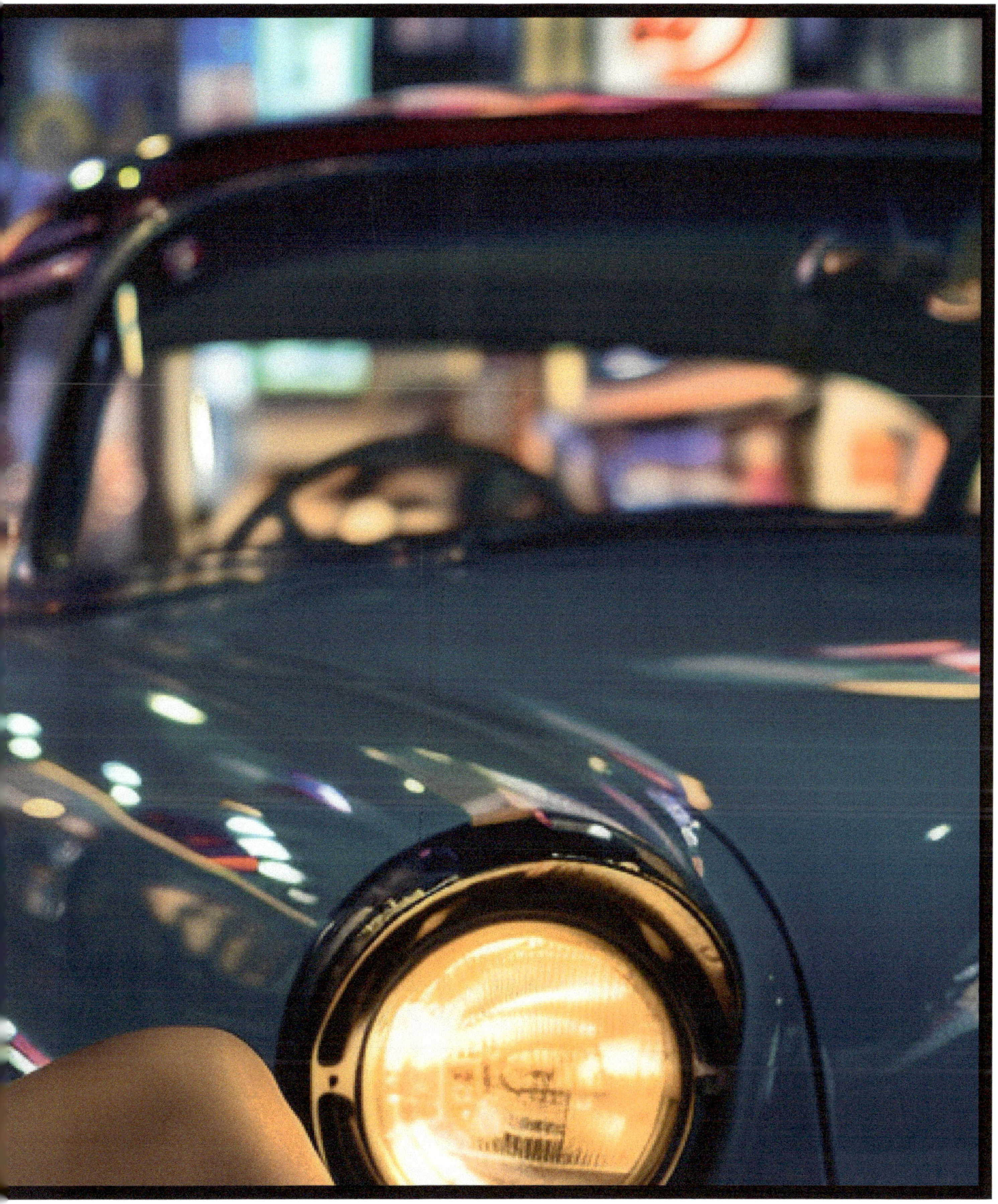

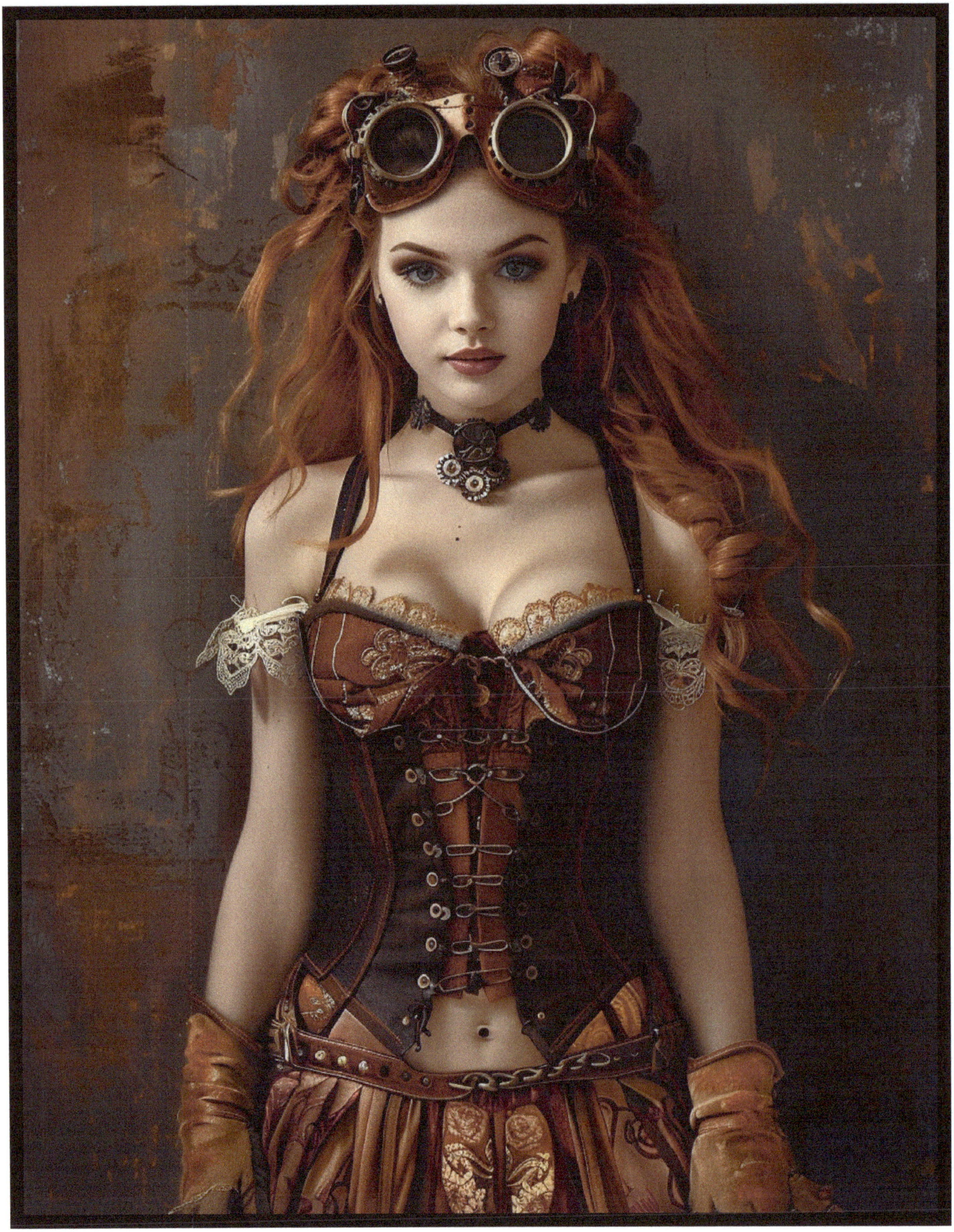

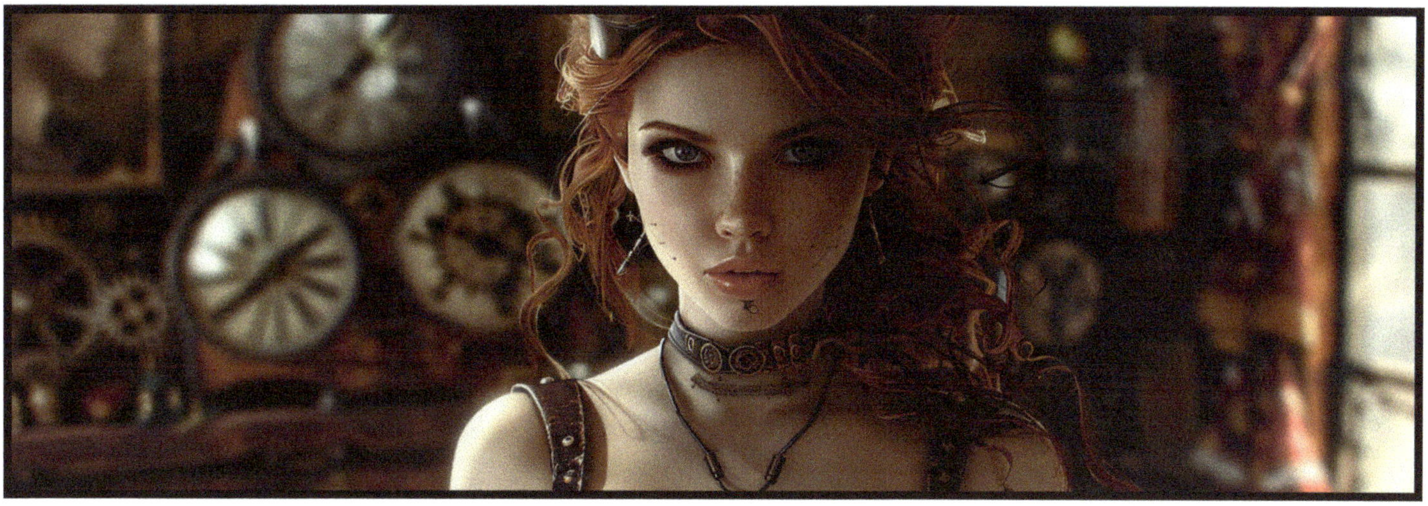

INFLUENCE ON FASHION AND LIFESTYLE

Pin-up art has had a significant and lasting influence on fashion and lifestyle, shaping trends and inspiring various aspects of contemporary culture. This impact extends beyond mere aesthetics, influencing attitudes towards body image, personal style, and even social norms.

The fashion industry has long drawn inspiration from pin-up art, incorporating its distinct styles into mainstream and alternative fashion. The hallmark features of pin-up fashion—high-waisted skirts, form-fitting dresses, bustiers, and vintage swimwear—continue to be popular. Designers often draw from the classic pin-up silhouette, which emphasizes an hourglass figure, to create garments that celebrate and enhance the natural curves of the body. This retro-inspired fashion is characterized by bold colors, playful patterns, and feminine details such as polka dots, stripes, and floral prints.

Hair and makeup trends have also been heavily influenced by pin-up aesthetics. The iconic pin-up look includes victory rolls, pin curls, and voluminous waves, often paired with red lipstick, winged eyeliner, and perfectly groomed eyebrows. These vintage beauty trends have experienced a resurgence, with many people adopting them for both everyday wear and special occasions. Beauty influencers and makeup artists on social media platforms frequently showcase tutorials on achieving the pin-up look, further cementing its place in contemporary fashion.
The pin-up influence extends to accessories as well. Items such as cat-eye sunglasses, peep-toe heels, and bandanas tied in hair bows are staples of the pin-up style. These accessories not only complement the clothing but also add a touch of vintage charm to modern outfits. The use of such accessories allows individuals to incorporate elements of pin-up fashion into their daily wardrobes, making the style accessible and versatile.

Pin-up fashion has also fostered a sense of body positivity and self-acceptance. The genre's celebration of curvaceous figures challenges the often unrealistic and narrow standards of beauty prevalent in the fashion industry. Pin-up art and fashion emphasize the beauty of diverse body types, encouraging individuals to embrace their unique shapes and sizes. This message of inclusivity and confidence resonates with many, contributing to a broader movement towards body positivity.

Lifestyle choices and subcultures have also been influenced by pin-up art. The rockabilly scene, for instance, combines elements of 1950s rock 'n' roll culture with pin-up fashion. Rockabilly enthusiasts often dress in vintage-inspired clothing, attend car shows featuring classic cars, and participate in swing and jive dancing. This subculture celebrates the music, fashion, and lifestyle of the mid-20th century, keeping the pin-up aesthetic alive and vibrant.

Pin-up culture has made its way into home decor as well. Vintage-inspired designs, such as mid-century modern furniture, retro kitchen appliances, and pin-up posters, are popular choices for those looking to infuse their living spaces with a nostalgic touch. These elements create a sense of timeless style and charm, bridging the gap between past and present.

The influence of pin-up art on fashion and lifestyle is also evident in the entertainment industry. Television shows, movies, and music videos often incorporate pin-up elements to evoke a sense of nostalgia or to pay homage to the era. Celebrities and public figures who embrace pin-up fashion help to popularize the style, bringing it to a wider audience and ensuring its continued relevance.

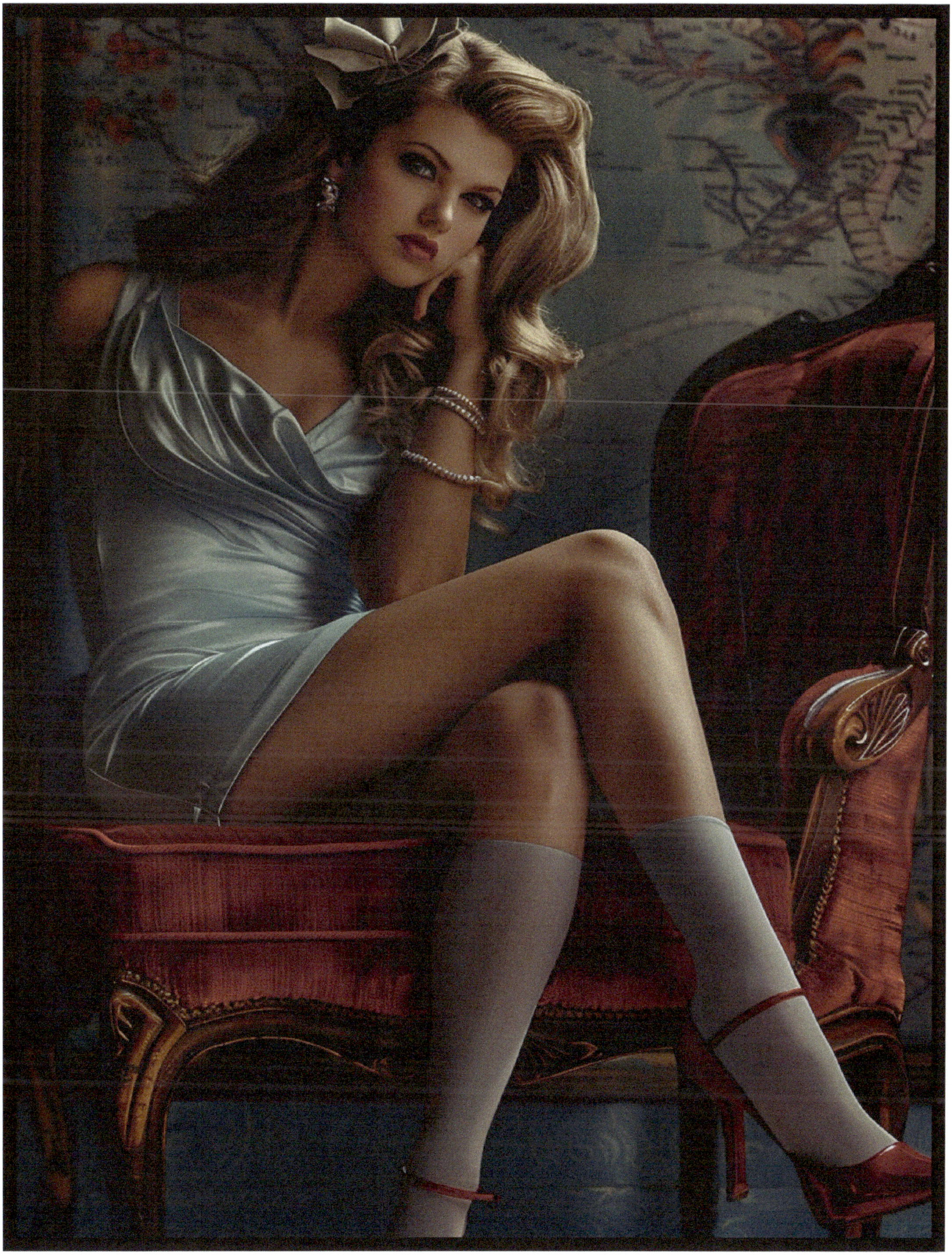

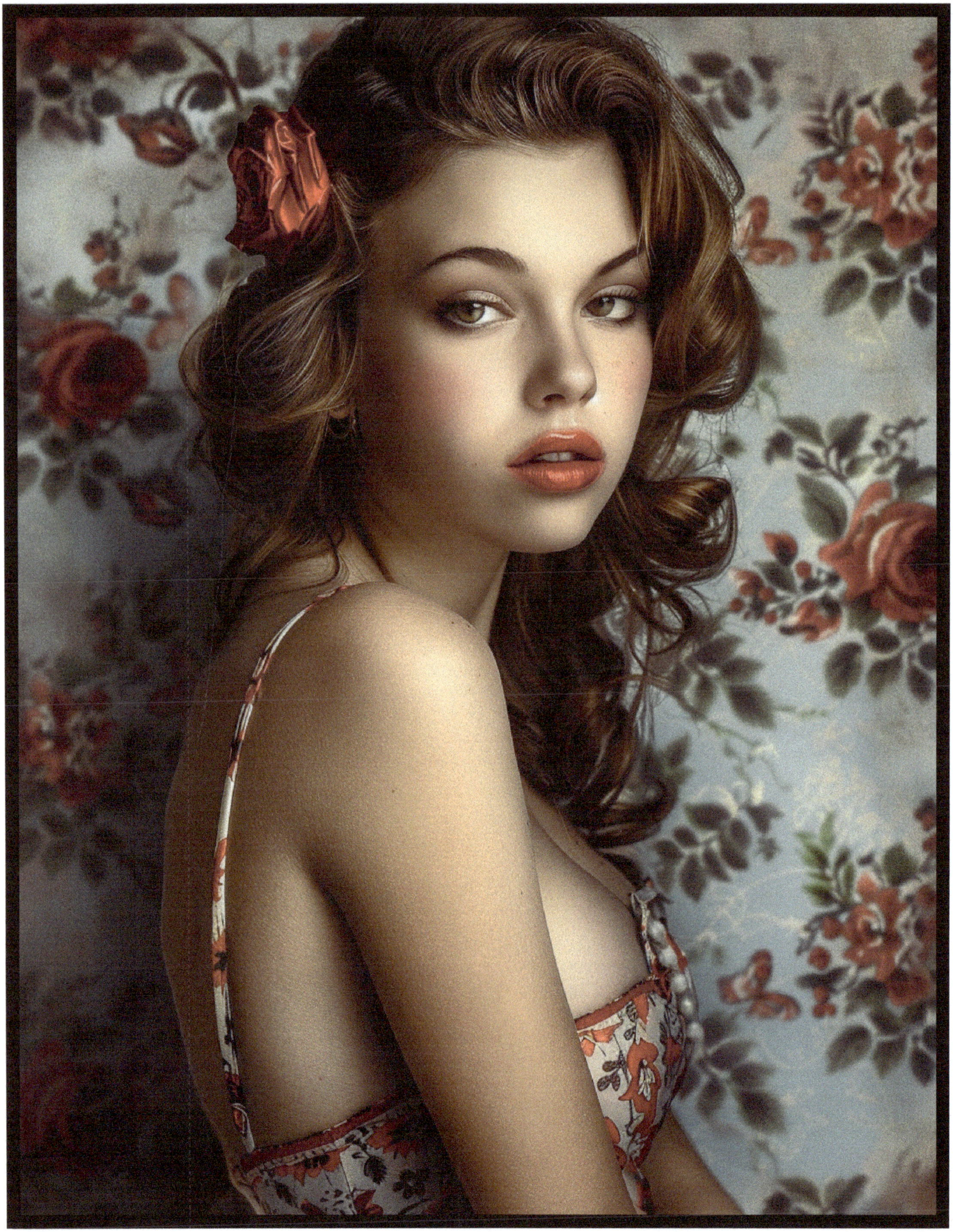

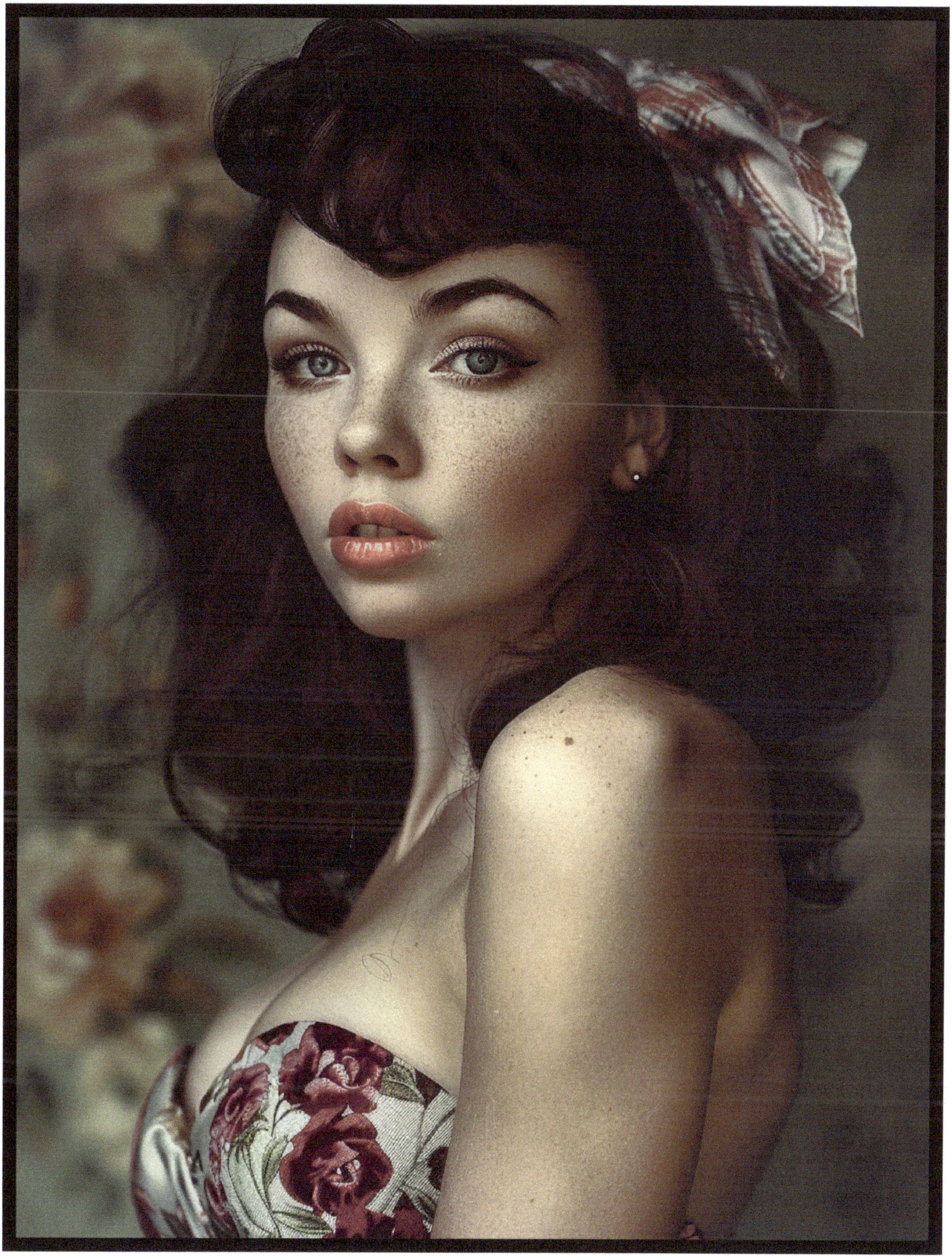

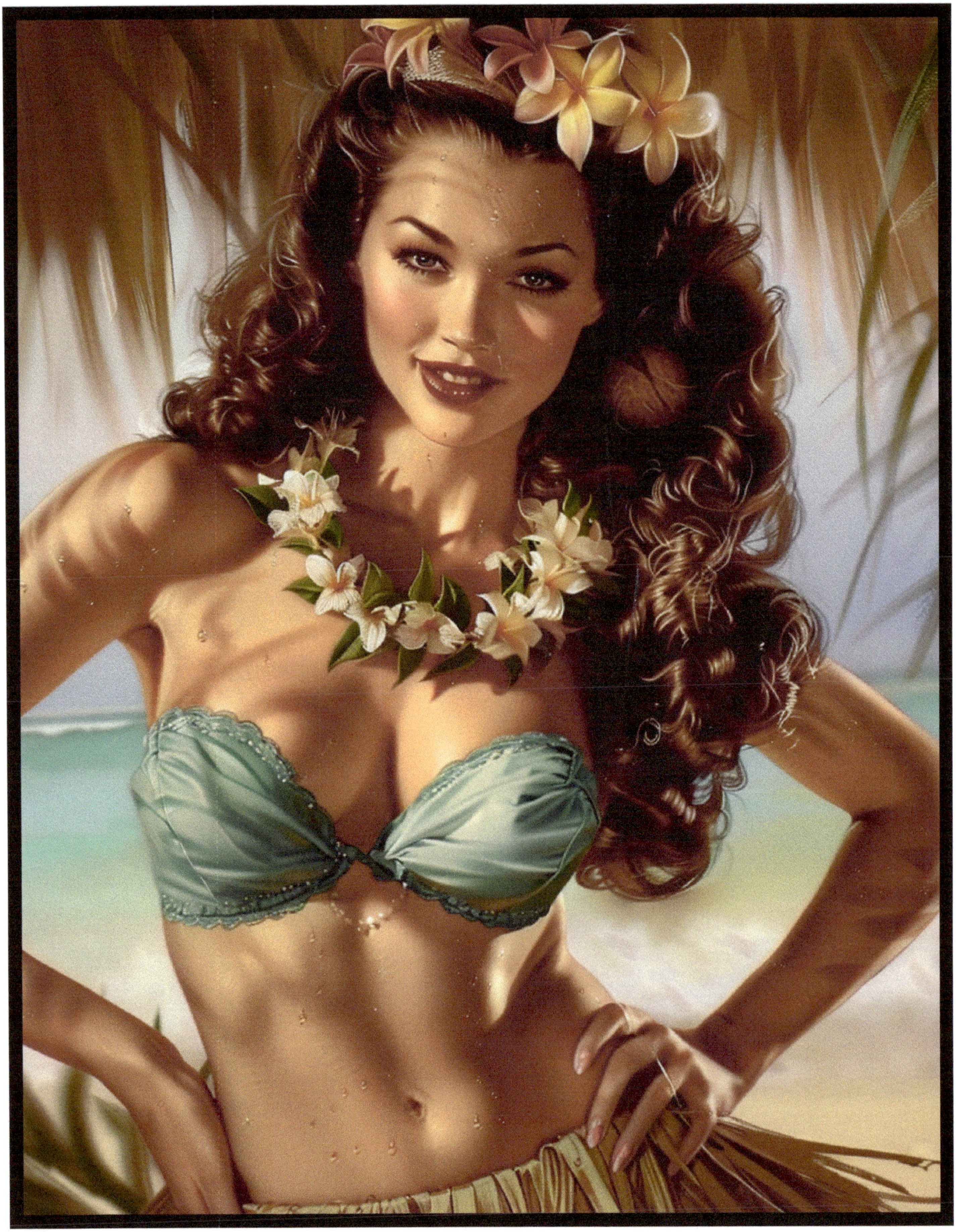

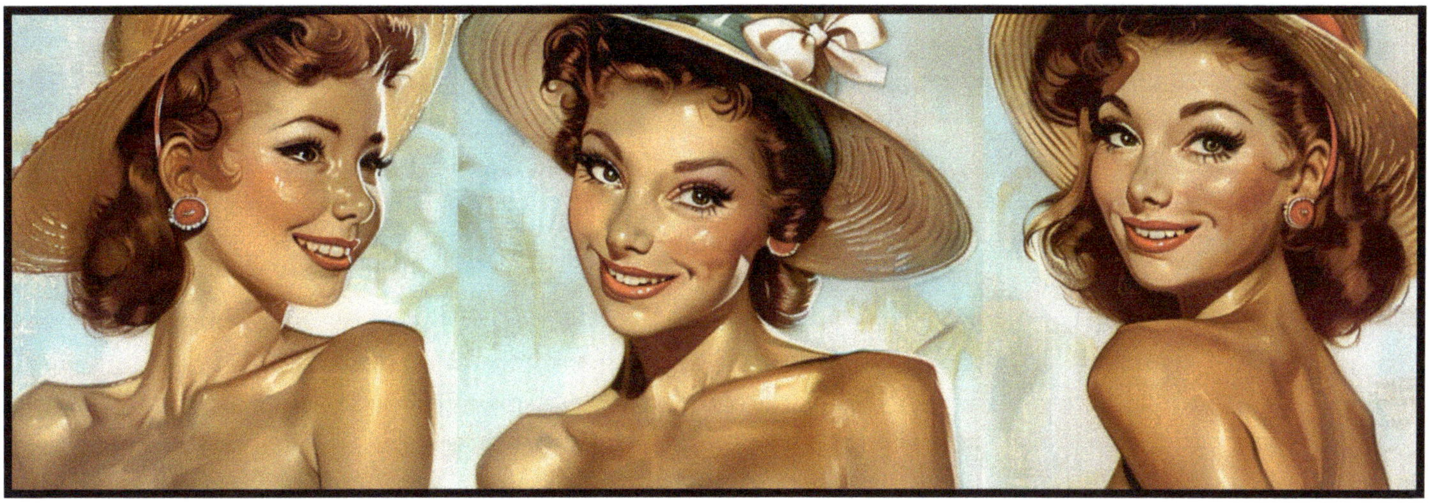

PIN-UP ACROSS DIFFERENT CULTURES

Pin-up art, though deeply rooted in American culture, has found resonance and unique expressions across different cultures around the world. As the genre has evolved, it has been adapted to reflect diverse cultural aesthetics, values, and traditions, demonstrating its universal appeal and adaptability.

In Latin America, pin-up art has blended with local cultural elements to create a distinct style. Latin American pin-up imagery often incorporates vibrant colors, floral patterns, and traditional clothing styles. Artists in countries like Mexico and Brazil have embraced the pin-up genre, infusing it with a regional flavor that reflects their rich cultural heritage. For instance, Mexican pin-up art may feature motifs inspired by Dia de los Muertos, with models adorned in traditional folk art elements, such as sugar skull makeup and colorful dresses. This fusion of pin-up aesthetics with local traditions celebrates both modern and historical aspects of Latin American culture.

In Japan, pin-up art has intersected with the country's own unique artistic traditions and contemporary pop culture. The Japanese pin-up scene often features elements from anime and manga, blending the sensuous and playful characteristics of Western pin-up with the stylized and dynamic qualities of Japanese illustration. This cross-cultural integration has led to the creation of a vibrant subgenre that appeals to both domestic and international audiences. Additionally, Japan's rockabilly and retro subcultures have embraced pin-up fashion and aesthetics, organizing events and gatherings that celebrate mid-20th-century Americana with a Japanese twist.

European interpretations of pin-up art have varied significantly across the continent, influenced by each region's historical and cultural context. In the

United Kingdom, pin-up art often reflects the post-war era's nostalgic charm, with a particular emphasis on the glamour and elegance of the 1940s and 1950s. British pin-up models and artists frequently draw inspiration from the country's own rich history of fashion and illustration, creating works that blend classic pin-up aesthetics with a distinctly British sensibility.

In France, pin-up art has been influenced by the nation's strong tradition of fashion and fine art. French pin-up imagery often emphasizes sophistication and sensuality, reflecting the country's renowned chic and artistic flair. French artists have contributed significantly to the evolution of pin-up art, creating pieces that balance playful eroticism with refined elegance. This unique approach has helped to establish a distinct French pin-up style that resonates with both local and global audiences.

In Australia, pin-up culture has developed a unique identity, blending influences from American and British traditions with local elements. Australian pin-up art often celebrates the country's outdoor lifestyle, featuring models in beachwear and summery settings that highlight the nation's natural beauty. The Australian pin-up scene is also closely linked to the vintage and rockabilly subcultures, with a strong community of enthusiasts who organize events, photo shoots, and competitions that celebrate the style and spirit of the genre.

The Middle East and North Africa have also seen a growing interest in pin-up art, though often with a more conservative approach to accommodate cultural norms and values. Artists in these regions may focus on modesty and traditional attire, incorporating pin-up elements in a way that respects local customs while celebrating female beauty and empowerment. This adaptation demonstrates the flexibility of the pin-up genre to transcend cultural boundaries and resonate with diverse audiences.

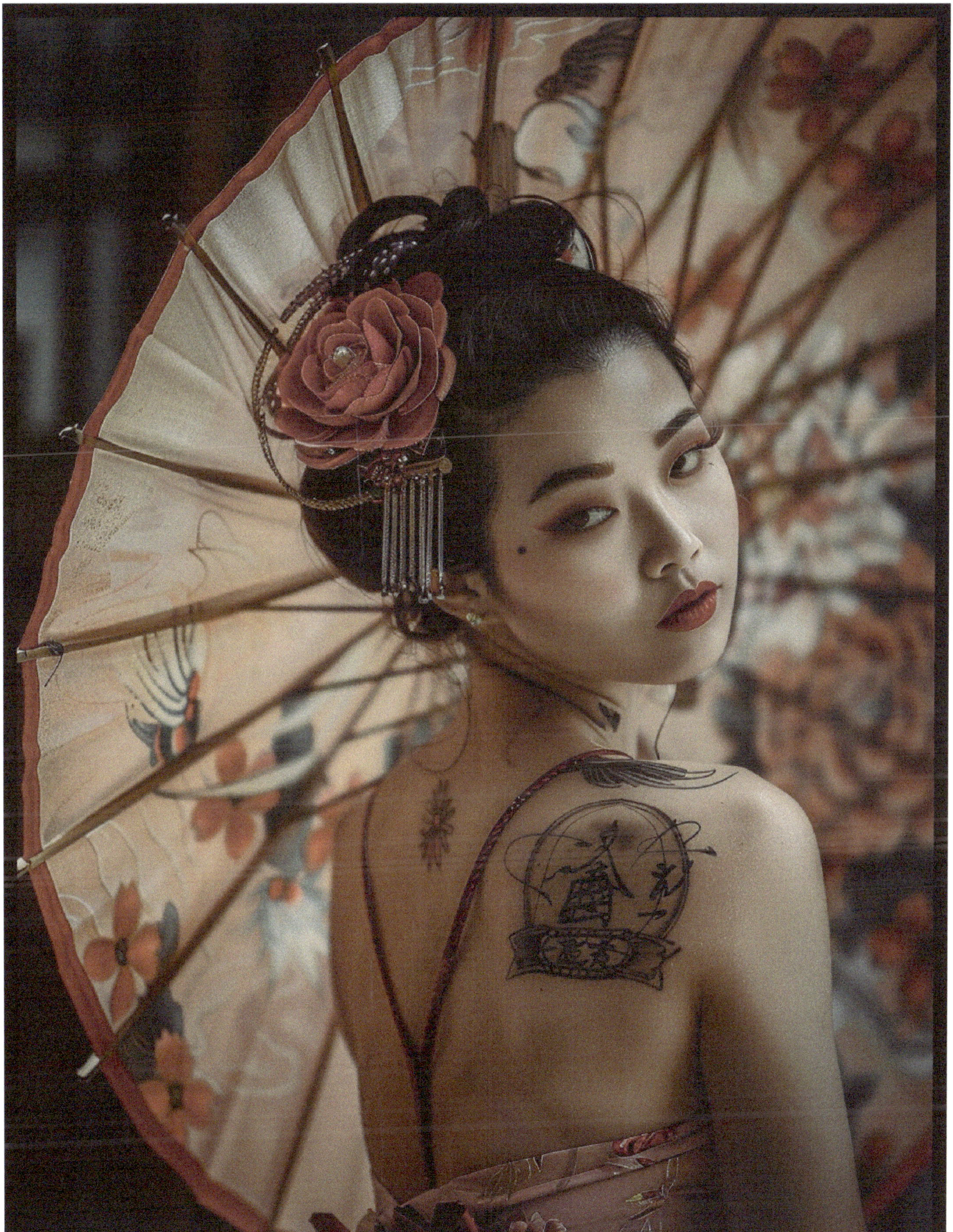

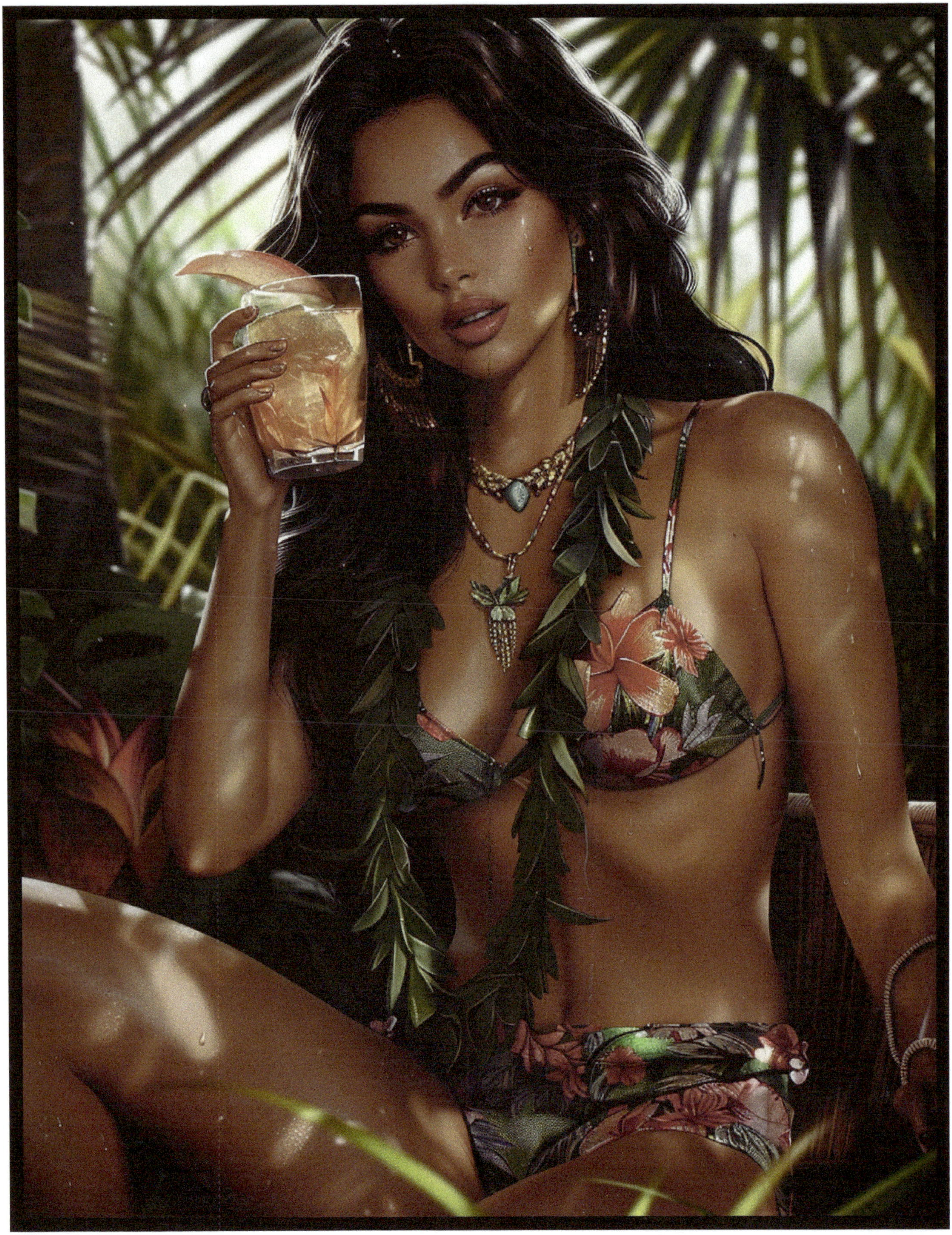

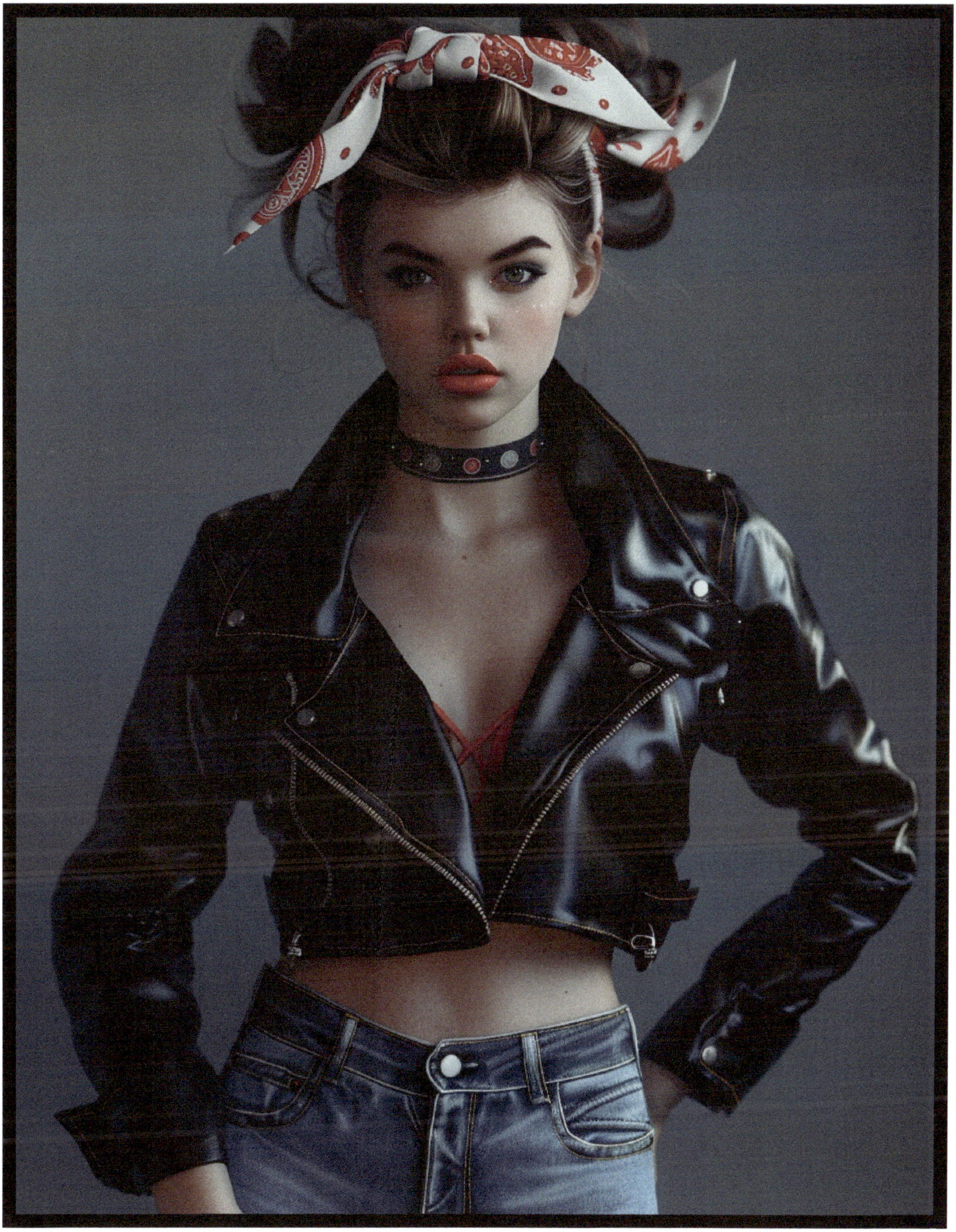

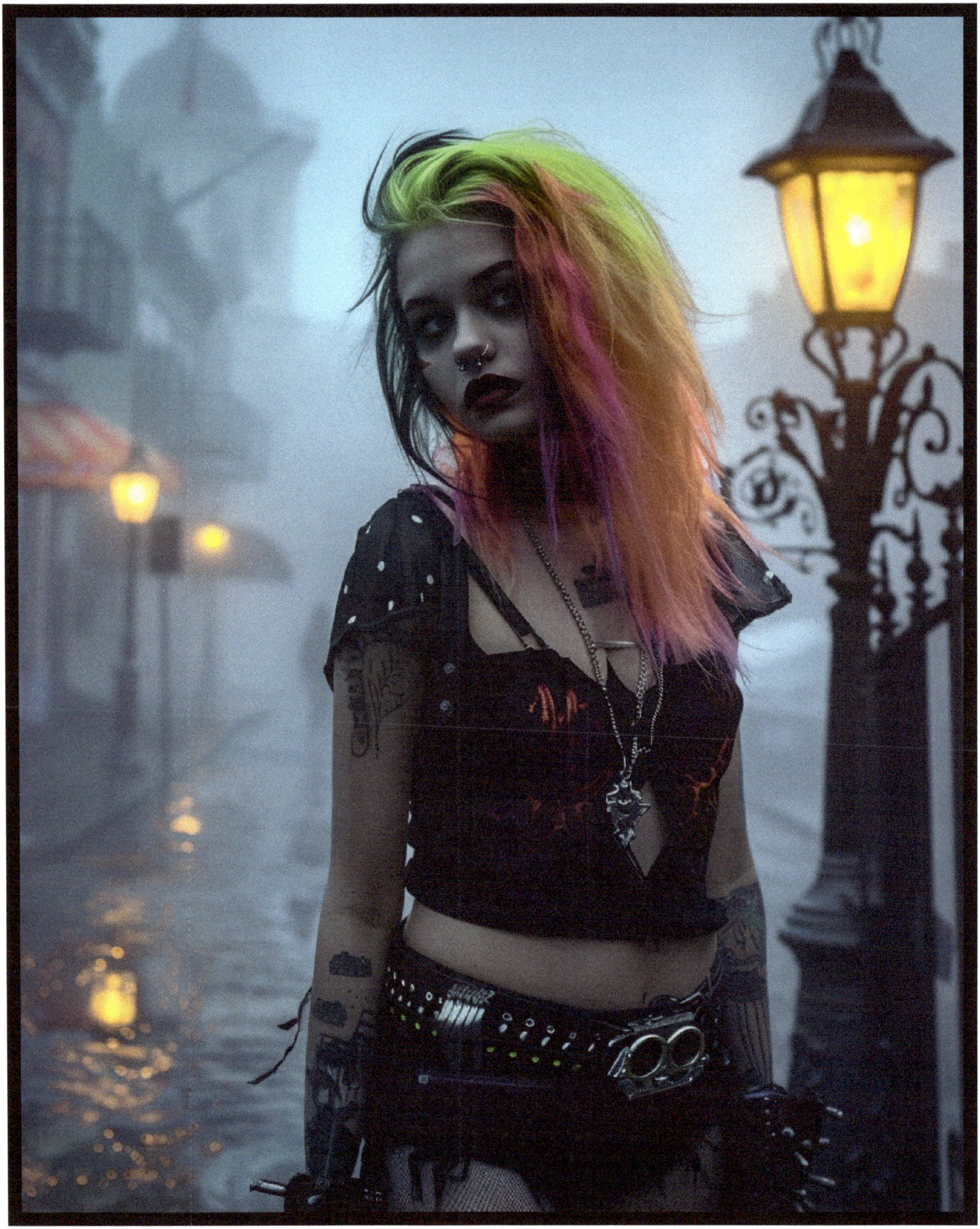

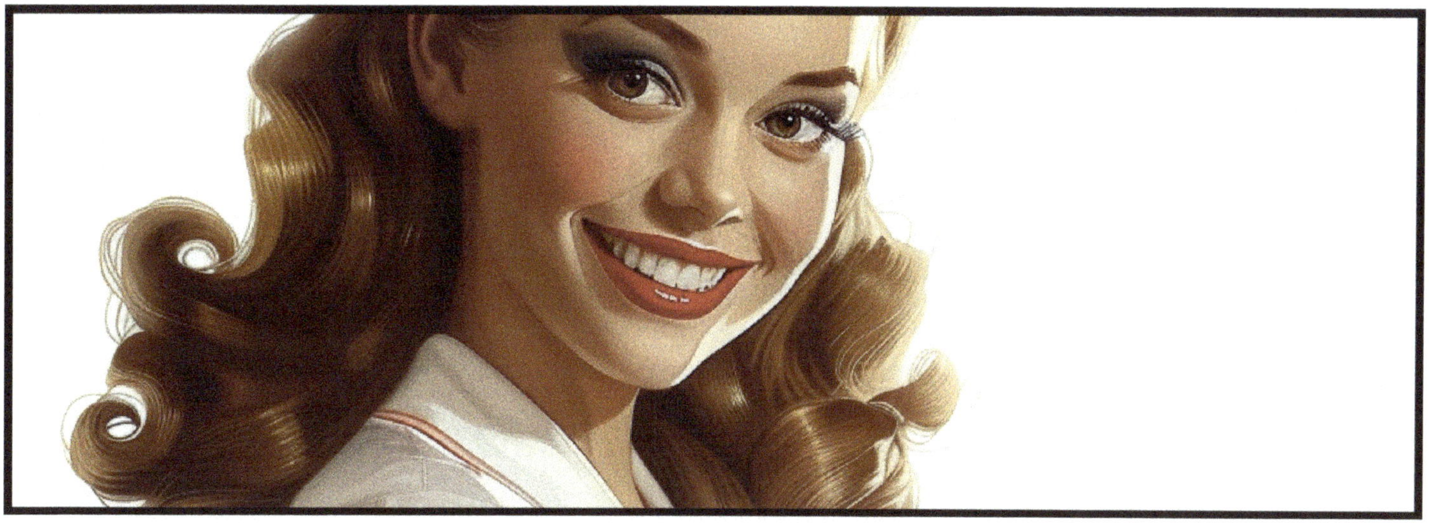

LEGACY OF PIN-UP ART

Pin-up art, with its rich history and dynamic evolution, continues to exert a profound influence on contemporary culture. Its legacy endures in various forms, reflecting its timeless appeal and its ability to adapt to changing societal norms and artistic trends.

One of the most significant aspects of the ongoing legacy of pin-up art is its influence on modern fashion. The pin-up aesthetic, characterized by high-waisted skirts, fitted dresses, and bold accessories, remains a popular choice for those seeking a blend of vintage charm and modern style. Fashion designers regularly draw inspiration from pin-up icons, incorporating elements like polka dots, cherry prints, and halter necklines into their collections. This retro-inspired fashion not only pays homage to the past but also resonates with contemporary audiences who appreciate its flattering and empowering silhouettes.

The beauty industry has also embraced the enduring appeal of pin-up art. Classic pin-up makeup, with its signature red lips, winged eyeliner, and flawless complexion, continues to be a go-to look for many. Beauty influencers and makeup artists frequently create tutorials to help individuals achieve the pin-up look, ensuring that this timeless style remains accessible and relevant. Hair trends like victory rolls, pin curls, and voluminous waves, iconic to the pin-up era, are regularly revived and adapted to modern tastes.

In addition to fashion and beauty, the spirit of pin-up art thrives in various subcultures. The rockabilly scene, for example, celebrates mid-20th-century music, fashion, and lifestyle, with pin-up aesthetics playing a central role. Enthusiasts of this subculture embrace vintage clothing, hairstyles, and accessories, attending events like car shows, music festivals, and dance parties that celebrate the retro vibe. Similarly, the burlesque revival has brought pin-up art to the stage, with performers drawing on the glamour and sensuality of classic pin-up imagery to create captivating and theatrical performances.

Pin-up art's influence extends to the world of tattoo culture as well. Vintage-inspired tattoos featuring pin-up girls, roses, and nautical themes are popular choices, reflecting the genre's lasting visual appeal. Tattoo artists often incorporate elements of pin-up art into their designs, blending traditional motifs with contemporary styles to create unique and personalized body art.

The digital age has also played a significant role in preserving and evolving the legacy of pin-up art. Social media platforms like Instagram, Pinterest, and TikTok have become hubs for pin-up enthusiasts, allowing them to share their passion for vintage aesthetics and connect with like-minded individuals. These platforms have enabled a new generation of artists, models, and influencers to reinterpret and celebrate pin-up art, ensuring its continued relevance and accessibility.

The ongoing legacy of pin-up art is evident in its impact on contemporary art and media. Modern illustrators and photographers frequently draw inspiration from the classic pin-up style, creating works that blend nostalgic elements with current trends. This fusion of old and new keeps the genre fresh and exciting, appealing to audiences who appreciate both its historical significance and its modern interpretations.

The empowerment aspect of pin-up art has also gained renewed importance in recent years. Originally celebrated for its celebration of female beauty and sexuality, contemporary pin-up art continues to promote body positivity and self-confidence. The genre's embrace of diverse body types and its focus on individuality resonate with current movements advocating for inclusivity and acceptance. By celebrating all forms of beauty, pin-up art remains a powerful tool for challenging conventional standards and promoting self-love.

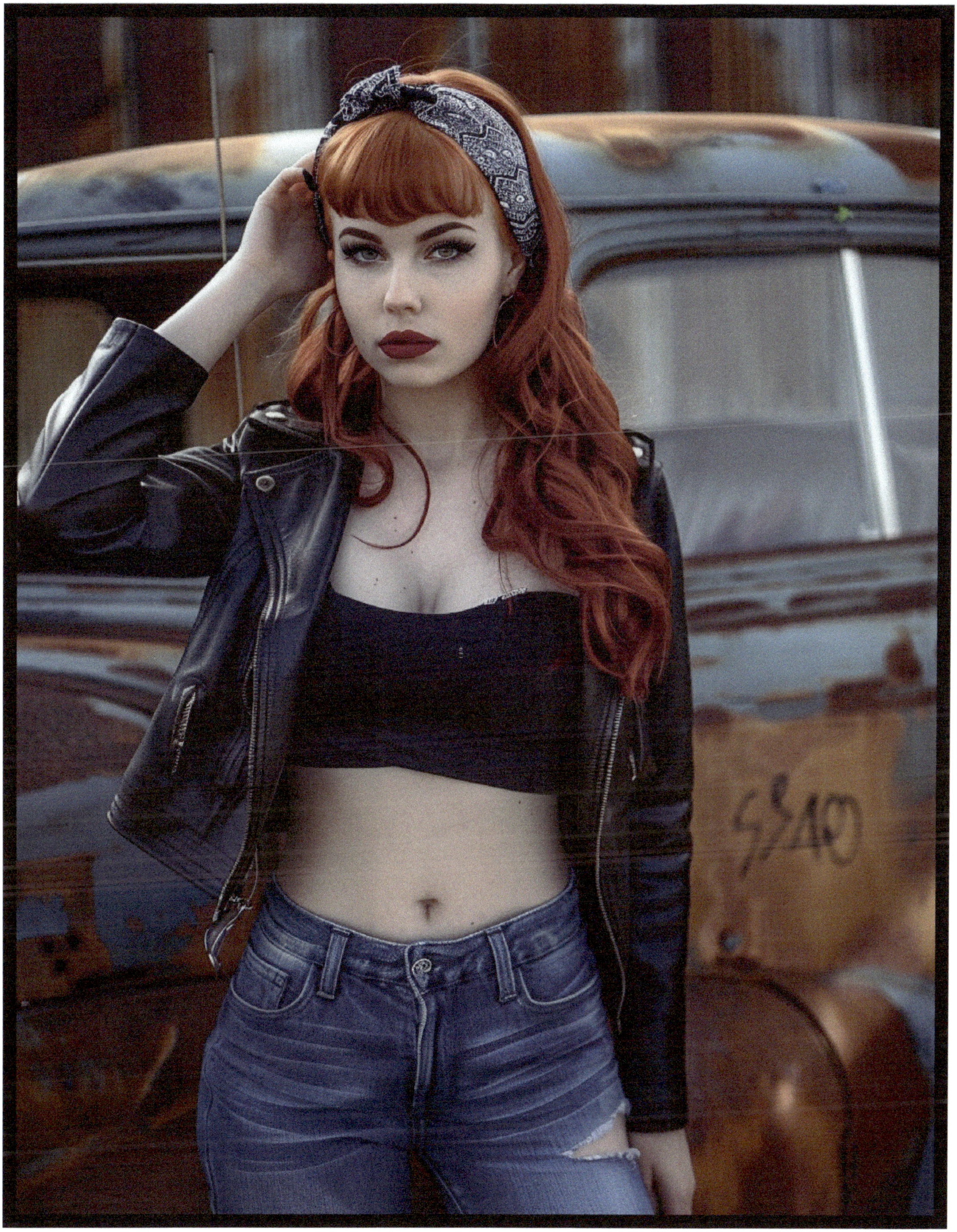

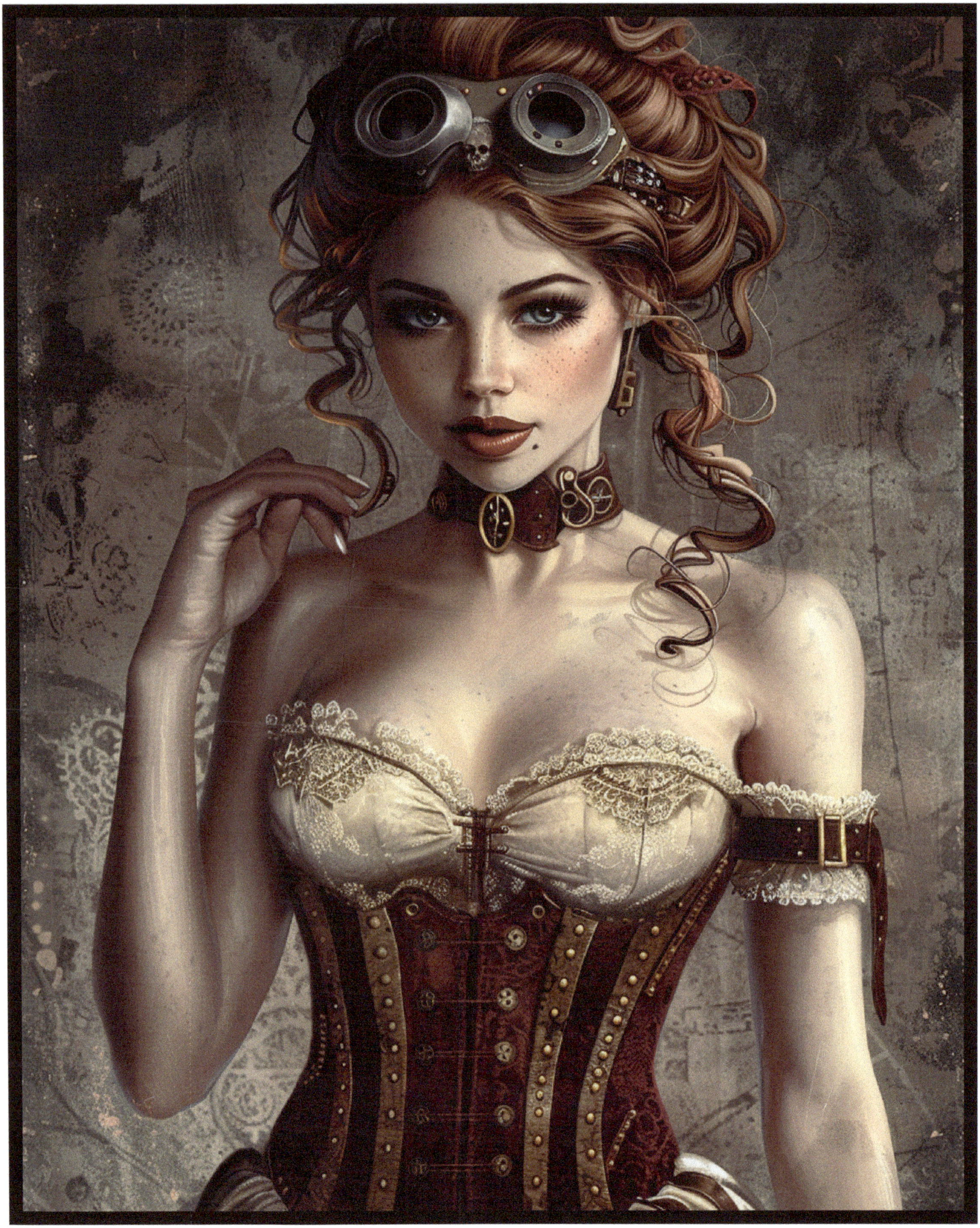

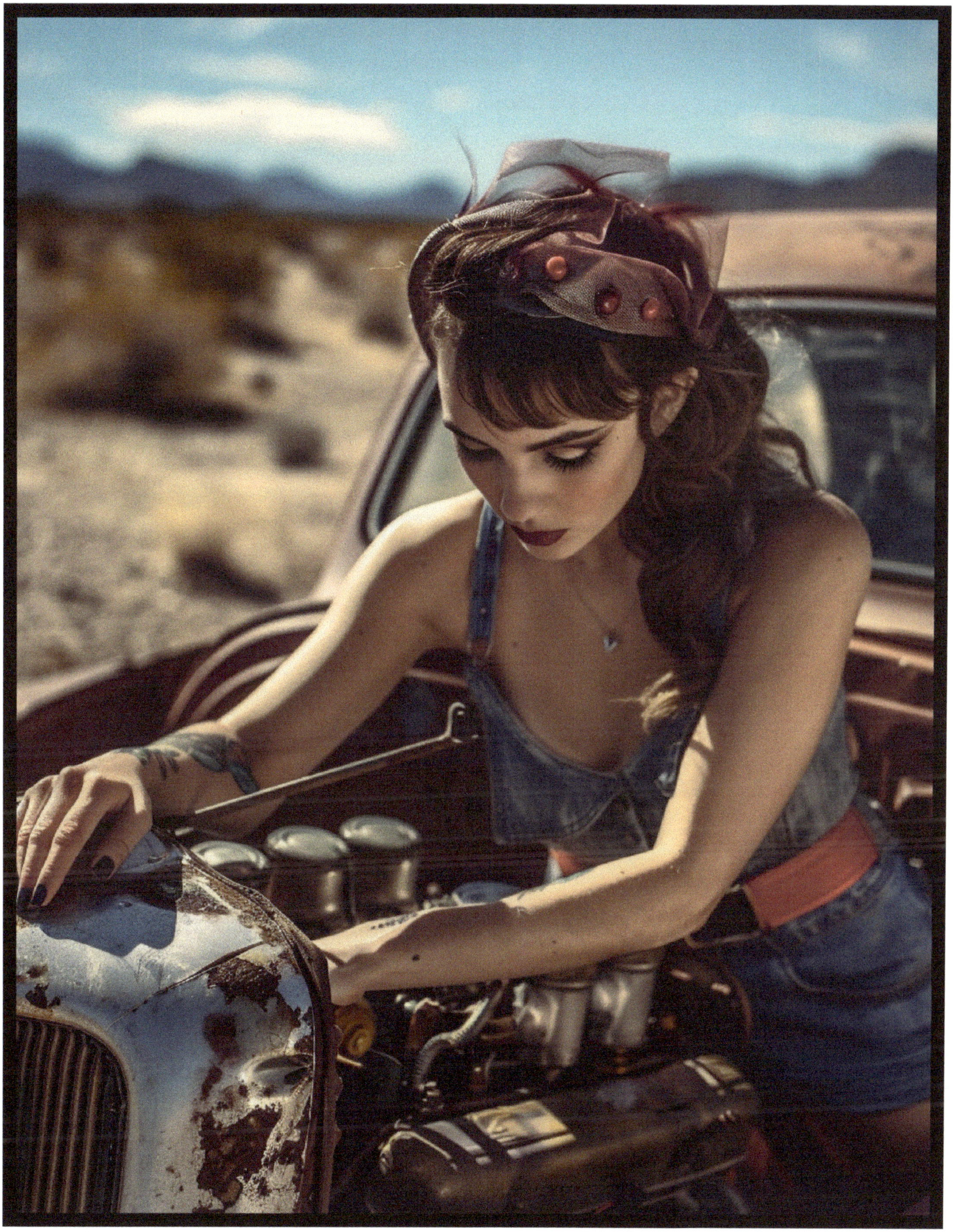

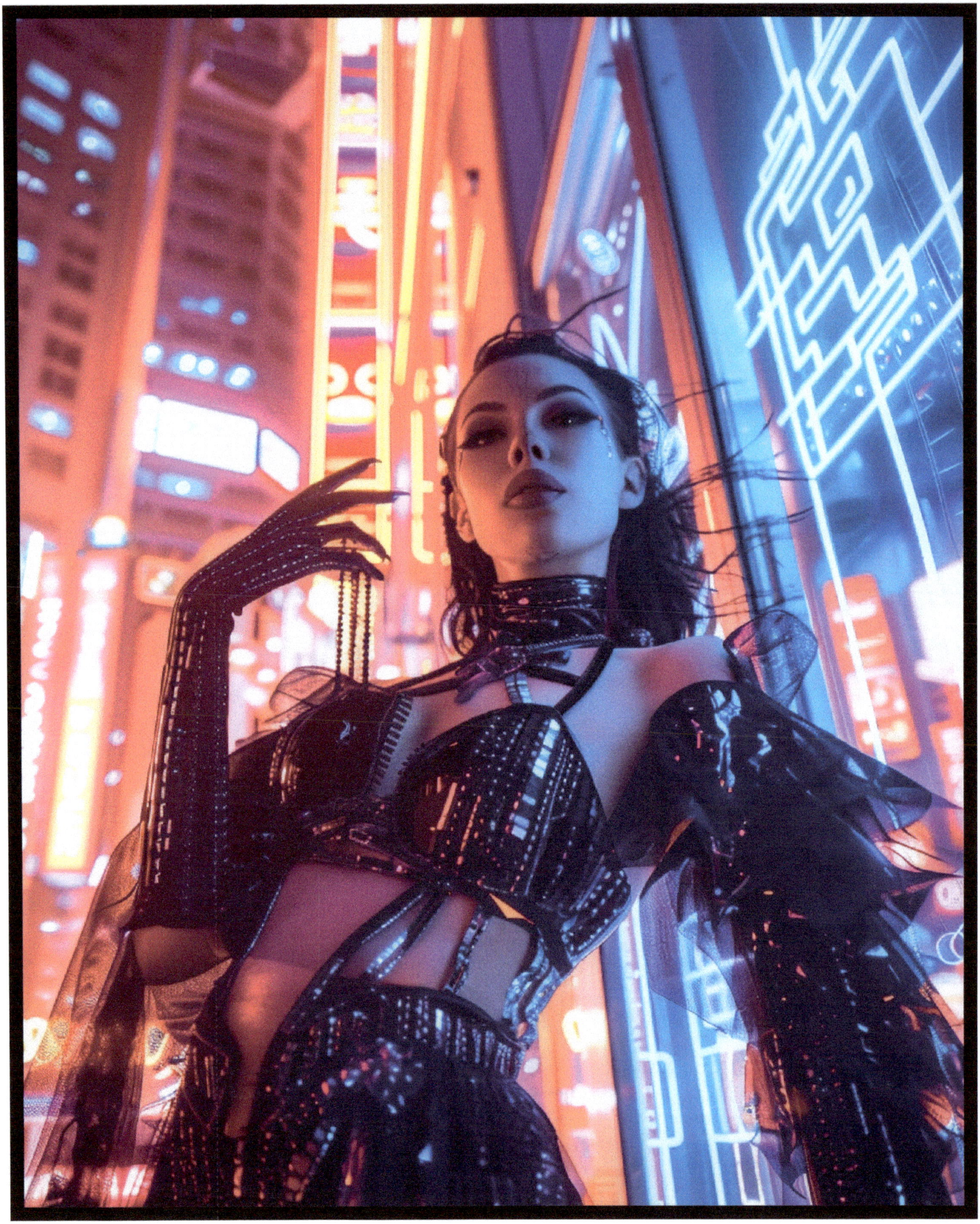

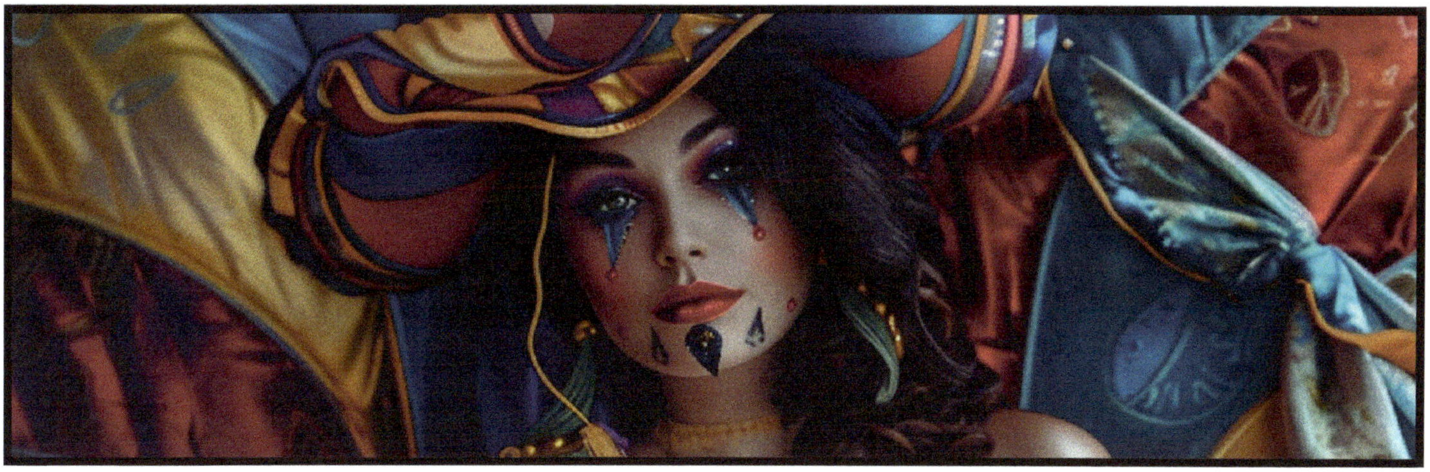

PREDICTIONS AND FUTURE DIRECTIONS

The future of pin-up art looks promising, with several emerging trends and directions indicating how the genre will continue to evolve and remain relevant in the coming years. As society and technology advance, pin-up art is poised to adapt and integrate new influences, maintaining its charm while embracing modernity.

One of the most significant future directions for pin-up art is its integration with digital and virtual reality (VR) technologies. As VR and augmented reality (AR) become more mainstream, pin-up art can transition into immersive experiences. Imagine interactive pin-up galleries where viewers can explore art in a three-dimensional space or virtual fashion shows that showcase pin-up-inspired clothing in a dynamic and engaging way. These technologies can bring a new level of interactivity and engagement to pin-up art, appealing to tech-savvy audiences and creating novel ways to experience the genre.

The trend towards inclusivity and diversity is expected to continue, with pin-up art embracing an even broader range of body types, ethnicities, and gender identities. As societal norms evolve, there will be a greater emphasis on representation and celebrating all forms of beauty. This shift not only aligns with current cultural values but also ensures that pin-up art remains relevant and relatable to a wider audience. Artists will likely continue to push boundaries, creating works that challenge traditional beauty standards and promote body positivity.

As sustainability becomes a more pressing concern, the fashion industry, including pin-up fashion, will likely shift towards more ethical and eco-friendly practices. This could involve using sustainable materials, promoting vintage and second-hand clothing, and supporting brands that prioritize ethical production.

The timeless appeal of pin-up fashion makes it well-suited for a slow fashion approach, encouraging consumers to invest in high-quality, durable pieces that can be cherished for years. This focus on sustainability will resonate with environmentally conscious consumers and ensure that pin-up fashion remains in step with global trends.

Pin-up art is expected to continue its fusion with contemporary art forms, blending traditional aesthetics with modern influences. Artists may experiment with mixed media, combining digital and traditional techniques, or incorporating elements of street art, pop art, and other contemporary styles. This fusion will keep pin-up art fresh and innovative, appealing to both nostalgic fans and those looking for new and exciting artistic expressions.

Social media will remain a powerful platform for the dissemination and evolution of pin-up art. Influencers, artists, and enthusiasts will use platforms like Instagram, TikTok, and emerging social networks to share their work, connect with audiences, and build communities. Social media's visual nature is perfectly suited to showcasing the vibrant and dynamic aspects of pin-up art, ensuring its continued popularity and relevance. Additionally, social media trends and viral content will influence the direction of pin-up art, leading to new styles and interpretations that reflect the zeitgeist.

There will likely be an increased focus on the educational and historical aspects of pin-up art. As interest in vintage culture grows, more efforts will be made to preserve and study the history of pin-up art, its cultural impact, and its evolution over the decades. This could involve exhibitions, documentaries, academic research, and publications that delve into the genre's rich history and its significance within broader cultural contexts. By exploring its past, pin-up art can provide valuable insights into societal changes and continue to inform and inspire future generations.

Collaborations between pin-up artists and other creative fields, such as music, film, and fashion design, will likely become more common. These cross-disciplinary projects can lead to innovative and unexpected results, expanding the reach and impact of pin-up art. For example, musicians might collaborate with pin-up artists for album covers or music videos, fashion designers might create collections inspired by pin-up aesthetics, and filmmakers might incorporate pin-up elements into their visual storytelling.

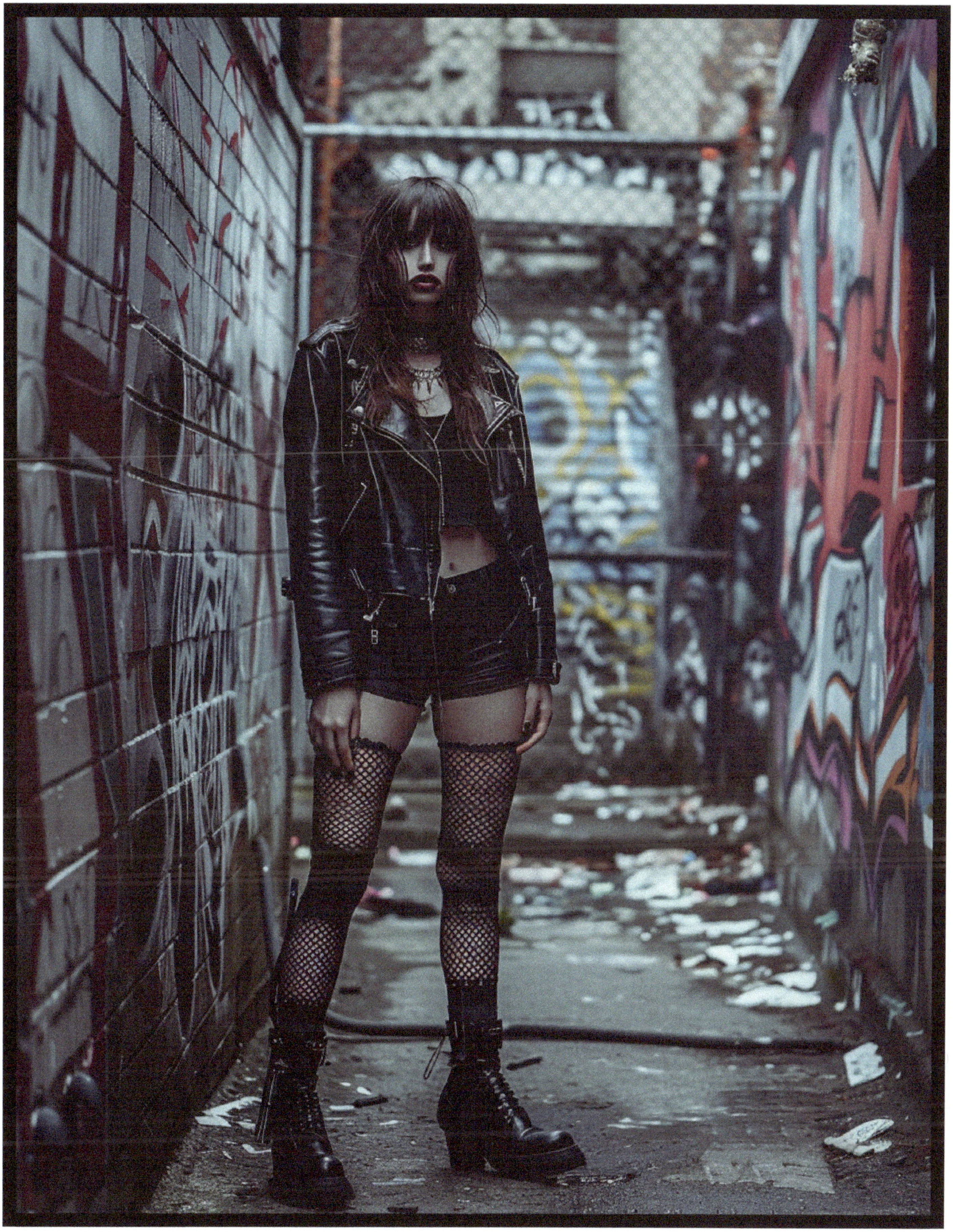

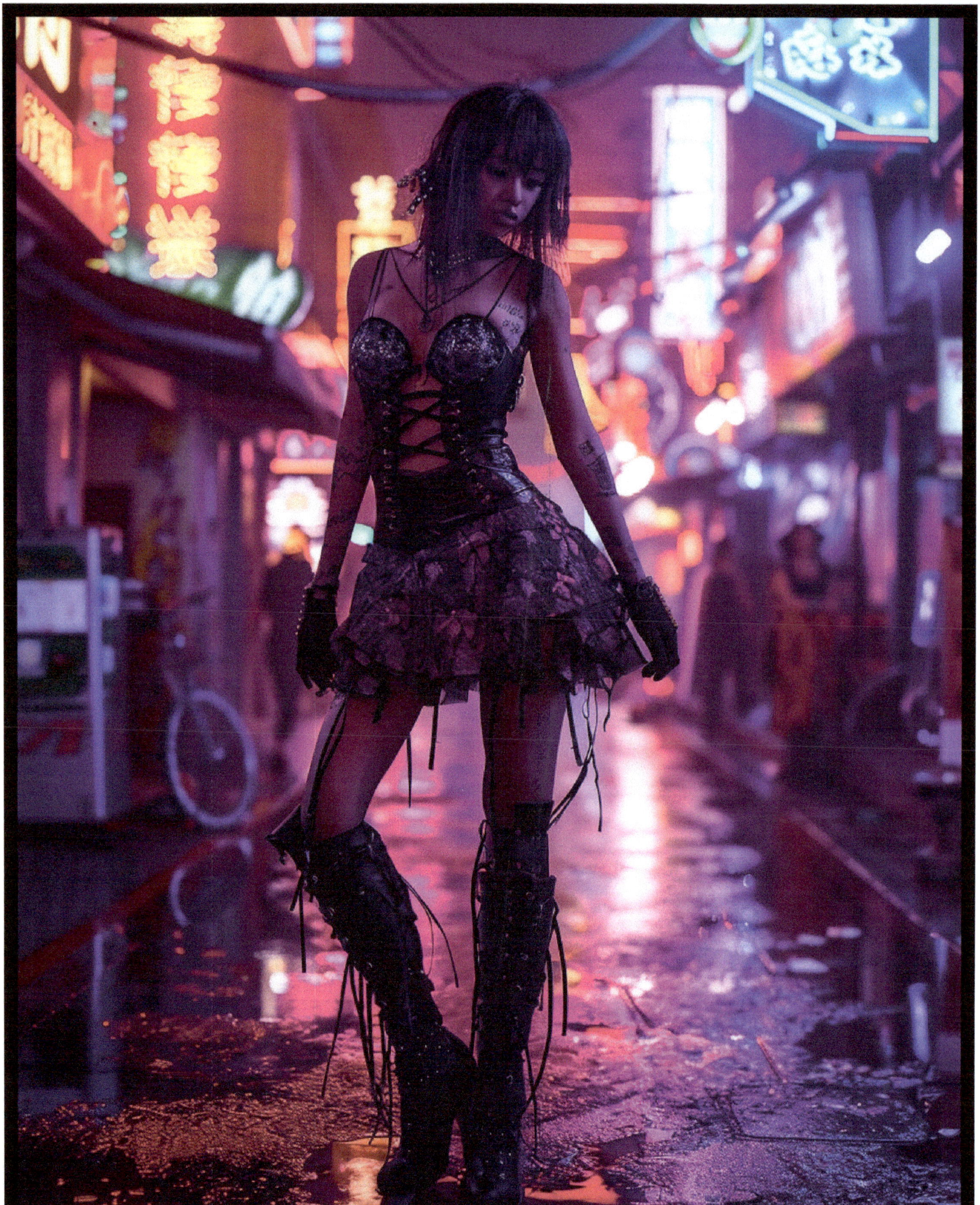

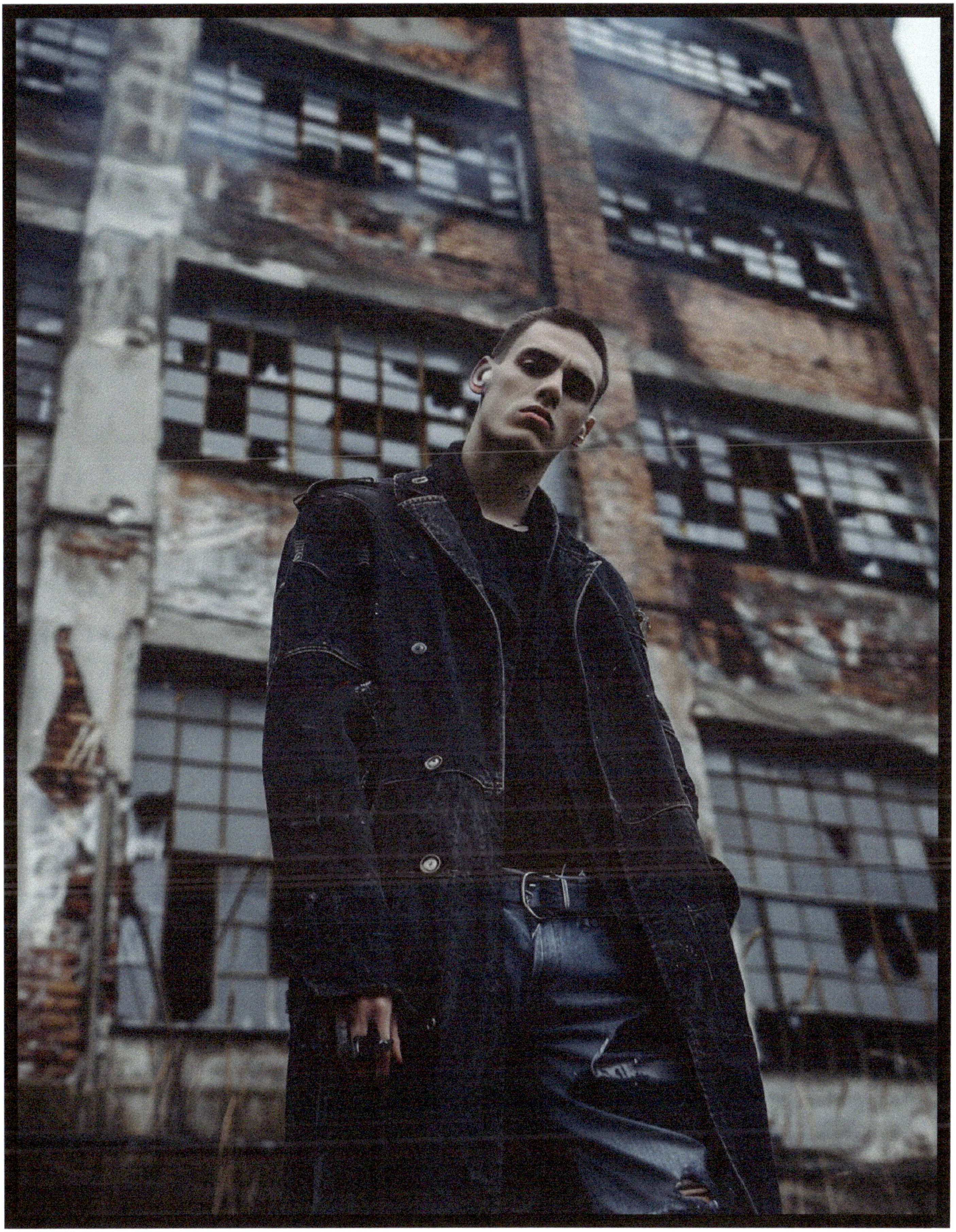

GARGOYLE
COLLECTIVE

www.ingramcontent.com/pod-product-compliance
Ingram Content Group UK Ltd.
Pitfield, Milton Keynes, MK11 3LW, UK
UKHW051458050625
6261UKWH00008B/35

9 786598 408220